The foe claims in error that a philosopher I am.
God knows I am not what he says I am.
But, having endured this sorrow's nest, I ask:
Why should I not know at least what I am?

—Omar Khayyam

HUMAN ARCHITECTURE
Journal of the Sociology of Self-Knowledge

Editor:
Mohammad H. (Behrooz) Tamdgidi
Associate Professor of Sociology
UMass Boston

Human Architecture: Journal of the Sociology of Self-Knowledge (ISSN # 1540-5699) is published by OKCIR: the Omar Khayyam Center for Integrative Research in Utopia, Mysticism, and Science (www.okcir.com, info@okcir.com) and printed by the Okcir Press, an imprint of Ahead Publishing House (APH), P. O. Box 393, Belmont, MA, 02478, U.S.A., tel/fax: 617.932.1170. Copyright © by Ahead Publishing House, 2002-2010. All rights reserved. *Human Architecture* is indexed in CSA Illumina's *Sociological Abstracts*® and complied in EBSCO's SocINDEX with Full-Text®, ProQuest's *Social Science Journals* full-text database, and Gale's *Academic OneFile* and *Expanded Academic ASAP*.

Submissions: *Human Architecture* publishes both submitted and invited manuscripts as well as the working papers of OKCIR: the Omar Khayyam Center for Integrative Research in Utopia, Mysticism, and Science—an independent research and educational project. Contributors extend permission to *Human Architecture* for the publication of their work in the journal. They retain copyrights to their work and may publish them elsewhere. If the submitted manuscript has been published elsewhere before, written permission from both the author(s) and publication(s) where it earlier appeared should accompany submission to *Human Architecture*.

Editorial decisions: *Human Architecture* adheres to the peer reviewing principle for advancing scholarship—seeking innovative ways to meet the need in favor of liberatory scholarly practices most conducive to the aim and purpose of the journal. Selection of papers from submitted or invited manuscripts are based on their substantive relevance and the coherence and innovativeness of their argument in consideration of the mission of the journal. Views expressed in the journal by contributors are those of their authors and may not necessarily coincide with one another, or with the views of the editor, members of the Editorial Advisory Board, or the institutions with which any of the above are affiliated. Authors are solely responsible for the accuracy and integrity of factual, bibliographic, and referential materials used in their own articles, and for obtaining permissions for using copyrighted material in their manuscripts. Methodological, theoretical, historical, empirical, practical, as well as literary and artistic contributions relevant to the mission of the journal are all encouraged. The primary language used is English, but material in other languages may be included if relevant to the purpose of the journal.

What to submit: All manuscripts should be submitted in electronic format. They should preferably be double-spaced in Times 12 typeface., with 1 inch margins all around. Footnotes, endnotes, or reference lists may be single-spaced. In general, authors should follow a consistent bibliographic and citation style of their choice throughout the manuscript. Using the ASA (American Sociological Association) style is preferred by the editor.

Where to submit: The Editor, *Human Architecture*, Okcir Press, P. O. Box 393, Belmont, MA, 02478, U.S.A., tel/fax: 617.932.1170, e-mail: mohammad.tamdgidi@umb.edu

Subscriptions: *Human Architecture* is a quarterly publication, published in either single-issue or double-issue formats, all issues for each volume becoming usually available concurrently at the end of every summer. Individual and institutional rates are $15 and $30 for single-issues and $30 and $60 for double-issues respectively. *Individual and institutional subscription rates* per year beginning from the most recently published issue (when subscription order is received) are $60 and $120 respectively. Back issues or additional copies of the journal are available upon request at the same rates as indicated above. Rates include domestic shipping and sales tax, where applicable. For international or bulk orders please inquire for special rates & shipping charges. Make checks payable in U.S. dollars to Ahead Publishing House, and send payments to Ahead Publishing House, P. O. Box 393, Belmont, MA, 02478, U.S.A. Contributors each receive one free copy of the issue in which their articles appear. Rates are subjected to change without notice.

Advertisements: Current rates and specifications may be obtained by contacting the Okcir Press, P. O. Box 393, Belmont, MA, 02478, U.S.A.; tel/fax: 617.932.1170, e-mail: mohammad.tamdgidi@umb.edu

Inquiries: Address all correspondence and requests to *Human Architecture*, Okcir Press, P. O. Box 393, Belmont, MA, 02478, U.S.A.; tel/fax: 617.932.1170, e-mail: mohammad.tamdgidi@umb.edu

Changes of address: Six weeks' advance notice must be given when notifying change of address. Please include both the old and the new addresses in your request. **Postmaster**: Send address changes to Ahead Publishing House, P. O. Box 393, Belmont, MA, 02478, U.S.A.

ISBN 978-1-888024-42-5

Human Architecture:
Journal of the Sociology of Self-Knowledge
Volume IX, Issue 4, Fall 2011
ISSN: 1540-5699
ISBN: 978-1-888024-42-5

Editorial Advisory Board

In Honor of

Jesse Reichek (1916-2005)
Professor Emeritus of Design
U. C. Berkeley

Terence K. Hopkins (1918-1997)
Professor Emeritus of Sociology and Founding Director of the Graduate Program in Sociology
Binghamton University

David Baronov
Associate Professor of Sociology
St. John Fisher College

Anna Beckwith
Lecturer of Sociology
UMass Boston

Jay Dee
Associate Professor of Higher Education
UMass Boston

Estelle Disch
Professor of Sociology
UMass Boston

Alicia Dowd
Associate Professor
Rossier School of Education
University of Southern California

Leila Farsakh
Assistant Professor of Political Science
UMass Boston

Benjamin Frymer
Assistant Professor of Sociology
Hutchins School of Liberal Studies
Sonoma State University

Michal Ginach
Psychoanalyst
The Institute for the Study of Violence
Boston Graduate School of Psychoanalysis

Lewis R. Gordon
Laura H. Carnell Professor of Philosophy, Religion, and Jewish Studies
Temple University

Panayota Gounari
Assistant Professor of Applied Linguistics
UMass Boston

Ramón Grosfoguel
Associate Professor of Ethnic Studies
U.C. Berkeley

Terry-Ann Jones
Assistant Professor of Sociology
Fairfield University

Philip Kretsedemas
Assistant Professor of Sociology
UMass Boston

Winston Langley
Provost and Vice Chancellor for Academic Affairs
UMass Boston

Neil G. McLaughlin
Associate Professor of Sociology
McMaster University, Canada

Jonathan Martin
Assistant Professor of Sociology
Framingham State College

Bruce Mazlish
Professor Emeritus of History
Massachusetts Institute of Technology

Askold Melnyczuk
Associate Professor of English
UMass Boston

Aundra Saa Meroe
Senior Researcher of Sociology
University of Chicago

Eric Mielants
Associate Professor of Sociology
Fairfield University

Martha Montero-Sieburth
Professor Emeritus of
Higher Education Administration and Leadership
Graduate College of Education
UMass Boston

Dorothy Shubow Nelson
Senior Lecturer of English
UMass Boston

Dylan Rodriguez
Associate Professor
Department of Ethnic Studies
U.C. Riverside

Khaldoun Samman
Associate Professor of Sociology
Macalester College

Emmett Schaefer
Senior Lecturer of Sociology
UMass Boston

Ingrid Semaan
Director of Women's Studies
Univ. of Connecticut, Stamford

Tim Sieber
Professor of Anthropology
UMass Boston

Santiago E. Slabodsky
Assistant Professor of Judaic Studies
University of Saskatchewan, Canada

Rajini Srikanth
Associate Professor of English
UMass Boston

Shirley Tang
Associate Professor of
Asian American Studies
and American Studies
UMass Boston

Aleksandra Wagner
BA Program Core Faculty, Sociology
The New School for Social Research

Reef Youngreen
Assistant Professor of Sociology
UMass Boston

Samuel Zalanga
Associate Professor of Sociology
Bethel University

Vivian Zamel
Professor of English
UMass Boston

Student Advisory Board

Ayan Ahmed
B.A., Sociology
UMass Boston

Keilah Billings
Undergraduate Student of Sociology
UMass Boston

Bart Bonikowski
Doctoral Student of Sociology
Princeton University

Bryan Gangemi
Alumni and Activist
UMass Boston

Chris Gauthier
Doctoral Student of Sociology
University of Michigan

Jenna Howard
Doctoral Student of Sociology
The State University of New Jersey at Rutgers

Tu Huynh
Doctoral Student of Sociology
SUNY-Binghamton

Jennifer McFarlane-Harris
Doctoral Candidate
English and Women's Studies
University of Michigan, Ann Arbor

Emily Margulies
Graduate Student of Sociology
SUNY-Albany

Anthony Nadler
Service-Learning and
Outreach Coordinator
Massachusetts Institute of Technology

Donna M. Rafferty
B.A., Sociology
UMass Boston

Annie Roper
B.A., Sociology
UMass Boston

Frank Scherer
Doctoral Candidate
Social/Political Thought Program
York University, Toronto, Canada

Peter Van Do
M.A., American Studies
UMass-Boston

Rika Yonemura
Doctoral Student of Sociology
U.C. San Diego

A Peer-Review*ing* Journal

Contributions to *Human Architecture: Journal of the Sociology of Self-Knowledge* pass through a rigorous selective process with respect to their fit, relevance, coherence of argument, and innovativeness in consideration of the scope, nature, and intended purpose of the journal. The journal adheres to the peer-reviewing principle for advancing scholarship, but aims to design and build new scholarly avenues to meet this requirement—seeking mechanisms that foster openness of inquiry and evaluation; mechanisms that invite constructive judgments subject to free, open, and mutually interactive, not blinded and one-sided, peer reviewing practices; mechanisms that can be employed as widely and dynamically as possible among specialist and interested scholars in the field who value the need for the proliferation of new, critical, and innovative personal and global insights and transformations.

To meet the highest standards of scholarship, liberatory editorial practices need to transition from static peer review*ed* to dynamic peer review*ing* models that de-couple publication from defective pre-publication peer review requirements, and engage in alternative peer review practices that remain open to all those wishing to review a manuscript at any time in the post-publication phase—encouraging expanded and deepening exchanges among scholars, authors and readers alike. They need to invite critical thinking about prevailing and dominant paradigms and inflame creative spirits to forge new scholarly horizons and intellectual landscapes. And they need to embrace the subaltern voices in the academia and beyond, voices of those who have been deprived of cultivating their sociological imaginations through formal scholarly publishing avenues.

Human Architecture warmly invites contributors and readers to peer review the articles herein and to openly share their critical and constructive insights with one another in the future chronicles of this journal.

Contents

HUMAN ARCHITECTURE
Journal of the Sociology of Self-Knowledge

Volume IX   Issue 4   Fall 2011

vii   **Editors' Note: De-Museumizing Migrations Without and Within**
Mohammad H. Tamdgidi, University of Massachusetts Boston

1   **Museum and Migration: An Introduction**
Issue Co-Editors: Ramón Grosfoguel, University of California at Berkeley; Yvon Le Bot, Ecole des Hautes Études en Sciences Sociales, France; Alexandra Poli, Ecole des Hautes Études en Sciences Sociales, France

5   **The Museumization of Migration in Paris and Berlin and Debates on Representation**
Andrea Meza Torres, Humboldt University, Berlin

23   **Danishness, Nordic Amnesia and Immigrant Museums**
Lia Paula Rodrigues, Roskilde University, Denmark

35   **"African, Chinese and Mexican National Museums in the United States": Did You Say "National"?**
Cristina Castellano, University of Paris 1, Sorbonne, France

49   **The Challenge of Cultural Diversity in Europe: (Re)designing Cultural Heritages through Intercultural Dialogue**
Estela Rodríguez García, Centro de Estudios Diálogo Global, Spain

61   **Immigrant Communities, Cultural Institutions and Political Space: The Success of the Immigration Museum in Melbourne, Australia**
Ilham Boumankhar, University of Paris 1, Panthéon-Sorbonne, France

93   **"Indépendance!": The Belgo-Congolese Dispute in the Tervuren Museum**
Véronique Bragard, Université catholique de Louvain, Belgium

105   **Representation of Africa and the African Diaspora in European Museums**
Artwell Cain, National Institute of Dutch Slavery Past and Legacy, The Netherlands

117   **Slavery, Colonialism and Museums Representations in Great Britain: Old and New Circuits of Migration**
Stephen Small, University of California, Berkeley

Editor's Note: De-Museumizing Migrations Without and Within

Mohammad H. Tamdgidi

University of Massachusetts Boston

mohammad.tamdgidi@umb.edu

Abstract: This is the journal editor's note to the Fall 2011 issue of *Human Architecture: Journal of the Sociology of Self-Knowledge*, entitled "Contesting Memory: Museumizations of Migration in Comparative Global Context," including papers that were presented at an international conference on "Museums and Migration" held on June 25-26, 2010, at the Maison des Science de l'Homme (MSH) in Paris, co-organized by the issue co-editors Ramón Grosfoguel, Yvon Le Bot and Alexandra Poli, with the support of MSH Director and President of the International Sociological Association, Michel Wieviorka. Appreciating the important comparative studies in the volume regarding the contested representations of global migration history by migrants and officials organizing migration museums, the editor suggests that it may be helpful to maintain a dialectical epistemic framework and vantage point here—using which the seemingly separate categories "museum" and "university" are rendered more or less identical and one in which the identity of the studied object and the studying subject of the studies undertaken is consciously recognized and maintained. In this light, then migration can be experienced and studied in its broader and multifacetted meanings, de-museumized to encompass all migratory experiences without and within.

This, Fall 2011 issue of *Human Architecture: Journal of the Sociology of Self-Knowledge*, entitled "Contesting Memory: Museumizations of Migration in Comparative Global Context" includes papers presented at an international conference on "Museums and Migration" held on June 25-26, 2010, at the Maison des Science de l'Homme (MSH) in Paris. Co-editors Ramón Grosfoguel, Yvon Le Bot, and Alexandra Poli—who also served as the co-organizers of the conference with the support of MSH Director and President of the International Sociological Association, Michel Wieviorka—have done an excellent job summarizing the contributions of each author in the volume in the introduction that follows this editor's note.

My purpose here is to briefly reflect on the contributions and the co-editors' reading of them as well, seeking to further understand the seemingly novel idea of "migration museums" in light of the purpose and mission of the present journal and my own substantive interests as framed by the sociology of self-knowledge and what C. Wright Mills called the sociological imagination—that is, the sociological perspective which enables its beholder to relate one's own and others' personal troubles to larger public issues.

Mohammad H. Tamdgidi is associate professor of sociology, teaching social theory at UMass Boston. Most recently he has been the author of *Gurdjieff and Hypnosis: A Hermeneutic Study* (Palgrave/Macmillan 2009), *Advancing Utopistics: The Three Component Parts and Errors of Marxism* (Paradigm Publishers 2007/2009), and "Decolonizing Selves: The Subtler Violences of Colonialism and Racism in Fanon, Said, and Anzaldúa" (in *Fanon and the Decolonization of Philosophy*, edited by Elizabeth A. Hoppe and Tracey Nicolls). Tamdgidi's writings have appeared in *Review* (Journal of the Fernand Braudel Center), *Sociological Spectrum*, *Humanity & Society*, *Contemporary Sociology*, and several edited collections.

"It belongs to a museum" is an adage used in popular culture. It can have a double-meaning when used seriously, or sarcastically. Seriously uttered, it means that something is too rare and has too much value to belong to someone or someplace specific and is of a broad public significance, so belongs to a museum for all to see, experience, teach about, learn from, and simply enjoy. When used sarcastically, it is usually uttered when people think something has lost its current, practical use-value and is too "old" in the mundane sense of the word; so it belongs to a museum. In either case, when the object is museumized, it usually leaves the sphere of practical use for what it is, and turns into a more or less inanimate object of greater, or lesser, value, and simply put on display, passive to its surrounding, and for others to use for seeing, learning, teaching, experiencing, and enjoying—more or less.

Applied to people themselves and their inter/intra/subjective experiences of self or others in social life, one may then think of a third, but related, meaning for the adage: becoming "museumized" can have this inter/intra/subjective meaning of one's or another's losing a sense of what one or another is or is worth—too much or too little—such that one finds oneself of no practical use or value when it comes to active participation in whatever one is currently engaged in, becoming merely a display object for oneself or others to—more or less—see, teach about, learn from, experience, and/or simply enjoy.

Would one put something, someone, or a self/social experience in a museum, if it is already actively out there, and/or in here, everywhere, if one cares and learns to notice and see it as it is present and takes place everyday, everywhere—world-historically, and in the here and now? Would one then need a museum to show it, to teach it and learn about it, or more or less enjoy it? Does "migration" belong to a museum, for one or another reason?

In addressing the above questions, we also need to recall that the English word "museum" comes from Latin, which itself originates from a Greek word (pronounced as *Museion*) named after Muses, who were regarded as patron goddesses of the arts and literature. "Museion"/"Museum" denote a place set aside for study and the arts and literature.

While today the terms "museum" and "university" refer to different institutions, the identity of the purpose of modern-day museums and that of universities is apparent from the word's meaning as noted above. You go to both to learn, to "guide"/teach, and to educate yourself or others about something. You may have to pay a fee or receive a wage or salary, but at times it may be free and state-sponsored, using hired or "free" and volunteer work. While there, you can read the literature about artifacts yourself, and/or attend a class, seminar, or workshop, organized by a "guide." Lectures and learning may be in person, or via audiovisual, or nowadays online, media. Objects to examine may be on the floor, in special rooms such as libraries, in "labs" inside, online, or experienced during field trips outside, accompanied by "tour guides." Granted, admittance to museums is presumed to be much easier, targeting wider public audiences for education, and universities may be more or less difficult to be admitted into. Museum visits can take at most a day or two to accomplish. University "visits" months, years, or decades. But all these do not do away with the basic commonality of the two seemingly different, and nowadays separately housed, institutions. Moreover, with the advent of the information age and the Internet, both institutions have extended their reach to virtual reality, and offer their resources and services online to an unprecedented extent. Furthermore, some universities now have permanent museum collections, and museums offer permanent teaching and learning resources and facilities.

Museums have historically taken many forms and are now specializing in many fields. So do universities. And, so, a new museum type, or field or concentration of scholarship and research today, has emerged having to do with global migration. As scholars are increasingly becoming interested in migration studies, thanks in part to the deepening and widening reach of globalization today, so we find a new type of museum is emerging that sets its specific goal to educate the public about global migration, as experienced by specific peoples in specific international contexts. The purpose in both migration studies and migration museums is to critically explore and understand the historical processes through which specific migration experiences, forced or not, have taken place, and how various sides involved in the process come to terms with the nature of the migration process, its causes, and its consequences and outcomes—appreciating (or not) what immigrants have lost, found, or newly contributed in the course of their migratory experience. Obviously, as the migration experiences themselves were or still are contentious, the university studies of migration and the museum exhibitions of migration and what transpired are contentious and contested.

But, then, we should still go back to the earlier mentioned double-meaning of "it belongs to a museum" and the question we posed. It now sounds somewhat irrelevant, if not absurd, to think that studies of global migration (including those of migration museums) do not belong to universities, or migration exhibitions and workshops to museums. One way to address this seeming irrelevance in favor of understanding is to ask: can studies of migration in universities, or exhibitions of migration experience in museums be conducted in such a way that teaching or learning about "migration" as an everyday, everywhere, living experience—one that is experienced by "others" and by oneself, including the researcher or museum curator him/herself—turns into a more or less isolated, frozen, lopsided, inanimate, object "out there," intellectually or figuratively concentrated on, displayed as a concentration program or exhibition project, and then, second-handedly contested? Can museums and universities have this rather odd effect of turning the subject matters of their study or exhibition into lifeless, rigidified objects of lesser or greater value, frozen inside or outside or across equally rigidified disciplinary boundaries or exhibition styles, and simply put on display to more or less effectively teach, learn from, experience, and enjoy?

The reason for the above introductory notes is to encourage the reader to keep in mind a double-meaning of the nature of contributions collected in this journal issue, *including* this editor's note. On the one hand, the contributions aim to shed light on the nature of what may be called the contested museumizations of migration taking place in a comparative global context, focusing particularly on several Western migration museums. On the other hand, this publication itself is an exhibition of intellectual artifacts, produced by university educated/affiliated scholars who—one may safely argue, depending how far back we go and how we define "migration"— are personally or ancestrally immigrant themselves. I hope that by the end of this editorial note, I succeed in clarifying why it may be helpful to maintain this alternative, dialectical epistemic framework and vantage point being proposed here—one in which the seemingly separate categories "museum" and "university" are unfrozen and rendered more or less fluid, interpenetrating, and identical—ones in which, moreover, the identity of the studied object and the studying subject of the studies undertaken is also consciously recognized and maintained.

The issue co-editors plausibly point out that while studies of migration and of museums proliferate separately, academic studies of the phenomenon loosely called "migration museum" have been rare—and for this reason consider the present journal issue a first of its kind directly focusing on the topic and containing new studies by specialists on the field. One reason for this lack of research on the topic may have to do with the fact that migration museum as a museum type is rather recent, and its advent itself reflective of the increasing significance of migration in the rapidly globalizing world of the past several decades.

When my colleague Ramón Grosfoguel approached me with the idea of publishing the proceedings of the previously held conference on such a theme—an invitation of which the current volume is now a product—the idea of migration museums was new to me and I found it rather odd that I had not heard of it as such previously, especially given that I am myself a naturalized "immigrant" from Iran living in the US. I can't say that I am an avid museum-goer, but every now and then, when friends visit us in Boston, we take them to museums, and I have been to some museums in Iran, Greece, and elsewhere as well, ones of the usual nature and character as far as museums are traditionally concerned. I realize that many small or large sections of museums are devoted to displaying the cultural heritage or artifacts of "other" or one's own cultures and peoples, and that annually people of different cultural or ethnic heritage in the US, including Iranians, take to the streets and hold marches and events celebrating their ethnic and migratory background and cultures and displaying their arts and crafts and customs to people of other backgrounds and traditions.

Reading the rich contributions which then Grosfoguel shared in preparation for editing and eventual launching of this journal issue, however, exposed me not only to an ongoing, and in fact increasing trend in building and organizing such migration museums particularly in the Western parts of the world, but also to the rich and critical academic studies of the phenomenon as exemplified by the contributions in this journal issue. Having the dialectical epistemic lens on, as described previously, I now saw reading these manuscripts themselves in terms of examining museal artifacts, their authors themselves as academic migrants, and myself, being the issue editor, a curator for their museal exhibition in the form of this publication. Now, not having even attended a migration museum "out there," I realized I have been living and working in one, that is, the university 'museum," for years. I think this bridging across what seems to be alienated or alienable spaces or categories such as "migration museums" to one's own everyday and everyplace life experiences is very important, as I hope this editor's note will make further clear.

Andrea Meza Torres compares the contrasting museumizations of migration in Paris and Berlin and the politics of how building such centers challenges or accommodates the broader national identities in France and Germany. Lia P. Rodrigues explores a similar theme, but this time in the context of the Danish national identity and its "Nordic amnesia" of its racialized history of colonialism. Christina Castellano, comparatively explores Asian, Mexican and African migrant community museums in Chicago and how they articulate their mission with the larger, imagined identity of US as a nation. Estela Rodriguez García studies a similar theme in the context of Spain, and the Cultural Heritage designs in Europe as represented in the Forum Universal de las Culturas in the Barcelona and Catalonia's History of Immigration Museum. Ilham Boumankhar reports in detail on her study of the Immigration Museum in Melbourne, Australia, including many photos, one of which appears on the cover of this journal issue—a mock-up of a ship in a large room of the museum, representing the mode of transportation of migrants. Véronique Bragard studies the representations (or lack thereof, as far as Congolese migration to Belgium and its diaspora therein are concerned) of Belgium's colonial history in Tervuren Museum's exhibition, and Artwell Cain and Stephen Small, in their respective studies, explore the problematic representations of African diaspora in Europe (particularly in The Netherlands and in the United Kingdom, respectively).

The studies report in detail on the conduct of audiovisual workshops teaching and sharing immigration experiences, and whole sets of organizational innovations and challenges, including fiscal budget considerations, in order to make possible for people and visitors to have a museum experience of what it took and is still taking for migrants to move (or be forcibly and violently moved, as the painful history of slavery is concerned) from one place to another. The museum then becomes an agent of its own, linking with the immigrant communities outside, and finding ways of articulating what actually went on historically in the course of migration, the challenges faced and still facing the migrants, and highlighting as well the ongoing politics and contestation of remembering and historical and personal memory construction and representation, especially as emergent in the process of organizing and curating the museum itself.

A whole series of institutions, large or small, are then set up, the sole purpose of which is to represent, amid much contestation over both substance and form as well as organization and budgets, the "true" nature of what went on in the histories of migrations of peoples. What these migration museum do, perhaps with more creative sets of means—audiovisual, tangible, and sensible—than those offered at the universities, is essentially the same as what the authors of these contributions (and the co-editors, and this editor as well) essentially do in constructing particular memories, discourses, retrospectives, prescriptions, and forecasts of the migration experience worldwide—narratives in which, as noted above, all those published in this volume are also implicated in terms of their own personal or ancestral migration experiences. Having our dialectical epistemic lens in mind, in studying the process of museumization of migration in a comparative global context, in other words, we should be also reflecting, in a world-history context, on our own personal experiences as more or less recently immigrant "professors" and "scholars."

When considering the nature and types of migration museums studied in this volume, it is important to note that they predominantly represent and study a particular form of migration, that is, migrations across national borders, involving movements of people with particular ethnic backgrounds from one place to another, from what they regarded as their old home(s) to what they expect to experience as their new home(s). They give up one set of senses of belonging, to acquire a new set of senses of belonging. The question, though, is to realize this is just one type of migratory experience. Once we limit, consciously or not, the migratory experience to one particular form, we create insiders/outsiders associated with that particularly frozen and typified form of migratory experience. The "native" people who arrived earlier, then begin to feel a sense of entitlement that those newly "arriving" do not (yet) feel. Migration museums, as such, would then be visited by people who feel they identify or not with particular types and histories of migration—forced or not, violent or not, enjoyable or not. However, to the extent that "migration" becomes defined more broadly as any experience of moving from one home to another, from one inner state or self to another, from one family to another, from one group or organization to another, from one university or museum to another, then suddenly the imagination and conception of the migratory experience, of what constitutes migration, its short-term or long-term history, its micro or macro dynamics, etc., is suddenly unfrozen, such that the concept and the experience becomes inclusive for all. This way, basically, all secondary socializations become interpreted, seen, taught, learned, and enjoyed (or not) as migratory experiences. Then a so-called recent "native" can begin to identity with the experience of a differently experienced migratory experience by other "strangers" because the "native" has experienced the sense of loss, finding, belonging, or stigmatization, stereotyping, humiliation, and outsiderness, in his or her own way. So, migration museums can be much more than just displays and/or experiences of cross-national migratory experience. They can be museums of all types of migrations without and within to more to and find new home(s). And, once this broader conception is acquired, then, the objectivation of learning and exhibition places to universities, museums, and particular journal issue publications loses its frozen significance, because now anyone, anyplace, and anytime can see, experience, teach about, and learn from, and more or less enjoy one's own experiences of migration in one's life-time.

One can go to "migration museums" out there to learn about and partake in the contested memory of migration experiences in a global context. However, provided that one maintains a non-binary epistemic lens, it should not escape our attention that we can also reflect on our own experiences, as more or less recent (personally and/or ancestrally) immigrant professors and scholars, and migrants of different kinds (and not just cross-national types), on the "museum" floors of our own selves and (for us as academics) universities, the "places" where we also seek to study, teach, and advance the sciences and the humanities. We are, ourselves, also global migration artifacts and textbooks, in need of self-understanding and re-experiencing of the nature of global and world-historical processes that have shaped who we are, and how we go about knowing the world and ourselves. I can't speak about the contributors' own personal experiences, but can briefly speak about my own, for the purpose of illustration. The advantage of migration museum visits—such as now, as you read this journal—is, after all, to study the migratory artifacts and experiences closely and by direct example.

Recently a colleague of mine kindly invited several faculty members, including me, to share and reflect on our experiences as "immigrant professors" by way of a forum on campus, one that is going to continue via a second forum next semester. I appreciated the invitation and considered the topic very timely and interesting. However, personally, as I expressed this in the forum itself, I had this discomforting sense of being put on display as an "immigrant (professor)," when, ironically, this has never been a part of my self-identity as a person—even though, based on all textbook definitions, I am an "immigrant." The "personal trouble" of being labeled an "immigrant professor" hit me as both odd, and interesting. I say "again," because this was not the first time I was confronted with the line of fault between how I experience my self-identity and how others view me. I recall editing another issue of *Human Architecture* a few years ago, one co-edited by Terry-Ann Jones and Eric Mielants (Vol. VII, Issue 4, Fall 2009), when at the time I reflected on the same experience in my editor's note to the issue, noting that "[w]henever the topic of migration and its studies come up, somehow, as far as I am concerned, the term does not personally ring an identity bell in me immediately. For some reason, the status of being an immigrant to the U.S. does not strike the core of my identity and sensibility. I have always wondered why, given that obviously I am, for all practical purposes, an immigrant from another region of the world (Middle East, Iran in particular) …" (p. viii).

There, I argued that what explained this discrepancy between the "objective" circumstances of my life, and my "subjective" identification with it (or not) has much to do with the negative connotations associated in the public discourse with migrants as "not belonging" in par with other citizens. The co-editors of the present volume also raise this important point in their introduction when they observe,

> ... the term "migrant" itself has been contested by "minority" groups that happen to have a long colonial history in the metropolitan society and are today formal metropolitan citizens born and raised in the metropoles but still perceived as "foreigners" and "immigrants." (p. 2)

In other words, the very term "migration museum" may sound offensive to some because it turns a secondary aspect of their identity as a human being into a primary identity marker, a marker that has at times been associated with otherness and outsiderness. They may also find it offensive that particular peoples are singled out as having had a migratory experience, when in their view all have had the experience, depending on how the term is defined, the type of "migration" experienced, and how one defines the spatiotemporal co-ordinates of the migratory experience. This is how I have been interpreting and experiencing migration.

I think such feelings as noted by the co-editors in the above quote may not be limited to long-established migrant families and persons, but to recent migrants as well, particularly those who have earned citizenship in their "host" nations or institutions. What seemed paradoxical to me—as I had reiterated in my Fall 2009 editor's note—is that from another point of view and standpoint, I regarded and still regard being a "migrant"—in the sense of not being bound to any particular national, cultural, spiritual, academic culture and disciplinary tradition, and being in turn "nomadic" and "migrating" across the borderlands of false dichotomizations and binaries—as being crucial for understanding and transforming social and self realities in favor of more just and egalitarian outcomes.

A further complicating consideration is that who is a migrant or not depends on the extent to which we come to realize how much of our subjective realities today have been intricately shaped by diverse cultural, ethnic/racial, spiritual, gendered, etc., elements such that for those who care to carefully observe and study their thoughts, feeling, sensibilities and biographies, they will find that there is literally no way one can find purely "native" or "migrant" selves within. Here, Gloria Anzaldúa's notion of our inner lives being populated with all sorts of selves and representations of people comes to mind. In other words, as soon as one begins to realize the extent to which what one has regarded as his or her "home" identity—be it a religious belief, cultural identity marker, disciplinary or intellectual tradition, theoretical orientation, etc.—is in fact an amalgam of many different ideas from a diverse set of traditions, belief systems, and cultural or aesthetic values, one suddenly may awaken to the fact that one has been, subjectively, a "migrant" all along and never at home with anything specific. It is just that one's personal, cultural, or ideological amnesia had prevented one to see the fluid and migratory nature of one's subjective belongings and understandings.

The reason being labeled an "immigrant" and an "immigrant professor" is troubling to me personally, therefore, is less that of being in denial of my own objective identity as an immigrant, and more that of being singled out as if others, the so-called "natives" in particular, are presumed to be any less of a "migrant" than those readily more apparent and on display on the museum or university sites—and this, in the racialized and xenophobic (in my case also Islamophobic, even though I do not belong to any single spiritual tradition) context of "not belonging" being a negative value associated with the label "migrant" acquires its added significance.

It would therefore be quite limiting to focus our studies of migration and its museumizations on macro processes, and especially its cross-national forms, and thereby lose sight of how the contestations of memories of what migrants can contribute to their new home (but in turn be denied acknowledgment for it) can take place in micro dynamics of our everyday academic lives. Exploitations of migrant labor do not take place just on agricultural fields or industrial shopfloors, needing then to be displayed second-hand on separately organized museum stands. These practices can take place on our university floors as well. And the exploitations should not be seen as ones simply belonging to lecturers.

Let me illustrate the above with an example. I know of a full-time faculty who "migrated" to his new university a while ago, where three then-colleagues eagerly approached him with the idea of starting a conference series. Two of these colleagues had been there for decades, and one had arrived a year before. Obviously, they had not initiated such a project until then, and were encouraged by the arrival of the new faculty to his new home to seek his contribution. It happens that the new faculty took the initiative in launching the conference series, always acknowledging, in writing, perhaps more than deserved, the input of his other colleagues in the process. The new faculty coined the conference series' name, listing its principles, took initiatives in establishing the basic structures of its annual operation, seeking funding supports, and serving as a principal organizer and proceedings editor of four of the annual conferences. Then, given conflicts already underway in the department before even he arrived—some of which these very same colleagues had drawn him into amid much fanfare and late night sloganeering and don quixotic plotting—when the conference series later acquired an international reputation and a good name, it just occurred to them that the conference series could be a wonderful item on their academic cv's, associated solely with their own names to support their own promotional, service, and other ambitions. So, with the aid of another faculty who oddly used the excuse of a poster's design to belittle the new faculty's many years of work, they took over the project from the fifth annual conference on—to which, the new faculty of course willingly consented to let go of the troubles, amid a personal illness he was undergoing at the time. It just then happened that in the foreword to the published proceedings of the fifth conference series they then organized on their own, when commenting on the nature and background of the conference series, there was no "memory" of the new faculty and his name in sight—and this, despite the fact that in an internal memorandum a year before, announcing the take over, one of these then-colleagues could not avoid reluctantly acknowledging that the "migrant professor" who had newly arrived from another university, had been a co-founder and principal organizer of the series for the previous four years. The "tradition" of the organizing committee of the conference series as spelled out in the foreword to the fifth proceeding simply "lost memory" of the "past" co-founder, principal co-organizer and proceedings editor of the conference series.

Contested memories of migratory experience take many shapes and forms and can happen anytime and anyplace.

It is precisely these sorts of subtler violences, and contestations of memory of migratory experiences—experiences that do not have to always take the form of cross-national migrations—in our everyday, including academic, lives that may escape our attention in the large halls of our global migration museums and departmental concentrations. We may then build magnificent migration museums and global migration studies for display on our websites and in our departmental posters, but in the very process of living our university lives end up subtly violating (even when apologies are offered) and belittling the integrity of colleagues and their labors for no good reason, in what they had thought to be their new academic homes.

When we speak of contesting memory in the context of establishing and running migration museums, we should therefore not lose sight of the fact that the processes of museumization of migration, on the one hand, and of academizations of migration experience, on the other hand, run the risk of transforming real and living symbolic interactive experience of agencies in everyday life into institutionalized contestations of second-handed, frozen, identities and scholarly projects that are further and further removed from the actual personal and historical experiences of actors in everyday life. So, we end up not seeing the trees for the forests of our academic or museal ambitions and busy-bodied strategic plans.

The question remains, however, as to whether the new advances in digital technologies in the Age of the Internet are making it more necessary, or obsolete, to rely on traditional and highly hierarchical and institutionalized forms of memory and knowledge construction in general, and more specifically as far as the experiences of global migration is concerned. Perhaps the very traditional notions of museum, and of the university, are being increasingly replaced as relics of the past belonging to "museums" with new modes of direct representation and expression via new digital and travel technologies that can make the building of formal museums and universities redundant in time.

In his "The University at a Crossroads,"[1] Boaventura de Sousa Santos asks:

The idea of a knowledge society implies that knowledge is everywhere; what is the impact of this idea on a modern university which was created on the premise that it was an island of knowledge in a society of ignorance? What is the place or the specificity of the university as a center of knowledge production and diffusion in a society with many other centers of production and diffusion of knowledge? (p. 9)

One can readily ask similar questions in regard to the process of museumization of migration and its consequent contestations as creatively and critically studied by contributes in this volume. In the context of a globalizing knowledge society, what and whose purpose does the museumization of migration in their current forms serve? In what way does the accommodation of historical memory of migration, as such, deprive people of real experience of other cultural heritages and traditions, and of alternative epistemic and knowledge traditions? To what extent the institutionalizations of migration museums and migration studies accommodate or inhibit our abilities to reflect on the museum floors or university campuses within our own intra- and interpersonal lives, and develop the necessary skills and know-how to understand the subtler migratory experiences we undergo everyday, wherever we are?

As an artificial ship in the midst of a great museum hall cannot capture the pain and the suffering the migrants faced in making the journeys from one home to another, the displays of "migrant professors" on campus forums, or belittling of their work after they arrived in their new home, or token inclusion of "other" faculty in de-

---

[1] See *Human Architecture: Journal of the Sociology of Self-Knowledge*, vol. IX, Special Issue, 2011, pp. 7-16.

partments while not respecting their contributions and integrity, cannot do justice to the complex realities of their subjectivities and to the appreciation of the subaltern voices they intend to contribute to the academic discourse.

Otherwise, both such museums and universities end up serving as legitimating vehicles for the status quo, their real prejudices becoming hidden behind the glamour of "diversity"-friendly and -fronted institutions that seemingly respect and equally appreciate different and pluriversal epistemic traditions and cultural heritages, when what actually passes as "true" memory and knowledge of how they belonged to the places and how their fared in making their contributions are those sifted through the "tolerable" assessments of powers-that-be, busily preoccupied with other important things.

Museum and Migration: An Introduction

Ramón Grosfoguel, Yvon Le Bot and Alexandra Poli

University of California at Berkeley • Marie Curie Research Fellow, Center for Research in Ethnic Relations (CRER), University of Warwick, UK • Ecole des Hautes Études en Sciences Sociales, Paris, France

––

grosfogu@berkeley.edu • ylb@ehess.fr • polialexandra@yahoo.fr

Abstract: This is a co-editors' introduction to the Fall 2011 issue of *Human Architecture: Journal of the Sociology of Self-Knowledge*, entitled "Contesting Memory: Museumizations of Migration in Comparative Global Context," including papers that were presented at a conference on "Museums and Migration" held on June 25-26, 2010, at the Maison des Science de l'Homme (MSH) in Paris. The co-editors were able to organize this event thanks to the support of MSH Director and President of the International Sociological Association, Michel Wieviorka. The focus of the present collection is on questions of representation and social agency of both migrants and museum officials. The purpose is to explore in a comparative perspective the complex and conflictive articulation between how migrants are represented by themselves and by museum institutions. The topic of migrants as social actors is one of the key issues explored in this collection. Migrants are not passive toward their lives and representations. They are social agents actively involved in their communities and socially vigilant of the way they are treated, perceived and represented by the host society. They produce also their own narratives and representations that are many times in conflict with Western hegemonic perceptions of their cultures and identities. Their strong presence in global cities and metropolitan societies today confronts the dominant society with issues of racial/ethnic discrimination and historical memory otherwise ignored by the hegemonic views in the mainstream of Western societies. Museums dealing with the history of slavery, the history of migration and the colonial history emerged as spaces of contestation. Moreover, the term "migrant" itself has been contested by "minority" groups that happen to have a long colonial history in the metropolitan society and are today formal metropolitan citizens born and raised in the metropoles but still perceived as "foreigners" and "immigrants."

––

The articles published in this Fall 2011 issue of *Human Architecture: Journal of the Sociology of Self-Knowledge* were presented at a conference on "Museums and Migration" held on June 25-26, 2010, at the Maison des Science de l'Homme (MSH) in Paris. We were able to organize this event thanks to the support of MSH Director and President of the International Sociological Association, Michel Wieviorka. He encour-

––

Ramón Grosfoguel is Associate Professor of Ethnic Studies at the University of California, Berkeley, and a Senior Research Associate of the Maison des Sciences de l'Homme in Paris. He has published many articles and books on the political economy of the world-system and on Caribbean migrations to Western Europe and the United States. **Yvon Le Bot** is a sociologist in the CADIS-Centre d'analyse et d'intervention sociologiques (Ecole des hautes études en sciences sociales/Centre national de la recherche scientifique). He participated in this project as a Marie Curie Intra European Fellow within the 7th European Community Framework Programme. He is the author of several books, including *La guerre en terre maya* (1992), *Violence de la modernité en Amérique latine* (1994), *Le reve zapatiste* (1997), *Indiens: Chiapas, Mexico, Californie* (2002) and has participated in numerous collective publications. He analysed wars between and within communities in M. Wieviorka (ed), *Une société fragmentée?* (1997); the relationship between armed conflict and movements based on identity in P. Hassner et R. Marchal (eds), *Guerrs et sociétés. Etats et violence aprés la guerre froide* (2003); the ambiguity of forms of behaviour in Mexico in the face of globalisation in M. Wieviorka (ed), *Un autre monde …* (2003). His most recent book is *La grande revolte indienne* (Robert Laffont: Paris, 2009). **Alexandra Poli** is a researcher in the CADIS-Centre d'analyse et d'intervention sociologiques (Ecole des hautes études en sciences sociales/Centre national de la recherche scientifique). Her work is focused on Racism and Public Policy against Discrimination. For a list of her many published articles see: http://cadis.ehess.fr/document.php?id=1150

aged us from the beginning to organize an international conference on this topic. This publication is the result of his strong support to our project for which we are very grateful.

When we started to organize this event, we were surprised by the fact that there is not much done in academic circles on this topic. There is an industry of publications about migration and another industry about museums. What we found was a scarcity on publications that link the two topics. Although there are some seminal works in the field of Museum Studies and in the field of International Migration, there is not much done in terms of research, publications and events related to the link between migration and museums. This collection is the first one of its kind presenting a broad comparative perspective on museums and migration. It focuses fundamentally on Europe but includes articles on Australia and the USA as well. Most of the contributors are specialist on international migration.

The focus of the present collection is on questions of representation and social agency of both migrants and museum officials. We want to explore in a comparative perspective the complex and conflictive articulation between how migrants are represented by themselves and by museum institutions. The topic of migrants as social actors is one of the key issues explored in this collection. Migrants are not passive toward their lives and representations. They are social agents actively involved in their communities and socially vigilant of the way they are treated, perceived and represented by the host society. They produce also their own narratives and representations that are many times in conflict with Western hegemonic perceptions of their cultures and identities. Their strong presence in global cities and metropolitan societies today confronts the dominant society with issues of racial/ethnic discrimination and historical memory otherwise ignored by the hegemonic views in the mainstream of Western societies. Museums dealing with the history of slavery, the history of migration and the colonial history emerged as spaces of contestation. Moreover, the term "migrant" itself has been contested by "minority" groups that happen to have a long colonial history in the metropolitan society and are today formal metropolitan citizens born and raised in the metropoles but still perceived as "foreigners" and "immigrants."

Questions of "national" identity are inevitable in these debates. Who belongs and who does not belong are crucial questions and the boundaries defining them are related to the foundational myths of the "nation" as well as problems of racism.

As part of the challenges posed to national identity by migration, Andrea Meza Torres does a comparison between Paris and Berlin in terms of what she calls the "museumization of migration." She compares two migration museums: the Cité nationale de l'histoire de l'immigration in Paris and the experience of migrant representation in Berlin. Her article documents how both locations served to link with the immigrant communities and to "stage a transformed revival of the colonial heritage." She addresses issues of representation of migrants in relation to each country's national identity.

Similarly, Lia P. Rodrigues analyzes the Danish Immigration Museum (DIM) in relation to Danish national identity discourses. Her article shows the blind spots and forgetfulness of Danish national identity. The DIM itself is a space that highlights this historical amnesia. Colonial subjects and some immigrants of color are not represented in the museum. History of Danish colonialism and present racialized subjects inside Denmark form parts of what Rodrigues calls Nordic amnesia linked to questions of racism.

Cristina Castellano also looks at the

way the US national identity is constructed in relation to ethnic/minority groups. She explores Chicago as a laboratory of diverse museums built by the ethnic/racial communities themselves from Asian, Mexican and African origins. Contrary to other countries, the United States has a tradition of national museums co-existing with small community museums. Her article discusses how these small community museums, built by ethnic communities whose origins are elsewhere, relate in contradictory and complex ways to the representation of the US as an imagined nation. We see here the strategies developed by the communities of color to negotiate the complexities of incorporation to the metropolitan society. At the same time she shows the limits of community self-representation in their own museums. While Castellano acknowledges the community museums in the US as a "political practice of free representation in institutions…," she goes on to note that "this does not guarantee a real social change in the ways of seeing practiced by people in every day life; this does not change the racial prejudices" in the metropolitan societies (p. 47).

An important dimension in studies of museums and migration is the role of the media in the representation of migrants. Estela Rodriguez's article analyzes the Cultural Heritage designs in Europe in relation to media representations and takes as a case study the city of Barcelona. She criticizes the myths of cultural hegemony and whitening of European cultural heritage. Rodriguez states that "…immigrants, who have lived among us for decades, receive scant attention from the media, which often associate them with situations of criminality, underdevelopment or subalternity, reinforcing the cultural imaginaries that negatively affect our perception of other cultures" (p. 50). These negative representations are constitutive of the way immigrants are perceived in European societies. She ends her article with an analysis of the Forum Universal de las Culturas organized by the city of Barcelona in 2004 and Catalonia's History of Immigration Museum where she deals with questions of education and interculturality.

As a promising note, the works of Ilham Boumankhar on Australia and of Véronique Bragard on Belgium emphasize positive aspects in the museum representation of migrants. Boumankhar examines the concept of immigration in Australia using as a case study of the Immigration Museum in Melbourne. She shows the role of the museum and its link to immigrant communities, showing the interaction and social agency of both. She uses this case study to show positive aspects that could serve as an example to other countries. Based on a survey of the visitors and interviews to Museum officials, Boumankhar offers a fascinating empirical research.

Véronique Bragard's important intervention in this collection is on Belgium's colonial history and its representation in the old colonial Tervuren Museum's exhibition "Independence 50 ans d'indépendance racontés par des Congolais." After looking at the history of Congolese migration to Belgium, she looks at the denial of Belgium's colonial past and the conflictive relationship with Congolese diaspora in Belgium today. Then she moves on to discuss in detail the exhibition and characterizes it as an important step in Belgium's recognition of its colonial past.

Further, we can see the search for justice and the active role of racial/ethnic communities in building museums in the work of Artwell Cain and Stephen Small. Artwell Cain documents the conflictive and problematic representation of African Diaspora in European Museums. His article reveals the active role of African Diasporic communities in The Netherlands as social actors in building a museum that does justice to its heritage and memory while confronts stereotypes and racism.

Finally, Stephen Small analyzes the

links between colonialism, Black migration and Museums in the United Kingdom. In particular he looks at the role played by Black agency in the formation of the slavery museum in Liverpool. He ends his article with the following statement that reflects the spirit of this volume and that should be taken seriously by analysts in the fields of international migration and museum studies:

> Because museums are racialized institutions; because they continue to house so many precious and sacred artifacts that were stolen or illegitimately acquired; because they are one institution among many in which contestations over grand narratives of national history occur; because museums about Black people arose primarily because of multiple patterns of migration; and because they reflect issues of access to resources, of power and inequality, then the link between museums and migration must remain an important issue of concern to social analysts. (pp. 125-126)

This volume should be of interest in several fields of scholarship such as social sciences, history, museum studies, international migration and postcolonial studies. We hope it will contribute to the decolonization of memory, knowledge and metropolitan spaces.

The Museumization of Migration in Paris and Berlin and Debates on Representation

Andrea Meza Torres

Humboldt University, Berlin

meza77@gmx.de

Abstract: In this article, the author takes an ethnographic approach to the museumization of migration in Paris and Berlin by focusing on the French migration museum, the *Cité nationale de l'histoire de l'immigration*, as well as in various examples in Berlin—such as neighborhood museums, art institutions and ethnographic museums. By looking at these examples through the perspective of social movements which have taken place in the United States and which unleashed debates around civil rights, the representation of racial/ethnic minorities, knowledge formations and the design of academic curricula, this article explores the ways in which actors engage in representing migration in museums and exhibits. The ethnographic cases show arenas of conflict and interaction between "makers" and "participants," in which the making of representations is contested. At the same time that the topic of "migration" in a museum can be used for a politics of multiculturalism, it can also open up spaces for political interventions "from below." The first part of the article discusses the strategies employed by the *Cité nationale* to represent migration "from above," showing the internal fractures and the conflicts which emerge when "immigrants" appear as visitors in the museum. The second part of the article shows ethnographic cases in Berlin, focusing on how the body of the "immigrant" as well as "immigrant communities" are used by museum curators as objects of display in neighborhood and ethnographic museums. The third part explores an exhibit in Berlin, which shows how actors of an immigrant association represented themselves and their community in an art institution and in their own terms. The last part compares the exhibits on migration in both cities and describes the political intervention of the Sans Papiers movement, which took the *Cité nationale* between October 2010 and January 2011 to fight for their legal status from within the museum.

I. INTRODUCTION

In this article, I will focus on the museumization of migration in Paris and Berlin as a continuum of debates on representation, which had a focal point (but not only) in the cannon battles that took place in the United Sates of the '80s (Cusset 2003). These "battles," which are closely related to issues of migration, unleashed important debates in all fields concerning representation: the formation of academic knowledge and teaching curricula (Fassin 1993; Beverley 1999), the practice of ethnographic writ-

---

Andrea Meza Torres is a PhD candidate at the "Institute for European Ethnology" at the Humboldt University, in Berlin. Her topic is "The Museumization of Migration in Museums and Exhibits in Paris and Berlin." Her work focuses on migration, representations and knowledge production. She has previously engaged with the institution of the Cuban National Ballet, the role of the "non-white," male body in the staging of representations of the "Cuban," and its migration and integration in Opera Houses in Europe and North America. Since January 2010 she is a member of the French-German Graduate College "Thinking Differences" ("Unterschiede Denken. Construire les différences"). She is author of the article "The postcolonial debate in France. Circulation of Knowledge and Social Dramas," which appeared in German, in the *Revue Trajectoires* (CIERA), in 2010. **Andrea** Meza Torres, "Die Debatte um das 'Postkoloniale' in Frankreich," *Trajectoires* [En ligne], 4 | 2010, mis en ligne le 15 décembre 2010, Consulté le 04 janvier 2011.

ing (Kaschuba 2006), debates on citizenship, migration and racial/ethnic minorities (i.e., Chicano and black movements), as well as on "national" identities. These debates reflect the battleground within the "ethnic studies" in the United States which is nowadays caught between multiculturalism, disciplinary colonialism and de-colonial studies (Grosfoguel 2007). They have reached the domain of museums and have naturally impacted the making of representations (Chakrabarty 2002). Museum landscapes worldwide have become important fields of research, as they are arenas where the crisis of the nation is discussed face to face with demands of social representation of immigrant and non-immigrant minorities as well as diasporas, and with questions arising from the fields of post-colonial and de-colonial studies. In my view, the migration museum in Paris, as well as exhibits on migration in Berlin, are examples of how these issues and debates from the other side of the Atlantic have emerged and become "visible" in both European cities. They also show the potential of the debates which can be unleashed around the museum which, in the case of both countries, concerns also the creation of images of Europe and of a new politics of migration.

I will present ethnographic cases in progress, which are the result of my travelling back and forth between Paris and Berlin from July 2009 to October 2010. During this period I have mainly conducted interviews with the actors involved in the museums and exhibits, aimed at finding relevant arenas of conflict. The cases presented here can be regarded as "objects" which have emerged through my interaction with the field of migration in museums and its actors. These objects are related to spaces in which established knowledge formations and social representations are contested.

II. THE "ENTRANCE" TO THE *CITÉ NATIONALE DE L'HISTOIRE DE L'IMMIGRATION*

My research began with the *Cité nationale de l'histoire de l'immigration*. Inaugurated in Paris in 2007, it is the first national migration museum in Europe. The museum is actually an enormous institution in which visitors can lose themselves as if in a labyrinth. Instead of offering answers about migration issues, the museal space opens up a field for infinite questioning regarding the making of representations in contemporary societies. After two years of observation, all I can grasp at the museum are notions of the complex dynamics of the institution. This can be due to the fact that the museum has no "centre" and it is made up of fragments: it is loaded with different contents, actors and controversies, and its structure is very weak. To give an example, neither President Sarkozy nor other important representatives attended the museum on the day of its opening, on October 9, 2007. In France, all national museums are inaugurated by the prime minister and the representatives of the ministries which financially support the institution.[1]

The *Cité nationale de l'histoire de l'immigration* has a very liminal, or marginal, existence, since it is a project to represent immigration—which is complex enough—unfortunately landing in a very difficult historical and architectural context: at the "Palais des colonies," at Porte Dorée, which was specially built for the colonial exhibition in 1931. I think such a heavy history carved in such huge stone confronts visitors with a complex juxtaposition of elements. And this occurs way before visitors enter the museum. Visitors are either encouraged to go on asking questions, or they are blocked by the historical overload.

---

[1] In this case, the ministries of immigration, culture, education and scientific research.

I will begin by showing an example of how confusions may arise: on Monday, the 21st of June 2010, I attended the "Fête de la musique," at the *Cité nationale*. The museum had announced its participation and engaged two groups to perform outside the building, in the courtyard of the "Palais des Colonies." When the "Fête de la musique" started, at around 7 p.m., the access to the exhibits and the museum was already closed. All that visitors could see was the entrance made of huge stone carvings and the logo of the *Cité nationale*.

The first group performed a piece about "dressing up" and, just after that, there was a music group. Both came from "Africa" or were associated with "Africa." The music was "African," the representation "African," and the visitors saw these evocations of "Africa" just outside the building, so the only thing they could link to it was the colonial history. The project of the *Cité nationale*, the permanent exhibit "Repères," which strives to change the images of immigrants in France, was hidden in the second floor of the (closed) museum. Thus, the logo of the *Cité nationale* was associated with the colonial history (the building and its stone carvings) and to contemporary diasporic and ethnic images of "Africa."

Beyond this example, it is important to say that, when the museum is open, visitors are immediately confronted with huge colonial frescoes—just behind the reception, on the first floor of the former Palais—depicting images of colonization, which justified the enterprise at the time. These frescos have been declared world-heritage by *UNESCO*. At both ends of this first floor, visitors can see the former working place of two colonial officers in the style of "art deco." Third, if visitors decide to go to the basement before climbing to the second floor, they land in the aquarium, where the fish are classified and contextualized in their habitats in ways that are reminiscent of how "non-European" peoples were displayed during colonial exhibits (Blanchard et al. 2002). With this, I would argue that the project of the *Cité nationale* is surrounded and oppressed by the history whose meaning it is supposed to change.

The scientific committee behind the *Cité nationale* (i.e., the historian Gérard Noiriel) had the aim to transform the meaning of colonial heritage through the making of a new project—by juxtaposing the exhibit and museal activities with the building, thus transforming the oppressive historical patrimony into a positive reflection of the past. Nevertheless, this history proves to be all too big and maybe unchangeable. Although there are actually activities in which schoolchildren, students, and other visitors are introduced into the history and the project, thus having very positive results (Gaso Cuenca 2010), the venue of the "Fête de la musique" was, in my eyes, a good example of how the project of the *Cité nationale* tends to disappear, eaten up by the building.

Nevertheless, if we do arrive at the museum's upper floor and look closely "inside" the project, we can see that the *Cité nationale* embodies the convergence of many departments—history, social organizations, art, anthropology, museography, cultural activities and pedagogy—which seem to work quite independently from each other. The project is quite large and open and, at the same time, the coexistence of such different departments and areas renders its existence very conflictive. During my fieldwork, I have talked with most of the main actors behind each department / area: with historians who took part in the scientific commission to make the *Cité nationale* and who decided to resign their duties in mid 2007, due to the opening of the "Ministry for immigration, national identity and co-development"—which, until November of 2010, financed half of the budget of the museum.[2] Further, I spoke with staff engaged by the museum and in charge of the departments / areas of history, anthropology, contemporary art, the collection of 19th and 20th century objects and with arguably the most important department of the museum: the network of immigrant and social associations (the "réseau"). There is huge work involved in each department, and the different backgrounds and aims of each section collide with each other at the moment of negotiation, thus provoking internal conflicts. This situation renders the tracing of a linear "history" of the museum's concept and trajectory very complex—but here lies also the great potential of this museal arena.

Below, I want to describe the small, temporary exhibit "Football et immigration. Les initiatives du réseau" which was organized by the network of social institutions and staged by the designer who was also in charge of the permanent exhibit of the museum. The exhibit "Football et immigration. Les initiatives du réseau" was located in the "Hall Marie Curie," which embodies the passage between the colonial frescoes and the "Médiathèque Abdelmalek Sayad"—the museum's library, which gathers works and key publications about migration. This small exhibit focused on social work. It was, actually, a miniature version of the main exhibit "Repères" in that its space worked as a platform for the intersection between many areas. The first area contained collaborative work of schoolchildren and art students: the schoolchildren had made up images of football and immigration, while art students had taken these images and fashioned a bigger collage—a representation—for the exhibit. The second area was made up of contemporary art works, which reflect also on the main topic. Objects of plastic art, photography, drawings, collages and video-installations were spread through the exhibit between the works of the other areas. A third aspect would be the representation of social projects in France and "development" projects in Africa, which intersect with football. Near the entrance to the "Médiathèque Abdelmalek Sayad," an electronic guest book, about one meter high, took the role of an object of the exhibit. Outside the "Hall Marie Curie," in the room with the huge colonial frescoes, visitors find two permanent brown cabins. One of them was bound to the exhibit. Here, visitors could access an intranet space to research about the social and immigrant organizations which participated in this exhibit.

The intersection between the areas was solved by the means of design—optic and spatial ways of organizing diversity and difference in the museal space. The exhibit was small, but elaborate. It showed the mixture between various representational techniques: first, avant-garde representations of depicting "otherness" (in this case, the images of "Africa"); second, "art deco" to organize heterogeneity in a national space (Rosenfeld 2005); third, baroque, as the representation of "migration" is bound to images of excess, proliferation and labyrinths—thus preferring curves rather than lines. Social work was also successfully incorporated to the design. By the way of repetition, this "design" elaborates a way to depict migration in the French context. This repetition has the potential to inscribe such images in the viewing practices and memories of the visitors.

Now, I will turn to the main exhibit "Repères." Here, design is worth mentioning, as it is not only what visitors might take in emotionally, through image viewing, representation techniques (installation in the space) and the audio-guide (which is also part of the spatial and visual ensemble), that needs to be considered. The

---

[2] The "Ministére de l'intégration, de l'identité nationale et développement solidaire" began its existence in 2007, thus being responsible of half of the budget of the *Cité nationale*. The ministry was abruptly closed in mid November 2010, and immigration affairs were transferred to the "Ministére de l'interieur" (Sperrfechter 2010).

design organizes knowledge and tries to fill up the voids of interdisciplinary work, discussions and (thematic as well as temporal) conflicts.

For example, concerning "history": chronologies and historical documents—like press articles, magazines, videos and migration laws—are organized in small tables, which correspond to the ten topics of the permanent exhibit, each one placed in the corresponding thematic area: "migrating," "facing the nation-state," "welcoming land, hostile France" "here and there," "living spaces," "at work," "roots," "sport," "religions" and "cultures." Important to note is that this strategy was adopted contrary to some historians' wishes, who would have preferred a chronological sequence to structure the exhibit's narrative. The designer, Pascal Payeur, worked much closer with the political representative of the museum, Jacques Toubon, than with the individual departments—the pressure to finish the museum in a period of political uncertainty was their main goal (Interview Payeur, 30.09.2010). This provoked tensions with different ways of documenting and displaying the collection.

Throughout the exhibit visitors can see personal objects and interview excerpts on video screens. These were collected by the anthropologist Fabrice Grognet for the permanent exhibit. Grognet has a perspective of defining migration which—contrary to historians who prefer the juridical definition—relies more in the self-representation and self-definition of people themselves as "immigrants." He did not only choose the objects as such, but he selected interview partners who were to leave their testimonies and biographies in the museum. He has a set of criteria through which he collects temporary or permanent donations (objects) from people for the museum.

Next, the art department would be engaged to choose contemporary art works for the exhibit. Throughout "Repères," visitors can see photography (artistic and documentary), painting, objects of plastic art, film and art installation. These pieces are inserted between historical facts (history tables) and the personal (immigrant's) objects. This department relies on other—aesthetic and thematic—criteria to choose what will be exhibited as art and naturally contrasts with Grognet's work, as it does not take people's self-definitions as the point of departure. Artist's origins or biographies are not supposed to play a role in the criteria. The department selects the works relying on the depicted themes and their relevance for the exhibit, and presents them to a higher commission, which attests their aesthetic quality and approves their inclusion into the museum (Interview Renard, 08.03.2010).

Having described this, I would like to comment on the difference between the work of the anthropologist and the art department. Based on a conversation with Grognet, I will show how conflicts arise between different (disciplinary) ways of collecting, displaying and producing knowledge.

In March of 2010, I met Grognet in one of the big meeting rooms of the *Cité nationale*. At one point in our conversation, he mentioned the temporary exhibit of contemporary photography, "Ma Proche Banlieue. Photographies 1980—2007," which was shown at the *Cité nationale* in 2009. This exhibit of Patrick Zachmann's photographic work in a specific banlieue had been organized by the art department. Grognet criticized neither the photographic works nor the exhibit as such, but the fact that it was placed at the *Cité nationale*. The exhibit showed pictures of a poor "banlieue," thus stigmatizing all "banlieues" and, further, the photographed people. The juxtaposition of the pictures' content with the *Cité nationale* proved to be counterproductive, as it puts the museum's aim at risk. Instead of changing prejudices against immigration, the museum would have actually achieved the contrary effect and thus reinforced the existing prejudices.

And here comes the interesting point, as exhibits do not end within the doors of the museum, but are also tied to people and to their bodies. With this exhibit, the museum was not showing contemporary artistic photography of anonymous people, but rather of real French citizens who live in Paris. So, what happened next? One day, according to Grognet, some of the photographed persons recognized themselves and complained to the museum. Why? Because they argued that they were not immigrants. They were, in administrative terms, "French," and did not want anything to do with the museum's narrative.

Here, artistic criteria had incidentally reversed the museum's aim: instead of taking immigrants out of mainstream discourses and making them look better in the French nation, it had turned "French" people into immigrants (!)[3]. This situation makes clear that the word "immigrant" has, in France, a negative connotation, which in turn makes the museum a political space of social struggle and contestation. Also following this example, we can say that the exhibit would go against the juridical / administrative definition of migration which, according to Amar (Interview, 02.2010) was agreed by the committee of historians at the *Cité nationale*. This is what Grognet meant when he expressed his unease that skin color might lead to false classification: immigrants are, as according to Amar, only those who are not "French" in juridical terms. This incident is very important, as it shows differences between anthropological collecting—which links images and objects to bodies and tries to reflect on this—and the dynamics of the contemporary art market and its difficulties when juxtaposed to the French migration museum. Grognet emphasized that, what troubled him, was that anonymous people were classified as immigrants because they had a somehow "different" skin color. He posed the following questions: "who was making them into immigrants? What if the photographed people came from the Antilles and were thus French? The museum is labeling people. And, unfortunately, the *Cité nationale* is not seen as a sacralized place like, for example, the *musée du Louvre.*"

This incident points to the role of immigrants as persons and bodies and their role in museums as images, objects and actors / performers. In the following examples I will go deeper into these questions.

III. MIGRATION AND MUSEUMS IN BERLIN: WHEN IMMIGRANTS BECOME PERFORMING ACTORS, COLONIAL HERITAGE AND / OR POSTCOLONIAL CURATORS

As I argued in the previous chapter, "people" and their "bodies" end up taking a central role in museal representations of migration—either as objects, as actors or, as we will see, as museum staff and curators—thus dissolving the border between established notions of "selves" and "others." In this second part, I will give three examples of the representation of migration in museal spaces in Berlin, which are closely related with this issue. I will take on three separate cases at three different levels, as Germany does not have a national migration museum and Berlin does not have a centralized space to exhibit migration. Nevertheless, there are numerous disseminated stages where migration is depicted—either directly or indirectly. In these arenas, the relationship between bodies, objects and museal stages becomes tense. The figure of the immigrant as a person who is represented in the museum,

---

[3] This reverses the title of Eugene Weber's book: *Peasants into Frenchmen. The Modernization of Rural France 1870–1914*, which appeared in 1976.

opens many questions concerning representations. Like in the case of the exhibit "Ma Proche banlieue," in the *Cité nationale*, the distance between represented images and represented persons tends to disappear, which means that the representations can be directly contested anytime. This "open field" leads me to think about the complexity of the crisis of representation, and about the social structures out of which this crisis possibly originates.

A. Immigrants as Curators and Performing Actors

The first example is a small museum in Berlin, the *Jugendmuseum Schöneberg*, which addresses children and young people in the district of Tempelhof-Schöneberg. The aim of the museum is to represent the history and contemporary society of the district together with two other small museums (Stadtteilmuseen) which make up a local museal complex. Since 2002, it shows the exhibit "Villa Global," which aims to represent the cultural diversity of the district's "neighbors." I take this exhibit because of the way it engages with the community of the district in its curatorial practices. Conceived from museum pedagogy, social work and intercultural dialogue, this exhibit has opened a small theatrical and social space, in which the display of "otherness" has acquired important dimensions.

"Villa Global" is a "house" with 14 rooms occupied by people of different origins who are residents of the area of Tempelhof-Schöneberg. To set up the exhibit, the museum worked with "real neighbors" of the area. The museum director and staff chose people with "migration background." The participants designed their own rooms, freely, choosing the topics, the objects and the representational strategies they wanted, and each participant made his/her own "installation." This opened very important questions about social participation in the museum. Moreover, this complexity increased at the moment in which some of the curators were incorporated to the museum as guides of "Villa Global."

In one of my visits to the museum in the Spring of 2010, I wanted to know more about the effect of "self-exotization" which had taken place in some of the rooms. For example, in the "Peruvian" room of "Mr. Rodríguez," I was confronted with many pictures of Machu Pichu hanging on the walls. The room was full of Peruvian and Latin-American symbols like Che Guevara, many CD's (salsa and afro rhythms), as well as a baroque altar with a saint. This particular room seemed more like a museum than a place to live. Also in "Mr. Odgesou's" room there was a great deal of tradition, but at least the visitor could sit down in a couch comfortably and watch a TV-series from Ghana.

Walking through the hostel, I asked the woman in charge of the exhibit about who exactly had curated each room and how. Her answer was: "well, many people… like, for example, myself." "Ms. Dubinina" had curated the "Ukranian" room. She showed me the objects and I had the feeling that I was actually in "her" room. We picked up the phone and listened to a conversation in her mother tongue. Afterwards, she told me where she had bought each and every object and the stories behind how she had taken them all the way to Berlin. As we went out of the room I asked her if I could see someone else. In that moment, a man who crossed our way turned to be the curator of the "Iranian/Persian" room. He had come back to the museum to check and replace some objects. We went into his room which was also full of many very traditional objects—which could also be, actually, pieces of an ethnography museum. "Mr. Bahadoran" made a performance with some of the objects while we talked about revolutions and exile.

Each room had a proper name. All names were pseudonyms, except for one:

"Layla," who also worked for the museum on the weekends. On the day of my next visit, "Layla" was standing at the entrance hall welcoming visitors, wearing an outfit with a headscarf—her usual clothing. She was not pretending to be someone else. She kindly showed me the exhibit and especially her room, which was a very intimate sphere, very elegantly decorated to display the story of her marriage and wedding party. She showed me a collection of headscarves, which she would usually show to schoolchildren and, also, her wedding pictures, one by one.

Afterwards, she took me to "Yücel's" room. This room is a very traditional, "Turkish" place, but at the same time very real—so it seemed to me. It had a little tea room, a bed, and objects and pictures of a circumcision ritual and feast of "Yücel's" own son. After the visit, Layla agreed to make the contact between "Yücel" and myself and, as "Yücel" was not engaged by the museum, I went to visit her boutique in another district of Berlin. There, we met and talked for some time about the display of intimacy and other topics. For example, it turned out that her son, some years after the opening of the exhibit, had kindly asked her to dismount the circumcision ritual, as this was beginning to become too intimate for him as an adult. We kept on chatting about how immigrants develop different personalities. The personality she had left in the museum's room was only one aspect of her; it was her traditional self, through which she lives some aspects of her life. But this image did not wholly describe her being. And, for this reason, she had her boutique, which offered a modern image of an independent woman. But this was also just one aspect among others. When she was asked to make the room for the museum, she had thought that the best would be to show a compact version—a collection—of her "traditional" self.

My trip to the museum brought me closer into the intimacy of people's lives and took me all the way to the other side of Berlin. Entering the museum in Schöneberg, I came out in the district of Wilmersdorf-Charlottenburg. I was quite surprised by this journey which started with coming into contact with a display of the real. The bodily presence of the makers in their own rooms opens up a contact zone, a space of performance between the spheres of curation, of the represented objects, learning processes, and every-day life. This is a stage in constant movement.

During an interview with the museum's director, Petra Zwaka (11.08.2010), we discussed the risks and advantages of this stage. The risk of self-exotization and the over-display of intimacy could become a problem, as the makers can easily lose the sense of the border of what to display and where to display it: a "carnival" effect. A further and very important problem was the generational gap. While the older generations tended to focus on tradition, young people showed other ways to represent their memories. This was visible in the selection of everyday-life objects, where older generations distinguished themselves by displaying traditional furniture while the younger ones preferred to bring items from Ikea. This generates an inter-generational tension between different ways of displaying otherness and images of the self.

Zwaka had tried to bring change in the exhibit by asking new people to move in as other participants moved out. Nevertheless, she was not happy with this and has plans to change the project.[4] The exhibit at

---

[4] This statement is very similar to what the director of the museum of the district of *Friedrichshain-Kreuzberg*, Martin Düspohl, told me in Nov. 2009 regarding the permanent exhibit "ein jeder nach seiner Façon? 300 Jahre Zuwanderung nach Friedrichshain-Kreuzberg" ("everyone his/her own way? 300 Years of Migration to Friedrichshain-Kreuzberg"). Although it has been successful, he is also unhappy about it: something has to change. The exhibit was officially closed at the end of 2010.

the *Jugendmuseum Schöneberg* has existed for nearly eight years, and the representations and performances are beginning to look dated. This instability is partly related to the generational gap, but also to the nature of migration exhibits, which have to be in constant transformation in order to make sense. Migration exhibits might have a short life, especially when they are closely tied to communities which are in constant change. Changes in identity and in the relations between transnational spaces mean also changes in representation.

B. Colonial Imaginations in Liminal Spaces: "Africa" at the "Carnival of Cultures" and at the Museum

The second example is a project of the Africa-department of the *Ethnologisches Museum* in Dahlem. This project stems from a bigger project specially conceived by Peter Junge, the head of the Africa-department, for Berlin's future *Humboldt-Forum*. In contrast to Paris, Berlin is a capital city "in the making," which is still re-organizing a whole range of representations and museal collections around the creation of the *Humboldt-Forum*, which will be located at the city's centre.

I see this re-organization through the perspective of the shifts which took place in France / Paris as collections moved prior to the creation of the *musée du quai Branly*. For it was this re-organization which, in Paris, paved the way for placing the *Cité Nationale* project at the building in Porte Dorée. As collections moved from Porte Dorée to the *musée du quai Branly* and to Marseille, the palais at Port Dorée was empty and could host the project of the migration museum. Now, a big contrast with Berlin is that the project for the *Humboldt-Forum* does not contemplate including the topic of "migration." Migration is, until now, a blind spot, a fact which has been heavily criticized in academic circles.

However, the topic of migration—although not mentioned—"filters" through the walls of the *Humboldt-Forum* by way of actors, bodies and objects. The Africa-department of the museum developed a project especially for the *Humboldt-Forum*, which is extremely interesting as it works with the notion of community, but under the image of a diaspora in Berlin. This project contrasts with other departments of the *Ethnology Museum* in Dahlem, which prepared projects for the *Humboldt-Forum* that engage with local, traditional, and ethnic communities in, for instance, Alaska or Mexico. The Africa-department seems to be working with a Nigerian community, but is actually working with people who moved demographically from Nigeria (their place of birth) to Berlin, that is, with immigrants who are officially associated in Berlin and engage in the cultural life of the city. Nevertheless, the museum does not want to name the immigrants. Junge explicitly rejects to make this shift, although he himself accessed a very important piece for his project in a place, which is permeated by migration processes: the *Karneval der Kulturen* ("Carnival of Cultures") in Berlin.

To transform the African colonial heritage of the museum for the *Humboldt-Forum*, some steps were taken since 2006: the first one was to present ethnographical objects as art ("Kunst aus Afrika"/"Art from Africa," 2006). The second, to extend the project with the exhibit, "Ijele. Zeitgenössische Kunst. Bamum. Benin" ("Ijele. Contemporary Art. Bamum. Benin") (September 2009). This new stage begins with a small room in which a big and colorful object is shown: the "Ijele Mask." This mask was made in Nigeria, especially for the "Carnival of Cultures" in Berlin and it is contextualized as part of the intercultural work of the association *Ikuku-Berlin*[5] at the Carnival.

---

[5] *Ikuku-Berlin's* aim is to promote Nigerian culture in Berlin/Germany. It was grounded in 2006 as a German/Nigerian initiative.

To acquire this mask, Junge had negotiated with John Durumba, the head of the Nigerian association *Ikuku-Berlin*. I was very surprised to know that the negotiation had taken place so easily, and that it had been the will of both—Durumba and Junge—that the mask be shown at the museum. Regarding this issue, I interviewed both actors and there seems to be no evidence of big tensions during the negotiations. During a conversation with Durumba (2009), which took place at *Ikuku-Berlin*, I asked him if he had gone to the museum or if the museum had called him. He answered the following:

> The museum saw the presentation during the carnival (…). So Dr. Junge (…) came to see the mask and took some pictures of it. And about three or four months later we had a contact, I got a call from (…) the "Karneval der Kulturen" director (…). So she called on me, then I went to her, we had a discussion, she brought the proposal, if it would be good to present it at the *Ethnological Museum*—and I said "actually that was my intention, that was my idea" (…). So that is how Herr Junge comes, and then we start a discussion (…). We lent it (the Ijele mask) to them for one year (…). (Durumba, Nov. 9, 2009)

Junge's version is similar. When I interviewed him on the 22nd of April, 2010, he narrated how he had seen the "Ijele mask" at the carnival and how he wanted to show it in the museum. This mask would be a rarity and he had only seen one outside of Nigeria. He had been surprised. Sometime after the carnival, while he was wondering how to get the mask, he had received a call from *Ikuku-Berlin*.

What is important here is the meaning of the institution of the "Carnival of Cultures" in Berlin as the contact zone between museums and social / immigrant organizations. The carnival was the place where the "Ijele mask" was shown for a Berlin audience. This means, that the object was already mediated for a specific public. And it was the carnival which made a quick contact possible between *Ikuku-Berlin* and the Africa department of the *Ethnologisches Museum*. The carnival played the role of a successful mediator between both takeholders.

Nevertheless, the ambivalence implied in the acquisition of the mask is what makes the representation of *Ikuku-Berlin* as "diaspora" very contested. The carnival is, on the one hand, an important place for social participation and for the display of cultural "differences." The roots of this type of carnival in Europe are usually traced back to the *Notting Hill Carnival*, in London. The *Karneval der Kulturen* in Berlin would embody its rhizomatic extension. But, on the other hand, it is also the place for self-exotizations in which objects made in Berlin could be seen as the "other." It offers a collecting platform for museum curators—among others. The carnival is thus a market of primitivism, which keeps representations in the stable place of "otherness." During the long weekend of celebrations, the carnival naturalizes participants and objects as "others." And it is in the context of this liminality in which the negotiation of objects begins. Besides the example of the Africa department of the *Ethnologisches Museum* I could grasp other examples, like the *Stadtteilmuseum Neukölln*, which displays a carnival mask from Colombia in its newly opened exhibit. And it is also in the context of the carnival in which Nigerian culture can be linked to Germany's colonial heritage—by the way of an object.

In the example of the "Ijele mask," I think people who have lived a long time in Germany are presented as a diaspora and in juxtaposition with colonial collections, thus silencing migration processes which anyhow threaten to emerge at any moment.[6] When migration lies at the background of a cultural process, it tends to leak through the representations and emerge in the margins of cultural politics or cultural productions, even in the contexts where it is not wanted. It can always emerge and make the whole ensemble of representations very unstable. This point has been criticized with regards to the *Humboldt Forum*. In her work, ethnologist Beate Binder describes how the planning of the *Humboldt Forum* announced a "dialogue of cultures" with a picture of an exotic woman dancer of the *Karneval der Kulturen* (Binder 2009:292). The carnival seems to have the most important role in regard to the representation of images of "otherness" in the *Humboldt Forum* project, and will thus acquire important visibility in Berlin and Germany. Emerging in Notting Hill, London, and travelling to Berlin, the carnival dynamics have been appropriated by local/national projects. The *Karneval der Kulturen* might fulfill the role of making and securing a peripheral space for the display of otherness, and of making this place stable enough to stage "temporary" performances—in which acts of participation can be simulated.

This is a very important phenomenon, because it can be compared to the dynamics of the contemporary art market which has been flourishing in Berlin for years. Returning to the exhibit "Ijele. Zeitgenössische Kunst. Bamum. Benin": If we go beyond the small room where the "Ijele Mask" is placed, we land in a space called "Contemporary art / Africa." Here, there is a clear relation between the museum and the art market—galleries and art biennales. The latter mediate images of otherness and make the contact between artists and ethnological museums possible. In the work shown in the exhibit, it is not clear through which criteria this art is representative of "Africa." The art market is a process by which art is mediated into museums and thus plays a similar role as the institution of the carnival (simulating participation of "Africans" in the exhibit).

But, on the other hand, there also exist art institutions in Berlin which play an important role in changing these dynamics. As I will show in the next example, democratic art institutions offer a stage in which "new" actors (not the traditional museum curators) can depict community work, transnational identities and migration in their own terms.

IV. THE IMMIGRANT ASSOCIATION *KORIENTATION* AND THE *NEUE GESELLSCHAFT FÜR BILDENDE KUNST*

To focus on the role of artistic spaces for the representation of migration, I will describe an exhibit that took place in an art institution, the *Neue Gesellschaft für Bildende Kunst* (NGBK) or "New society for plastic arts."[7] The exhibit was called "Shared. Divided. United" and was inaugurated in October 2009. The exhibit embodied the convergence of the immigrant organization *Korientation* and this art institution, the *NGBK*, of which practically anyone can be a member. At the *NGBK*, the rule is that five members of the curatorial board have to support a project in order for it to be

---

[6] This silencing of "migration" is a constitutive part of Germany's nation-building process. Kaschuba (2008) describes how the dramatic experience of migration has been normally blended, migration thus being conceived as "otherness." The psychological and social problems related to it are silenced, and so remembering often becomes taboo, and memory a trauma (Kaschuba 2008:310). This silencing process—where migration and transformation are taken to be shameful—can be seen in the experiences of "German diasporas," "guest-workers" and the "integration" of the former GDR after "reunification" (see Ibid.:295-329).

[7] The *NGBK* has been financed by the *Stiftung* (Foundation) *Deutsche Klassenlotterie* since 1969.

approved. Five members of *Korientation*—"first" and "second" generation, some with academic backgrounds, who define themselves as German-Korean—joined the democratic art institution and worked out a concept for an exhibit. It was approved. With it, an interesting representation of their work came to life.

The exhibit was complex and carefully elaborated. It also showed a continuity with concepts and work done in Germany over the past few years. When I interviewed one of the curators, Sun-Ju Choi, she confirmed that she and another member of the curatorial board had been part of "Projekt Migration" (2005–2006). "Projekt Migration" has been the biggest exhibit on the topic of migration in Germany, which heavily relied on contemporary art as a medium of expression. The importance of "Projekt Migration" is huge, because it brought together actors from many different disciplines. An example is the enormous exhibit catalogue, where the international selection of authors represents the academic disciplines of sociology, history, post-colonial studies, gender, and art. The catalogue gives space to images of art and documents related to migration. The texts were published in the original languages with translations. The publication/catalogue *Projekt Migration* shows similarities with avant-garde magazines like *Documents, October* or *Lettre International*. "Shared. Divided. United" was a unique exhibit in terms of the representational strategies it showed. The exhibit's narrative was built in the way of an art installation, as it created history out of objects collected from the people themselves who had lived the migration experience between a divided Korea and a divided Germany. It mixed works of plastic art with documentary pieces (video) and relied on the epistemologies of post-colonialism and gender. This was visible in the style of narrating the history of Korean guest-workers to Germany and on pictorially representing the gender division of labor.

Nevertheless, the exhibit "Projekt Migration," which took place in the open urban space of the city of Köln, had lacked much more participation from "non-German actors" within German society or, using the mainstream political language, actors with "migration background." This was the statement made by Choi during our conversation on the 23rd of November 2009. I think this has to be noted and reflected upon, as this problem comes up very often when interviewing "non-German" actors, and the issue will intensify in the coming years. The members of *Korientation* had felt underrepresented at the time of the making of "Projekt Migration" and this would be one of the reasons which inspired them to make their own exhibit. Choi stated that, although they had played the role of scientific researchers in "Projekt Migration," the decisions—the selection of historical materials, the "look" of the exhibit—had been taken by the "Mehrheitsgesellschaft" (members of the German social majority).

Thus, "Shared. Divided. United" can be described as a project of "continuity in difference,"[8] as it stems from the "German" project *Projekt Migration* and takes its representational strategies and conceptual framings to depict their narrative. But, at the same time, it develops differences and specificities. As Choi pointed out, "Shared. Divided. United" was conceived by German-Koreans only—all coming from the socialization of postcolonial studies—and from its natural counterpart, gender studies. Also, the exhibit relies much more on post-colonial epistemologies[9], gender

---

[8] I take the phrase "continuity in difference" from Gayatri Spivak's conference at the *Freie Universität zu Berlin*, on June, 2010.

[9] This was clear in the terminology used at the exhibit: the emphasis in „in-between spaces" and "shared histories/narratives" refers to the work of Homi K. Bhabha and Shalini Randeria.

perspectives and art (installation) as representational strategies than "Projekt Migration" and is a statement about lack of participation, affirming difference.

To come to an end, I want to make two last observations. Surprisingly, this last example makes me think about phenomena which I have been observing in Paris. The first one is: "Shared. Divided. United" was inaugurated at the time of the commemoration of the 20th anniversary of the fall of the Berlin Wall. It could be seen as an example of the engagement of immigrant associations in representing their histories and their contributions in the context of national commemorations. This shows a big parallel to what happened in France as the preparations for the commemoration of the 200th anniversary of the French Revolution took place in 1989. The association and archive *Génériques*, in Paris, created the exhibit "France des étrangers, France des libertés. Presse et communautés dans l'histoire nationale" (1989), which was made specifically for the commemoration festivities. Here, we can see how immigrant associations have inscribed social and cultural work as well as their memories in the national landscapes / memories through participating in commemorations of the "history with a big H."

My second observation is that, in both countries, some of the political activists and representatives of immigrant associations I have talked to show not only affinities with post-colonial and gender epistemologies, but rely explicitly on the example of social movements, which took place in the United States: the civil rights movement, the Chicano movement, the "teatro campesino" (El Yazami, 31.05.2010) and / or take events like the Obama election as crucial acts concerning political representation—which are far away from taking place in Europe (Brandalise, 28.04.2010). In my conversations with members from *Génériques* as well as with the representative of the *Migrationsrat Berlin Brandenburg*, it was clear that their work is based in transatlantic bonds and transnational networks.

In the field of representation, these bonds are presented through the means of plastic art and performance to build up in-between narratives. This is the way "immigrant" ("non-German" or "non-French") actors have taken to represent migration, their communities and their transnational bonds, as well as to empower and become curators in the scene.

VI. Conclusions

The projects in Paris and in Berlin show important points of convergence when seen through the perspective of the debates on representation and, also, when related to the fact that immigrants, simultaneously understood as actors, bodies and objects of "western" history, have found different ways to act and change the established narratives of migration.

The *Cité nationale* (2007–2010) as well as *Projekt Migration* (2005–2006) have developed representational strategies which have established ways of organizing diversity. Nevertheless, these strategies are made up from the standpoint of national perspectives, as immigrant groups and individuals are hardly represented in the overall making of the exhibits. All museal staff holding relevant posts in France and Germany lack "migration background."

Plastic art and design are crucial to creating spaces of communication and to including "otherness" into national and European narratives. Also, interdisciplinary approaches and the de-centering of the museum—making exhibits outside the museum, in the urban city spaces (like in Paris and Köln)—as well as community work are relevant representational practices. The display of "migrations" is based on a mix of visual and auditory technologies and the representation of biographies and oral history; this type of work intersects with ethnographical interview methods. Further, two European traditions of depicting "otherness" and displaying images of the "avant-garde" play key roles in "filtering" images of migration. These are "white / European" representations of the history of "Jews" and the "Shoah," as well as "Africa," "blackness" and "slavery"—these two being the most dominant diasporic representations in Europe (Vergès 2007). All migration—or the performace of migration— tends to be filtered through these "white or European-constructed" perspectives, thus running the risk of freezing on their way to singularity.

Beyond design and frozen images of the "other," which are also related to the geopolitical construction of the "third world," we have seen how actors and communities empower, thus establishing a continuity in difference (as curators). One important actor in this field is the association and archive *Génerques*, in Paris, as it engages in collecting documents, safeguarding memories of immigrant associations, producing knowledge (as an ensemble) and displaying migration through exhibits—and always in tension with official representations. In Germany there exists a similar archive, *DOMID*[10], which is not located in Berlin but in Köln and strives for a similar aim as *Génériques* (with much less success). As I commented in regard to political activists and this type of archive, it is important to observe their transnational ties with minority movements and transatlantic transfers of knowledge. Although the exhibits (as final products) may be presented as "French" or "German"—as they are shown in national contexts, are partially or fully state-financed and even juxtaposed to national commemorations—they emerge from transnational and transatlantic exchanges.[11]

Although the main difference between Paris and Berlin is that France has a national migration museum and Germany does not (one field being centralized, the other fragmented), the fields are not so divergent if we take into consideration that, even if the *Cité nationale* embodies a "center," the museum has no stability and no linear narrative—nowhere to hold on. The building, the departments, the various ministries which finance it, everything points to a structural weakness. It seems as weak as the small and temporary projects in Berlin.

In both countries, we find work between the museum and the communities. Here, the *Cité nationale* and the *Jugendmuseum Schöneberg* (as well the other Bezirk or Stadtteilmuseen) converge in their aims to work with communities and to think new ways of participation. The *Cité nationale* has given the space of the small "Hall Marie Curie" for associations like the (now disappeared) Turkish cultural association *ELELE*[12] to organize temporary exhibits (in 2009). Also, the Spanish association *FACEEF* mounted an exhibit with the *Cité nationale* (in 2007), but in this case it happened "hors les murs." This means, that they re-routed their visitors to the premises of the Spanish association, thus extending the scope of the museum to the urban space (Gaso Cuenca, 04.10.2010). The association *Génériques* played a much bigger role at the *Cité* in the big gallery

---

[10] *Dokumentationszentrum und Museum über die Migration in Deutschland e.V.* („Documentation Centre and Museum of Migration in Germany").

[11] A networking between different fields of knowledge reminiscent of the international character of the avant-garde. For the linking between Migration and avant-garde see Römhild (2007).

[12] *ELELE* disappeared surprisingly in April of this year (2010), as the *Ministry of Immigration*, decided to cut its financial support. All associations have been affected by this abrupt and unjust decision, but not all have disappeared from one day to the other, like *ELELE*. (Petek, 29.09.2010)

space dedicated to temporary exhibits, located just beside "Repères." They managed to present a bigger narrative (in time) with the exhibit "Générations, un siècle d'histoire culturelle des Maghrébins en France" (2009–2010).

Overall, one can argue that while the *Jugendmuseum Schöneberg* showed individual self-representations in "Villa Global," the *Cité nationale* showed this process at the level of social and immigrant organizations (as cultural units). We can observe how the museal structures open special—rather small and temporary—spaces for the performance of migration. Although individuals and immigrant associations perform, they do not enter the big stage of decision-making, as the concepts are made and knowledge produced by representatives of the national societies. From another point of view, this is a very contradictory situation: in the national landscapes, migration museums and exhibits on migration—although made mostly by "nationals"—also occupy the most peripheral places within these landscapes and have the lowest budgets.

The second convergence between the fields Paris / Berlin is the re-organization of collections and projects to stage a transformed revival of the colonial heritage. In both cities, colonial heritage is sought to be transformed and prepared for a new era. At the *Cité nationale*, this concentrates at the "Palais the Colonies" and poses a big crisis of representation for the museum itself. In Berlin, the Benin collections (like the Benin bronzes) are also displayed in "transformed" landscapes—designed for the *Humboldt Forum*—but are also very problematic as they link the performance of an associated group of people to a colonial history which is not critically examined. Like in the case of the previous examples, the German-Nigerian association does not impact the concept or decision-making of the exhibit. The project does not show "immigrant" presence but rather links them to their mythical origins and thus displays frozen images of "otherness." With this strategy, controversy and debate around colonial issues and German colonial history are silenced, as the project cannot be linked to debates of contemporary migration.[13] Still, this debate threatens to emerge at any moment in the grounds of the coming exhibits in Berlin.

The *Cité nationale* has always existed in a very threatening context, imprisoned between the Immigration Ministry and the history of the palace.[14] Since its grounding in the Spring of 2007, the Immigration Ministry applied an aggressive migration policy in the national and, in 2008, also at a European level (as France took the European presidency for that year)—thus going against the work and the initial aim of the French migration museum. Towards the end of 2009 and until the beginning of 2010, the Ministry launched a debate on "national identity" which threatened to revive ideas and sentiments coming from the far right. Further, the plans to build a *musée de l'histoire de France* (Thiesse 2010) threaten to dismount the autonomy of the *Cité nationale*, should the financial support for the *Cité* be rerouted in another direction.

---

[13] Kaschuba explains how this silencing is linked with a process in which immigrants are kept only in the area of "communicative memory"—gathered around immigrant associations, sport clubs and ethnic restaurants—but out of the area of the production of "cultural memory" (Kaschuba, 2008:315). Like in the case of carnivals and some co-operations with museums, immigrants are in "in-between" and temporary spaces, in the periphery and in the areas of "communicative" (Halbwachs 1991) and "performative" memory, associated with bodily practices and rituals, as Connerton (1989) points out. But these spaces do not impact the production of cultural memory (Assmann 2007), which is closely related to museums and objects, or knowledge (as stressed by postcolonial theory). The breaking of these taboos would unleash new debates on subalternity, power and representation.

[14] Since the beginning, there have existed critical voices who have argued for the use the palace for a museum of colonial history (i.e. Pascal Blanchard).

In 2010, Sarkozy's racist campaign to expel the (European) Roma with the support of this / his Ministry, took the crisis of national representation to a European (regional) level. The Ministry closed abruptly in November of 2010. Consequently, the budget of the *Cité* will be administered by a different ministry.

Further, the *Cité nationale* was occupied between October 7th 2010 and January 28th 2011 by the labor union (*CGT*) and the Sans Papiers movement in their demands for the promises of regularization that were made to them. The *Cité nationale* became their political forum. The museum remained open and adjusted itself to its new "visitors" and, during this period of "occupation," the gap between museums, colonial history and civil society practically vanished. Compared to this major event, the examples described in this paper look minor. The 500 Sans Papiers experienced their everyday-life in the museum, inhabiting the *Cité nationale*—sleeping, eating, washing and organizing their "dossiers" in the museum—(Sperrfechter 2010). And they also played the role of visitors, as the staff seems to have prepared tours of the exhibit "Repères." As Sperrfechter (2010)[15] has noted, they made an important political and symbolic presence—as the men (mostly from Africa) as well as the women and children (mostly Asian) have been mainly photographed in front of the colonial frescoes—thus naturally going all the way to colonial history and reviving old debates on representation and exclusion.

During my fieldwork, it was clear that the *Cité nationale* was not pulling much public.[16] But it has a public which comes naturally to it. When exhibits open their doors they bring people in—their bodies and their political presence flow into the museal space. As the place of struggle and contestation, the *Cité nationale* became the forum for demands of labor and citizenship: these debates reached the museum and its staff, making it an explicit platform for demands on representation. Now, the solutions are no more in the domain of curators, but extend to the general field of social / national representations and to the domain of politics[17]. It might be that the most the important political activity of the museum has been to offer the *Sans Papiers* space and support to prepare their *dossiers*, demand their regularization and, hopefully, acquire a "legal" status.

BIBLIOGRAPHY

Assmann, Jan. 2007. *Das kulturelle Gedächtnis*. München: C.H. Beck.

Beverley, John. 2004. *Subalternity and Representation. Arguments in Cultural Theory*. Durham and London: Duke University Press.

Binder, Beate. 2009. *Streitfall Stadtmitte. Der Berliner Schlossplatz*. Köln/Weimar/ Wien: Böhlau Verlag.

Bancel, Nicolas, Blanchard, Pascal (et.al) (eds.). 2002. *Zoos humains. XIXe et XXe siècles*. Paris : La découverte.

Chakrabarty, Dipesh. 2002. "Museums in Late Democracies. *Humanities Research*. 1: 5-12.

Connerton, Paul. 1989. *How Societies Remember*. Cambridge: Cambridge University Press.

Cusset, François. 2003. *French Theory: Foucault, Derrida, Deleuze, & Cie et les mutations de la vie intellectuelle aux États-Unis*. Paris : La Découverte.

Fassin, Éric. 1993. Le chaire et le canon. Les intellectuels, la politique et l'Université aux États-Unis." *Annales. Économies. Societés. Civilisations.* 1 : 265-301.

---

[15] Ute Sperrfechter works at the *Cité nationale*, in the department which organizes the cultural activities and events. She reported on the experience between the museum and the Sans Papiers in a conference in Vienna on November 19, 2010.

[16] Some interview partners said that the public was made up by researchers and PhD students, like me. I would be the ethnographer, fan and public of the *Cité nationale*—all in one.

[17] The occupation opened important debates between the museum and the ministries. It was the first time that a museum remained open and engaged with the demands of the "occupants". Nevertheless, it did not have a "happy end"; it seems that the debates which were unleashed increased the conflicts between actors and institutions.

Grosfoguel, Ramón. 2007. " Los dilemas de los estudios étnicos estadounidenses: multiculturalismo identitario, colonización disciplinaria y epistemologías decoloniales." *Universitas Humanística* 63: 35–47.

Halbwachs, Maurice. 1991. *Das kollektive Gedächtnis*.Frankfurt a/M: Suhrkamp. .

Kaschuba, Wolfgang. 2008. "Deutsche Wir-Bilder nach 1945: Ethnischer Patriotismus als kollektives Gedächtnis?" Pp. 295-329 in *Selbstbilder und Fremdbilder. Repräsentation sozialer Ordnungen im Wandel*, edited by J. Baberowski, H. Kaelble und J. Schriewe. Frankfurt am Main: Campus.

Kaschuba, Wolfgang. 2006. *Einführung in die Europäische Ethnologie*. München: Beck.

Römhild, Regina. 2007. "Alte Träume, neue Praktiken: Migration und Kosmopolitismus an den Grenzen Europas," Pp. 211-222 in *Turbulente Ränder. Neue Perspektiven auf Migration an den Grenzen Europas* edited by TRANSIT MIGRATION Forschungsgruppe. Bielefeld: Transkript Verlag.

Rosenfeld, Lucy D. 2005. *Inside Art Deco*. Surrey: Schiffer books.

Thiesse, Anne-Marie. 2010. «L'histoire de France en Musée. Patrimoine collectif et stratégies politiques. " *Raisons politiques* 37 : 103-117.

Vergès, Françoise. 2007. "Maputo, Canton, Antananrivo, Port-Louis, Durban... Diasporas sud-sud. " *Diaspora : identité plurielle* 72 : 58—63).

Weber, Eugene. 1976. *Peasants into Frenchmen. The Modernization of Rural France 1870—1914*. Stanford, California: Stanford University Press.

Conferences

Ute Sperrfechter (department for cultural activities and events of the *Cité nationale*) ""Une certaine idée de la France" Hält die *Cité nationale de l'histoire de l'immigration* ihre Versprechen ?." At the conference: "Migration und Museum," *Österreichisches Museum für Volkskunde*, Vienna, 19th of November, 2010.

Gayatri Spivak. "Aesthetic Education in the Era of Globalisation," at the *Freie Universität zu Berlin*, Centre for Area Studies, History and Cultural Studies. 10. Juni 2010, Berlin.

Press Articles

Piquemal, Marie. "12 moins de grève et toujours rien," in *Libération*. (Société). 07 October, 2010 : http://www.liberation.fr/societe/01012294960-12-mois-de-greve-sans-argent-sans-rien. (last visit: 27.05.2010).

Gruson, Luc. "Notre mission: être un lieu de dialogue," in *Événement. Le Journal des Arts*, No. 334,, 5-18 Nov., 2010 : 4.

Sicot, Dominique. "Entretien avec Luc Gruson. Le gouvernement leur refuse d'entrer dans l'histoire," in : *Humanité Dimanche*. 3 – 9 Février, 2011 : 26-27.

Websites

Link to the exhibit "Villa Global": http://www.villaglobal.de/ (last visit: 27.05.2010)

Interviews (in chronological order)

John Durumba, head of the Nigerian Association *Ikuku-Berlin* (Berlin, Nov. 09, 2009)

Sun-Ju Choi, founding member of *Korientation* (Berlin, Nov. 23, 2009)

Martin Düspohl, Director of the *Bezirksmuseum Friedrichshain-Kreuzberg* (Berlin, Nov. 27, 2009)

Marianne Amar, "Responsable du département Recherche," *Cité nationale*. (Paris, Feb. 12, 2010)

Fabrice Grognet, anthropologist, *Cité nationale* (Paris, March 05, 2010)

Isabelle Renard, art department, *Cité nationale* (Paris, March 08, 2010)

Peter Junge, director of the Africa-department of the *Ethnologisches Museum*, (Berlin, April 22, 2010)

Elena Brandalise, founding member of the *Migrationsrat Berlin-Brandenburg* e.V. (Berlin, April 28, 2010)

Driss El Yazami, Director of *Génériques* (Paris, May 31, 2010)

Gérard Noiriel, historian (*EHESS*) and former member of the scientific commission for the creation of a migration museum in France (Paris, June 21, 2010)

Petra Zwacka, Director of the *Jugendmuseum Schöneberg* (Berlin, Aug. 11, 2010)

Curators and staff of the *Jugendmuseum Schöneberg*: "Dubinina," "Bahadoran," "Layla," "Yücel" (Berlin, between April and August, 2010)

Gaye Petek, former head of the Turkish cultural association *ELELE*—which disappeared in April of 2010 (Paris Sept. 29, 2010)

Gabriel Gaso Cuenca, head of the Spanish organization *FACEEF* (Paris, Oct. 04, 2010) Pascal Payeur, scenographer of the permanent exhibit "Repères" of the *Cité nationale* (Sept. 30, 2010)

Luc Gruson, Director of the *Cité nationale de l'histoire de l'immigration* (Paris, April 06, 2011)

Danishness, Nordic Amnesia and Immigrant Museums

Lia Paula Rodrigues

Roskilde University, Denmark

Lia@ruc.dk

Abstract: Museums' images and narratives play an active role in the construction of collective memories. Since collective memories are integral to the politics of social and group identity, most of the controversy surrounding museums' representational practices depart from the question of who "owns" memory and what form of remembrance ought to be presented (Prosise 2003). Through an exploration of the Danish Immigration Museum's website, in this article the author discusses the dynamics existent between DIM's representational practices and its politics of exhibiting other cultures. In order to render intelligible such dynamics, the politics of remembrance (of particular cultural elements) and oblivion (of other elements) within the museum's system of representation are scrutinized. Methodologically this means that questions concerning the "semiotics" of meaning production—how the museum classifies, categorizes, and represents other cultures—are not dissociated from the "politics" of meaning production—how the museum construct, through the objects it chooses to display and the narratives it chooses to tell, master narratives about itself. Accordingly, the representations of other cultures invariably involve the presentation of self-portraits, in that those who are observed are possibly eclipsed by the observer. The article's goal is to address how colonial legacies—with their epistemic and ontological violence—continue to inform, implicitly, current dynamics of representations in Danish museums.

I. INTRODUCTION

It has hitherto been the nation-state task to maintain the geographic territory as a regulatory element for the maintenance of its imagined community. History has been constructed from the idea of the national as organizing principle, and thus from a fixed location. It is this entrenched Western (read Euro-American) view of the world as organized in nations that territorial mobility is envisioned as abnormal, and the "postcolonial" immigrant as a "threat."

The immigrant subject has from this optic occupied a deviant position—neither completely inside nor completely outside the nation-state, constituting, within the nation state's own views, peripheral postcolonial narrations without historical impact to its memory.

Lia Paula Rodrigues holds a M.A. in Cultural Encounters from Roskilde University and a B.A. in Media and Communication from Rio Grande do Sul Federal University (UFRGS, Brazil). The theoretical and methodological framework for her work is based on concepts such as gender, Diaspora identities, ethnicity, racism, social change and Afro-Brazilian religion studies (Candomblé). Rodrigues has worked extensively on issues related to the body and spirituality in the context of African descendent cultures in Brazil. Her research experience also involves developing alternative research methodologies and concepts with particular emphasis on the methods and applications of non-written sources in knowledge construction.

The appearance of a museal culture devoted to symbolically and materially represent the history of immigrant cultures, contributes in many stances, I argue, to the multiple and subtle mechanisms of minimizing the historical importance of the nomadic, the "strange" and the ("ethnic") "other" within the nation-state's history.

The Danish Immigration Museum (DIM) in Denmark is not an exception. What we observe today represented in the museum's web documentation is a narrative of forgetfulness as a political feature of Danish national and public memory.

Despite vigorous institutional argumentation for immigration museums as sites of memory, the praxis shows us that such sites have often yielded paradoxically forgetful results. In this respect, the Danish Immigration Museum discloses a complicated national relationship to immigration and immigration politics: namely the question of colonial memory (Blaagaard 2010). A closer look at the museum's photo archives shows us an absence of any historical record related to the Danish former colonies[1] and their presence in the Danish territory.

Nordic history seems to show us that there is a collective purpose behind the suppression of memory. The intentional banalization of colonialism serves not only as a form of selective forgetting, but also as an ethical issue concerning the political relationship between Denmark and its former colonies.

The negation of intense participation in the European colonial administration has enabled and still enables the Nordic countries to carry on its fictitious humanitarianism. The silenced archives of the DIM contribute to this non-history of colonialism.

Furthermore, as part of a vehicle for integration policies, the museum fails to address historically important immigrant groups whose presence in the country today do not necessarily result from colonial history, but constitutes part of the Danish history, most notably, the Tamil immigrants from Sri Lanka.

A report published by the European Monitoring Centre on Racism and Xenophobia (2002), reveals that of all the Scandinavian countries, Denmark is the least interested in its minorities at the parliamentary level (Blaagaard 2010:107). Resonating with most European discourses on migrancy, the Danish discourse on immigrants is highly xenophobic and exclusionary in character. Descendents of immigrants are officially called new-Danes; however, the reality is that once an immigrant you'll stay an immigrant forever: "You're a first generation immigrant, a second generation immigrant, a third generation immigrant, a fourth generation immigrant—you're always an immigrant" (Gilroy 2006).

As I will argue throughout the article, the Danish hegemonic discourse on migration materializes itself in the overall structure of its one and only Immigrant Museum. In spite of its function as a memory site, the museum is oddly overdetermined by national blind spots, thus highlighting how colonial legacies and historical "forgetfulness" continue to inform current dynamics of cultural representations in Danish museums in general and in DIM, in particular. Paradoxically, the immigrant museum then becomes part of a master narrative that the Danish nation articulates about what it means to be "Danish" (and modern).

Accordingly, departing from the analysis of the DIM's website, the following article argues that there are two cultural constructions at work at the website, firstly,

---

[1] I am referring to Saint Thomas, St. John and St. Croix in the Caribbean, Ghana in Africa, Faroe Island and Greenland (Faroe Island is a former Danish colony and now self-governing part of the "Kingdom" of Denmark; immigrants from both Greenland and Faroe Island are not represented in the museum due to their Danish "citizenship").

the hidden construction of Danishness through the selective choice of exhibitions and topics related to migrancy, and, secondly, the "invisibilization" of some historical factors associated to immigration in Denmark including potential cultural memories.

In the first part of the article, I will be concentrating on the forms of knowledge constructed by the website. By highlighting how the site is given its meaning by the institution that creates it, I will discuss how representation connects meaning and language to culture (here expressed metonymically as "Danishness"). In this section, I will be also focusing on the museum's cultural narratives. That is, the stories that are reinforced through the function of the site. The article's last part intends to briefly examine the absence of the Danish colonial past in the museum's website. By examining why this past has been "forgotten" and how such forgetfulness continues to reproduce itself as discourses on Danishness, I will touch upon the the troublesome issue of race in immigration.

II. THE MUSEUM

I find the Danish Immigrant Museum's website to be interesting because its embodiment in electronic media brings to the forefront a multitude of issues that are informed by recent challenges to the definition of museums as memory sites. The museum has existed since 1987 and the website was constructed in July 2009. It is also important to note that, at the moment (June 2010), the museum's physical space is under construction, which makes its website the only means of public access.

The museum's goal to configure as a site of memory is evident in the structure of their exhibitions and the organization of their data; however, the site delivers basic information without really looking broadly at who might consume the information in the viewing public. That is particularly clear in the textual compositions of the website. Many of the links from the menu in the front page leads us to monological theoretical discussions of issues concerned with migration, without even presenting any artifacts or historical data on the issue being debated (see http://www.immigrantmuseet.dk/). It is evident that the site has a clear rhetorical preoccupation in engaging with the public debates related to migration in Danish media. This rhetorical urge seems to reflect the ideological interests of the museum staff more than it accommodates the needs of the audience.

In the following sections I will present a few selected links from the museum's website from which my discussions will depart.

III. THE MONOLINGUAL MUSEUM

"Language communicates attitudes, reflects traditions and conveys human relationships. On the one hand, language is an important part of an individual identity. On the other hand language marks affiliation to a group. Therefore language is often highlighted as an important element of integration." (DIM, June 2010 http://www.danishimmigrationmuseum.com/index.php?page=sprog)

The quote above is an example of one of the many discourses constructed by the museum. Language is the thematic subject under discussion in this link. I find the quote worthy of note because it reveals the twofold purpose of the text; the desire to articulate the use of mother tongues with identity politics, and the concealed message about the importance for immigrants to learn the host *country's language* for their successful integration. My argument in what follows is that the text above is inserted within the usual questions of politics of representation, placing, in this way, the juridical framework of identity politics—who has the right to speak? And who has the right to represent others?—right at the heart of the museum's signifying practice.

In order to contextualize the discussion, I can inform the reader that foreigners seeking residency through family reunification or political exile in Denmark are required to pay DKK 1406.00 for a Danish language test (Studieprøven) . In addition to testing Danish language skills, the exam also requires a residency applicant to know general facts about Danish culture and society.

 The test is composed of 200 questions in 11 areas ranging from the Danish royalty, local geography and the economy. Applicants have 60 minutes to answer 35 of the standard questions as well as five problems dealing with current events.

Applicants must correctly answer 28 questions to pass the test. And while they can re-take the test as many times as they wish, this particular test costs EUR 189.00 to take.

Reactions to the citizenship test have been mixed. A number of left-wing politicians and education experts have suggested it concentrates too much on obscure historical and political details that even Danes might have difficulty answering correctly. According to an article in Information, a Danish newspaper, several Danish university students struggled to pass the test. One student, Patrick, only managed to answer 29 questions correctly and admitted he found the test difficult: "I learned about a lot of the things it asks in school, but I've forgotten them again," he said. Another student, Natalia, felt that "the test concentrated too much on history" (Information 2006, June 28th).

I am arguing here that the website is a medium through which the museum's (and "Danish") thoughts, meanings and values are disseminated. The production of meaning in the text above seems to be telling us more about what the museum (and Denmark) consider important in terms of the relationship between language and integration, than the contribution of different mother tongues to Danish identity politics through the history of immigration in Denmark. Topics like the influence of foreign languages on the Danish language or the dialects and slangs spoken by the Arabic speaking urban youth are completely dismissed. Besides, the website does not give one single example of the multiple immigrant languages spoken in Denmark today (see http://www.danishimmigrationmuseum.com/index.php?page=sprog).

The politics of language, like religion, is highly ideologically charged—not least as a result of the national language ideology (as represented in the text above). The overall stance taken by Danish migratory policies is to discourage the toleration and promotion of immigrant languages due to the danger of ghettoification which, according to their rethoric, bears the risk of political fragmentation and community unrest. Such policies neither intend to promote the language rights of immigrant individuals, nor work to find a balance between the claims of individual language rights and the interests of the nation-state.

In the following I will tentatively discuss the mechanisms by which the museum constructs the "idea" of Danishness through the exhibition of objects brought by immigrants.

IV. Representing the Self through Others

Looking at the museum's collection, we find a curious interest in gathering traditional Christmas objects from Christmas around the world. This link is only found in the Danish version of the website (see http://www.immigrantmuseet.dk/index.php?page=alias-22). The most noteworthy about the link is its emphasis on the meaning of Christmas objects *for* Denmark.

In the translated Danish text below, we are informed about the history of the first Christmas tree brought by German immigrants to Denmark. The text's first paragraph bears quoting:

> "The Christmas tree is a European custom which came to Denmark from Germany. The first Christmas tree in Denmark was lit in 1808 at the Holsteinsborg property in Sealand (Sjælland in Danish). In Copenhagen, the first Christmas tree stood by the Lehmann family at New Kongensgade in 1811" (See http://www.immigrantmuseet.dk/index.php?page=juletret).

Christmas traditions are a very important element in the discourse on Danishness, and the "Christmas tree" can be considered to be the Nordic ethnographic object per excellence. The only problem, in the context of our discussion, is that discourses on the meaning of Christmas objects brought by immigrants for *Danes* tend to minimize the role material objects play for (non-Christians) immigrants to surmount the complex situations and emotional instability associated with the process of migration. The immigrant's material culture, their objects, plays a significant role in achieving self-remembering, self-representation and home (re)making.

This does not mean that I am arguing for the exhibition of immigrant's material culture as the only factuality of their sociocultural complexity. Rather what I am suggesting is that the over-representation of Christmas objects in the museum's collection tells us a lot about the manner in which the museum make certain objects meaningful, and how it constructs discourses through these objects display.

The website's emphasis on Christmas traditions speaks for itself bearing in mind that Islam is the largest minority religion in Denmark (statistics from august 2009: Blaagaard 2010). Nordic public and political debates often conflate the notion of "migrant" with the notion of "Muslim" (Jensen:2006). Norway's Constitution, for instance, requires that over half of the government cabinet are members of the state church (Human Rights Report 2008). In Denmark, a newly implemented migration law has created a quota that allows 500 refugees with a Christian religious background to access the country every year (ENAR Shadow Report 2004). Such political practices suggest that the Nordic nation-state's idea of integration/assimilation is powerfully informed by Lutheran-Protestant Christian classifications. As argued here, these (Islamophobic) practices point to the omission of other potential narratives, and omission of subjectivities that might generate cracks in the discourse about Nordic secular history and culture (Gullestad 2005).

It is uncontested that migration is not just about citizens crossing borders from homeland to host-countries; it also incorporates global movements of material and immaterial things. As I attempted to argue above, the museum's priority to select objects which seem the very epitome of the notion of mono-culturality (like the Christmas tree) and its concern in maintaining the idea of a "national language'" are part of a textual complicity which reveals a certain urge in communicating values concerned with the preservation of "Danishness." The multilingual, the pluri-religious and the intercultural society are still marginalized values in the museum´s discursive practices.

My main goal in this first part of the article has been to discuss what scholar

Jeanne Canizzo calls "museum as cultural text" (1998). Jeanne Canizzo sees the museum as a cultural text "that may be read to understand the underlying cultural and underlying assumptions that have informed its creation, selection and display" (Canizzo 1998:151). Resonating Canizzo's views, I have explored how implicit discourses of Danishness shape the museum's website textual content and the museums choice of exhibited artefacts.

In the following section the focus will be on the "silenced" archives of DIM. The general idea in this last section is to understand how the choice to "forget" or "look away" can function both on an historical level and on the level of representational practices.

V. THE "FORGOTTEN" IMMIGRATION: THE SILENCED IMMIGRANT GROUPS

By January 2009, the immigrant population in Denmark (though literally defined, referring to immigrants, refugees and descendants from all countries) made up 500,036, or 8.3%. of the total Danish population of 5,400,640 people (Danish statistics 2009). The term "immigrant population" includes in a statistical and formal manner people of both "Western" (29.2%) and "non-western" (70.8%) origins (Denmark statistics 2009). Immigrants with origin in Somalia, Lebanon, Afghanistan and Iraq have the lowest attachment to the labour market. The so-called original/working-immigrants; Turks, Pakistanis and Yugoslavs, are still among the largest immigrant groups in Denmark (Goli 2007:60).

The term 'immigrants' includes both foreigners and naturalized citizens. However, in the real world the term only refers to immigrant and descendants of non-western origin. The label 'descendants' means children born in Denmark, where at least one of the parents is foreign citizen born abroad—children born in other countries would be immigrants themselves.

40.4% or 178,491 of the total immigrant (including descendants) population in Denmark are Danish citizens of a different ethnic/national background (Goli 2007:61) who paradoxically are counted among immigrants, making the picture tremendously blurred. The complete survey of all immigrant groups existent in Denmark today would exceed the limits of this essay, suffice it to say for now that not all immigrants living in Denmark today are portrayed in the museum's website (http://www.danishimmigrationmuseum.com/index.php?page=grupper).

There is no apparent explanation for which criteria were used to choose these groups, other than other immigrant groups. Perhaps a look into the historical past may be helpful in order to understand why some stories are told over and over again and others are "forgotten."Among the immigrant groups represented in the website we find descriptions of what the museum calls the "potato Germans," the "Moravian," the "Somalis," the "Romani people," the "forgotten" Swedish workers, the "German-, Palestinian-, Russian and Hungarian refugees," and the "Turks" (Ibid.).

In his work "Silencing the Past: Power and the Production of History" (1995), the Haitian historian Michel-Rolph Trouillot uses the concept "silencing the past" to show how unimaginable or undesirable events are systematically written out of history—he highlights how "unthinkable" the history of the Haitian revolution was and still is. This forgetfulness can be seen, he argues, as an *activity* (Trouillot 1995) and not how we generally perceive it: as absence and motionlessness: a non-activity.

The case of the Danish Immigrant Museum is particularly illuminating. As an example of the "activity" of forgetfulness towards immigrants who generated cracks in the discourse about Danish self-perception, I will briefly introduce, in the following, one group of immigrants whose existence is not registered in the website, but whose presence provoked a heavy political havoc in Denmark: the group of immigrants and refugees from Sri Lanka.

VI. Nordic Amnesia I—The Tamil Case

According to official statistics 7,147 people of the origin of the island of Sri Lanka (Immigration Service 2009) live in Denmark today. The Sri Lanka Tamils came to Denmark in the eighties as refugees from the civil war. In 1987, the justice minister Erik Ninn-Hansen decided to decrease by law the number of Tamil family reunifications, which was justified by the improvement of the civil war situation in Sri Lanka. Nevertheless, the law clearly ensured the Tamil refugees the right to family reunification rendering Hansen's order, known as the Tamil case, illegal (Henrichsen 1993:10). When the case appeared in the media, several political parties opposed to the re-election of Erik Ninn-Hansen and others demanded an in-depth investigation, ultimately leading to the resignation of Erik Ninn-Hansen as justice minister in 1989 (Henrichsen 1993:10).

Four civil servants in the Department of Justice were charged and the justice minister was put before the court of impeachment, which led to the fall of the Poul Schlüter Conservative government in 1993. In 1995 Erik Ninn-Hansen was found guilty of three cases of power abuse and received a suspended sentence of 4 months of prison (Herichsen 1993:11). The official report on the "Tamil case"—a great work of 2218 pages (in addition, lawsuit 2782 pages and annexes 634 pages)—had a huge media repercussion during the 90s.

My point in bringing the "Tamil case" into light is that the Danish Immigration Museum's narratives does not emerge in a political vacuum, but rather reflects national blind spots. The Tamil case is one of the events that are well-known yet systematically and actively forgotten, considered unworthy of contemplation or unimportant in a museal context, even when it concerns an immigration museum.

VII. Nordic Amnesia II—Colonial History

When it comes to the history as well as the non-history or silence of Nordic colonialism, indifference occurs simultaneously with forgetfulness.

As seen in the previous discussion, there are groups who are remembered and those who are selectively forgotten. It is not common knowledge that Denmark was the seventh largest slave-trading nation during colonial times—the US being the sixth (Gøbel 1996). Information on colonial history is available in history books in Denmark but is not considered worthy or important for the country's understanding of their present (Blaagaard 2010).

In the following I will briefly present a list of the Danish former colonies (Gøbel 2002, Oommen 2005):

Europe
- Faeroe (1380/1536/1814 to present, although it exercises a large degree of autonomy from Denmark.)
- Iceland (1380/1536/1814 to 1918, after that fully sovereign state united with Denmark under a common king and since 1944 an independent parliamentary democratic republic.)
- Danish Estonia (1206-1645)
- Shetland Islands (1380-1469)
- Orkney Islands (1380-1469)

Arctic
- Greenland (1814 to 1979, since then largely autonomous)

America
- Danish West Indies (1666 to 1917)
- St. Thomas (1672)
- St. John (1683)
- St. Croix (former French West Indies Company) (1733)

Asia
- Danish East India
- Nicobar Islands (*Ny Danmark - Neu-Dänemark* 1756-1848/1868)
- Serampore (also *Frederiksnagore* in Bengal, 1755-1845)
- Tranquebar (Danish: *Trankebar*, sea port in India, 1620-1845)

Africa
- Ghana Denmark established several short term bases and fortresses at the Gold Coast in West Africa, today the coast of Ghana, in the 17th and 18th centuries.
- Ningo: Fort Fredensborg (1734-March 1850)
- Accra/Osu: Fort Christiansborg (1658-April 1659,1661-Dec 1680, February 1683-1693,1694–1850)
- Tshe: Fort Augustaborg (1787-March 1850)
- Keta: Fort Prinsenstein (1780-12 March 1850)
- Ada: Fort Kongensten (1784-March 1850)
- Amanful/ Amanfro: Fort Frederiksborg (1659-16 April 1685)
- Anomabu: Fort William (1657)

Despite the fact that there is no overarching master narrative in understanding the history of Danish colonialism, the list of Danish former colonies above certifies that the Danish kingdom had substantial colonial possessions.

Denmark has through its journalistic practices and educational and cultural institutions, privileged and prolonged a cultural amnesia through a silencing of colonial historical events.

This suspension of discourse kept Danes crimeless and irreproachable despite their continuous encounter with colonial subjects. Greenlanders are, for instance, an embodied presence of the colonial subject up to date in the country.

For the sake of our discussion on museums and their relation to migration we might ask: What are the political implications of the decision to perform historical events in the way it is done by eclipsing their existence as we see in the website of the museum? In short, who got to speak, who was heard and who was silenced? And, in what ways do colonial legacies continue to inform patterns of immigration policies, historical memory and museal representations?

VIII. Concluding: The Presence in Absence

I believe that the concept of "coloniality" as formulated by the Peruvian scholar Anibal Quijano (2000) may be a helpful analytic tool for understanding the modern/colonial Denmark and the questions posted above.

In my reading, coloniality shows us that modernity is not teleologically ordered; on the contrary, it carries the concept of coloniality within itself. If it has been the Western world's task to define modernity as living a present time continuous with the past, coloniality is a helpful concept because it cuts across the linearity of time, showing us another historical temporal logic. We find out that power relations in the present are not fundamentally different from power relations in the past. It is within this grammar, that *Quijano* uses the concept of *coloniality of power* to show the colonial elements in the model of *power* that today is globally hegemonic.

Two historical processes associated with the constitution of coloniality of power are important to mention: the social classification of the world's population around the idea of "race" (Quijano 2000), and the constitution of a new structure of control of labor which was also based on the ideology of racial classification. Coloniality of labor control determined the social geography of capitalism to be in the West (Quijano 2000:538).

Europeans in general, and Danes in particular, have astutely denied consciousness of those others who helped to accumulate the wealth through coloniality (wealth that, for instance, allowed Denmark to construct their modern welfare state). On the other hand, "coloniality of power" does not stand alone, besides coloniality of power there are "coloniality of being" and "coloniality of knowledge" (Maldonado-Torres 2007).

The basic assumptions behind "coloniality of being" and "coloniality of knowledge" is that the historical negation of the cognitive faculties of racialized others has provided the basis for their ontological negation (Maldonado-Torres 2007).

If we assume that European modernity or classical epistemology is built upon an anthropological colonial difference (as Maldonado-Torres argues) and that anthropological colonial difference is based on race, we are getting close to understanding racism as structural to the modern nation-state.

The irrational myth of modernity (de-linked from coloniality) (Mignolo 2000), and its epistemic and ontological violence, is the root, I argue, of the Danish social imaginary and its amnesia. These imaginary constructs "distorted ideas of common sense; an obscure *taken-for-grantedness*, which limits self-criticism by mystifying issues" (Blaagaard 2010:104). This is present in the public sphere; that is, social structures of representation such as libraries, architecture, museums, the press and publishing houses, public and government institutions.

Paul Gilroy uses the concept of agnotology in order to describe the patterned forms of ignorance present in the Nordic countries. Agno-politics is a form of structural blindness that produces a "new racism" (rather than a more easily condemnable overt racism) (Gilroy 2006).

The problem with concepts seeking to understand "new" forms of racism, as "recent" types of racism, is that they do not seem to assume racism to be structural to the concept of modernity. I do not believe in new forms of racism, particularly because lately the concept of new-racism emerged rhetorically in Scandinavia as if racism was a new phenomenon, as something that did not exist for a moment, and returns unexpectedly from an unknown past. The Nordic history shows us that the phenomenology of racism has always been racist, independently of its discursive morphology.

Lewis Gordon argues in "Bad Faith and Antiblack Racism" (1995) that everyone can succumb to ethnic hatred. In fact, this is predominantly what the concept of racism as bad faith communicate—"that racism should be understood as a permanent possibility (or even a permanent temptation) that is interwoven with the dynamics of human existence itself" (van Leeuwen 2008).

According to Gordon, the racist perceives himself as "presence," while the racial other is construed as "absence" or "emptiness" (Gordon 1995:35).

As I have argued throughout this article, the forms of knowledge constructed in the museum's website, the texts and artefacts it chooses to exhibit, discloses the strategies of a host country representing immigrants through a narrative of its own history and values as a norm. The history of migration that the Danish Immigration Museum presents to us is part of a master narrative of Danish modernity, wherein modernity is delinked from its colonial history. This is a statement that requires some unpacking.

Collecting Christmas objects from immigrants around the world, when the majority of immigrants in Denmark have a Muslim religious background, is a construction of an absence. In this way the website is also constructing a history of the good and the visible immigrant who brings the good objects, like Christmas trees, to Denmark. Through the lenses of Gordon's theories, I propose that Danishness is reified as presence in the website through the rhetoric of the "modern/colonial" world (Mignolo 2000); it is the racism inherent to this rhetoric that makes invisible the "bad" immigrant "other." The dynamics of presence/absence with regards to one's own location (ethnical, cultural and economic) are very complex in the context of DIM. As I have argued, the museum is not only representing the material and symbolic culture of immigrants; discourses on immigrant culture occur simultaneously with constructions of Danishness. Danishness, on the other hand, has also a racial dimension understood as the embodiment of universality and normativity. "Whiteness," in the context of the website, becomes the "axiom" as well as something invisible—"everything and nothing" (Dyer 1997).

This fictitious transcendental position is maintained, as I have argued, through the three colonialities: of power, of being and of knowledge; that is to say, the negation of the history and presence/existence of the colonial and immigrant "other."

The irrational myth of modernity is kept through master narratives told in various institutions, by different agents with multiple purposes, one of them, as we have seen above, been told through the invisibilization of potential cultural and historical memories while making national values and icons hyper-visible.

Resonating with Lewis Gordon's theory on racism, the racial other—in this case the "ethnic" immigrant—in the racist's universe is perceived as a lack of being (Gordon 1995:132), often in combination with the claim that the racist perceives him- or herself as universal presence of being.

REFERENCES

Blaagaard, B. Bolette (2010): "Remembering Nordic Colonialism: Danish Cultural Memory in Journalistic Practice." Kult 7 - Special Issue, *Nordic Colonial Mind* Spring 2010. Department of Culture and Identity. Roskilde University.

Canizzo, Jeanne (1998): "Gathering Souls and Objects: Missionary Collection" in *Colonialism and the Object: Empire, Material Culture and the Museum* (1998), Barringer, Tim (ed.). Routledge.

Denmark Statistic 2009: http://www.dst.dk/

ENAR Shadow Report 2004. http://cms.horus.be/files/99935/MediaArchive/pdf/Denmark2004_enOK.pdf

Gilroy, Paul (2006): "Colonial Crimes and Convivial Cultures" in *Rethinking Nordic Colonialism: A Postcolonial Project in Five Acts*. Coordinated by Kuratorisk Aktion. Nordic Institute for Contemporary Art: www.rethinking-nordic-colonialism.org.

Gøbel, Erik (2001): "De danske mennesketransporter over Atlanten" in Per Nielsen (ed.), *Fra slaveri til frihed. Det dansk-vestindiske slavesamfund 1672–1848*. Copenhagen: Nationalmuseet.

Gøbel, Erik (2002): *A Guide to Sources for the History of the Danish West Indies (U.S. Virgin Islands), 1671-1917*. Odense: University Press of Southern Denmark.

Goli, Marco (2007): "The Voice of Exit - Towards a Theory of Democratic Inconsistency." *Journal of Social Sciences* 3 (2): 60-68, 2007.

Gordon, Lewis (1995): *Bad Faith and Antiblack Racism*. New York: Humanity Books.

Gullestad, Marianne (2005): "Normalising racial boundaries. The Norwegian dispute about the term *neger*.î *Social Anthropology* 13: 1, 27-46.

Henrichsen, Carsten (1993): *Tamilsagen*. Retsvidenskabeligt Institut B, Copenhagen University.

Human Rights Report 2008. http://www.state.gov/g/drl/rls/hrrpt/2008/eur/119097.htm

Hussain, Mustafa (2002): "4.2 Denmark" in ter Jessika Wal (ed.): *Racism and cultural diversity in the mass media. An overview of research and examples of good practice in the EU Member States, 1995-2000*. Vienna, European Monitoring Centre on Racism and Xenophobia.

Jensen, Tim (2006): "Religion in the Newsroomsî in Johanna Sumiala-Seppánen, Knut Lundby, and Raimo Salokangas (eds): *Implications of the Sacred in (Post)Modern Media*. Gothenberg: Nordicom.

Maldonado-Torres, Nelson (2007): "On the Coloniality of Being." *Cultural Studies* Vol. 21, Nos. 2&3 March/May, pp. 240-270.

Mignolo, Walter (2002): "The Enduring Enchantment (or the Epistemic Privilege of Modernity and Where to Go from Here)." *The South Atlantic Quarterly*, Vol. 101, Nr. 4, pp. 927-954.

Oommen, George, and Hans Iversen (2005): "It Began in Copenhagen: Junctions in 300 Years of Indian-Danish Relations in Christian Mission." Delhi: Indian Society for Promoting Christian Knowledge.

Prosise, Theodore O. (2003): "Prejudiced, historical witness, and responsible: collective memory and liminality in the Beit Hashoah Museum of Tolerance." *Journal Communication Quarterly*: June, 22 2003. http://business.highbeam.com/4052/article-1G1-110575535/prejudiced-historical-witness-and-responsible-collective

Quijano, Anibal (2000): "The Coloniality of Power and Social Classification." *Journal of World-System Research* 6, no. 2, Special Issue: Festschrift Immanuel Wallerstein, Part 1 (Summer/Fall 2000), pp. 1-29.

Trouillot, Michel-Rolph (1995): *Silencing the Past: Power and the Production of History*. Boston, Massachusetts: Beacon Press.Richard Dyer (1997): *White*. London & NY: Routledge.

van Leeuwen, Bart (2008): "Racist variations of bad faith: a critical study of Lewis Gordon's phenomenology of racism." *Journal of Social Theory and Practice*. Florida State University. http://findarticles.com/p/articles/mi_hb6395/is_1_34/ai_n29415734/

African, Chinese and Mexican National Museums in the United States
Did You Say "National"?

Cristina Castellano

University of Paris 1, Sorbonne, France

cristinacastellano@hotmail.com

Abstract: This article explores how the model of the US cultural policies allows the creation of minority, racial and ethnic museums. It shows the difference between mainstreams museum and the community museums situated in peripheral neighborhoods in Illinois. It shows how the diaspora's recent museums in Chicago are questioning the imagined nations and how nomadic subjects are grounded and practicing a self-representation in US territory. The text places at the center of its analysis the case of National Museum of Mexican Art of Chicago and the contradiction of the assimilation of Mexican culture by the American hegemony. This article was originally presented in an international workshop about Migration and Museum in Paris, at the EHESS in 2009. The reader will find references to the French context throughout the text. This comparison is important because the French model of cultural policies doesn't allow a self-representation of minorities.

The political and cultural model of the United States allows the existence of national museums with an ethnic or racial character. The immigrant communities from African, Asian and Mexican origins have museums where they represent their own artistic and cultural heritage. But: what happens when the national assimilation project of the United States integrates as "national" the cultural treasures of immigrant communities? I will try to answer these questions briefly, based on case studies which I undertook in various museums in Chicago.

I. NATIONAL MUSEUMS

In the 19th century, the economic development of the United States not only accelerated the construction of industries and railways but also increased the emergence and development of museums. Criticized for their lack of historical tradition and heritage, the United States built up national museums with the aim of defining not only its economic power but also its cultural relevance to confront the cultural power of Europe. One of the instruments of the cultural power of the US is also the museum industry. In Europe[1], as well as in

---

Cristina Castellano, PhD, received her doctorate from the University of Paris 1. She researches processes of making meaning in contemporary exhibits and focuses on cultural theory, *métissage (mestizaje)* and on the national imaginaries exposed at the museums in France and US. She is editorial council member of the *Revue of Aesthetics Researches* at the *University of Guadalajara* in Mexico, and is as well member of *ICOM* France.

the United States, museums were developed to stimulate a national conscience and to build up a national imaginary. The idea of the national imaginary as a simple collective construction coincides with the theses of Benedict Anderson who characterizes "the nation" as an imagined construction:

> It is **imagined** because the members of even the smallest nation will never know most of their fellow-members, meet them, or even hear of them, yet in the minds of each lives the image of their communion.[2]

National museums appeared to show the images and symbols that expressed the pride and made up the identity of every nation. If in the United States the notion of "museum of art" did not exist before the American Civil War, it is important to stress that Ninety-five per cent of existing museums are said to have been founded since World War II.[3] But during the 20th century:

> [...] there was a proliferation of small, low-budget, neighborhood museums, often concentrating on the culture of everyday life or local heritage; at the other, corporate museums, the development of museums "franchises," "blockbuster" shows, iconic, "landmark" architecture, "superstar" museums, and "meta-museums" also flourished.[4]

Nowadays, the museum enterprises in the United States[5], which are emblematic of the national art and heritage, coexist with the small community museums which are run by the younger generations of immigrant descent. But, how can a national museum represent itself through a "foreign" heritage? How can the imagined nation represent itself through the images and symbols of another national imaginary? Isn't the fact of representing the American nation with museums and images of Chinese, Mexican or African origins a contradiction in itself?

II. COMMUNITY MUSEUMS

In the 20th century, museums with an ethnic or racial character have appeared all over the Unites States. The cultural heritage of the immigrant communities has become a museum object in exhibits, and an actual issue for shows as well. It is not a right exercised by the American State, but rather conquered by social minorities: Blacks, Jews, Asians, Hispanics, homosexuals and women, among others. These museums, named "community museums"[6] pick up in their exhibits the symbols of the groups or societies of origin which they represent. In this way, they show the contexts of their past, without forgetting the cultural mutations of the present.

---

[1] The French museums are very good examples of these thesis. See Dominique POULOT, *Une histoire des musées de France, XVIIIe – XXe siècle*, Éditions La Découverte, France, 2008.
[2] ANDERSON, Benedict. *Imagined Communities. Reflections on the Origin and Spread of Nationalism*, 1st edition 1983, Verso, revised edition, London, NY, 2006, p.6.
[3] MacDONALD S. *A companion to Museum Studies*, Blackwell Publishing, USA, UK, 2006. p.4.
[4] *Ibid.*, pp.4-5.

[5] Serge Guilbaut explains how the power of New York's cultural institutions has imposed itself to secure the "consecration and glory" of American art. See: *Comment New York vola l'idée d'art moderne*, Éditorial Jaqueline Chambon, Nîmes, France, 1996.
[6] The term to designate this type of museum changes depending on the language and/or country. In the United Kingdom, the term employed is *"neighborhood museum"*; in the United States, *"community museum"*; in French, the term employed is "musée de communauté"; in Italian, *"museo di quartiere"*; in Spanish, *"museo de una comunidad"* and, in Portuguese, *"museu comunitário, museu da comunidade."* See: *Dictionarium Museologicum*, edited by the working group "Terminologie du Comité International de l'ICOM pour la Documentation" (CIDOC), Hungary, Budapest, 1986, p. 62.

In the United States, one of the first community museums was the Anacostia Neighborhood Museum.[7] This museum appeared in 1967 due to the growth of national museums at the time. Originally, the Anacostia was an initiative run by the marginal and poor community in Washington. Since its beginnings, the community has participated in the museological tasks. For example, on demand of the young friends of the museum during the 70s, the first exhibit about jazz was staged: "This thing called jazz."[8] At the time, to choose "jazz" as a topic for an exhibit—a music so close to the popular Afro-American culture of the 70s—was without doubt an avantgarde gesture. For the first time, jazz was represented by the same community which saw the birth of this musical style. In contradiction to this, jazz is nowadays recognized as a cultural practice very close to "high culture."During many years and all the way to the present time, this museum has been working for a community that had been stigmatized in Washington. The African-American community was perceived as a "black ghetto."[9] Nowadays, the museum has a library and a multimedia centre. It is a place for the education in applied arts, a meeting place for the groups of the neighborhood and a cultural and artistic centre where it is possible to sing, dance, work and discuss social issues, to study and reproduce the practices related with Afro-American culture.

In France, Dominique Poulot mentioned the project of the urban museums (*museés de la ville*) as preliminary for the community museums. In his chapter *Le temps de l'histoire urbaine,* he writes that this type of museums appeared:

> [...] in the decade of 1970 in North America, because they wanted to give to misrepresented social or ethnic groups the possibility to rediscover their own cultures and to take in their hands the representation of their everyday lives (work, drugs, hygiene or their children's education.[10]

Actually, in the United States, the discourse of "neighborhood museums" did not only represent the communities or groups which were not represented by the national museums, but they opposed themselves as well to the hegemonic discourse of the "public museum." In these museums the object was to celebrate the visibility of the non-white community, the heroic past of peoples which had been ignored up to the present, the struggles of groups which found themselves outside of the mainstream and the democratic achievements acquired by the communities. It was important to stress this point because, for a long time, these communities had been ignored and despised by power structures.[11]

The affirmation of a "collective self" and the resistance to the assimilatory vision of the Occident was lived like a battle in the midst of the neighborhoods and the imagination of their leaders, which were backed

---

[7] Nowadays, the museum is called: *The Anacostia Community Museum.* http://anacostia.si.edu/

[8] George Henri Rivière analyses the pedagocial role of the museum in: "Rôle du musée d'art et du musée de sciences humaines et sociales," *Museum,* Vol. XXV, No. 1/2, revue trimestrielle de l'UNESCO, Presses Centrales, S.A., Lausanne, 1973, p.39.

[9] Stuart Hall has tried to understand the question of race and the elements which compose the category of the "black" subject beyond the positive representation which the communities have built up around them. Hall proposes the end of essentialisms and a concrete transformation of the politics of representation. See HALL Stuart, "Nouvelles ethnicités" dans *Identités et Cultures. Politiques des Cultural Studies,* Paris, 2008, p.290.

[10] POULOT, Dominique. *Musée et muséologie,* Éditions La Découverte, Paris, 2009, p.34. (My translation from French).

[11] Read this idea in the work of Karen Mary DAVALOS. *Exhibing Mestizaje,* University of New Mexico Press, Albuquerque, 2001.

up by the concerned populations. The communities put into place a new narrative and a new way of looking at themselves, which they told and showed. The museographic logic of the community museums in the United States, as well as their permanent collections, put in the narrative's centre the ancient history of their countries and continents of belonging. Also, they incorporated the new discourses that speak about their contemporary history. In this way, these museums are the containers of the conjunction of the present heritage of ambiguous identities, normally bi-national, fragmented and re-made. The community's actions recovered the chosen pieces of a past and at the same time they look forward to build up a narrative about the cultural and artistic identity of their own, which differs from the dominant national narrative and contests it. The clipping plane of exhibits in these kinds of museums was made to reconstruct a dignitary discourse for the younger immigrant communities.

In the context of a post-modern aesthetics of the world of global art, community museums reflect a turn towards the cultural materialism in the way of Raymond William's method:[12]

> Raymond Williams defines his method as a "cultural materialism": this means, that he approaches cultural facts not as figures of the mind or as simple objects, but as a whole of practices and institutions, which are in close relation to the social classes.[13]

Community museums display ethnicity not only with art objects but also with images, documents, photography and hand-made objects, which correspond to the popular culture. This method goes with the aim of bringing together the sense of identity and unity and to regard the community as singular but also as collective. Each community museum exercises, in its own way and with its own media, a politics of representation which allows them to locate themselves in a national category which has been remade: African-American, Chinese-American, Mexican-American.

III. CHICAGO AND ITS MUSEUMS

The city of Chicago is located in the state of Illinois in the northeast of the United States. It is situated in a border region with Canada. Chicago has a population of approximately three million people, including the peripheries. Chicago is the third most important city in the United States. On the 1st of January of 2006, the region had 1,331 French inhabitants registered in the region.[14] Chicago is a city six and half times bigger than Paris.[15] The history of immigration to Chicago is ancient. It begins with the European colonization and then with the African immigration resulting from the slave trade. In 1920, the immigrants came from Russia, Poland, Ireland, Germany, Italy and also from Scandinavian countries. The migration of the last 50 years consists mostly of Latin-Americans and Asians. Chicago is a territory which unites numerous racial and ethnic conflicts, and where "gang" violence is a

---

[12] WILLIAMS, Raymond. *Culture and materialism: selected essays,* Verso, New York, London, 1980, 2005.
[13] LÖWY Michael, *À propos de Raymond Williams,* Culture et Matérialisme, in: La Revue Internationale des Livres et des Idées web, downloaded 09/07/2010. Url:http:www.revuedeslivres.net/articles.php?idArt=550&page=actu

[14] The French community in Chicago. (Consulted in April 2010). http://www.france-expatries.com/Fiches/detail.asp?NewsID=4578&Nomcat=+Chicago
[15] HALBWACHS, Maurice. *Chicago, expérience ethnique,* dans Annales d'histoire économique et sociale, 4e année, N. 13, 1932. pp. 11-49.

"The Millennium Park." Downtown Chicago. USA.
© Cristina Castellano, 2006.

visible part of the long history of the city. This history of gang's violence or urban groups rivalry is still present nowadays and the fights take place every day and in different forms.

Chicago has one of the most important museum complexes in the United States. We find a concentration of museums of science and technology, museums of fine arts, museums of social history and museums of non-occidental cultures. A great part of these museums is concentrated at the heart of the city, which is named *"The Loop."*[16] The foundations, contemporary art centers, galleries, libraries and bookshops which strengthen the cultural life of Chicago can be found in that part of the city. The cultural agglomeration and concentration of Chicago is in tune with a modern and impressive architecture. Nevertheless, Chicago's architectural richness and the location of the museums in this part of the city is no coincidence because the architecture makes the museum. Architecture makes possible the way of seeing, conceptually and physically, and determines the visitor's experience.[17]

The architectural and urban context of Chicago's centre, as well as the monumental iron structures dedicated to the buildings of finance and cultural institutions show the interest that this city has for the architectural heritage and the museums.

There are eight museums built up in properties of city parks. They are administered by the project Grant Park. We find the *Adler Planetarium,* the *Art Institute,* the *Chicago Historical Society,* the *Du Sable Museum,* the *Field Museum of Natural History,* and the *Shedd Aquarium.*[18] Far from

---

[16] *The Loop* is Chicago's economic, historical and cultural centre. See *The Electronic Encyclopedia of Chicago* © 2005 Chicago Historical Society. http://encyclopedia.chicagohistory.org/pages/764.html (consulted on the 30th of May, 2010).

[17] GIEBELHAUSEN, Michaela. "The architecture is the museum," in *New Museum Theory and Practice, An Introduction,* Edited by Janet Marstine, Blackwell Publishing, USA, UK, 2006, p. 42.

[18] DAVALOS, Karen. "Exhibing mestizaje: the poetics and experience of Mexican Fine Arts Center Museum," in: *Museum Studies. An Anthology of Contexts.* Edited by Bettina Messias Carbonell, Blackwell Publishing, USA, UK, Australia, 2004, p.527.

the city centre, in the peripheries where a big part of the population lives, community museums have come to life. Although they have been conceived as monumental projects, they have been kept modest.

IV. THE AFRICAN COMMUNITY

The African-American Museum *Du Sable Museum on African American History*[19] is a constituent part of the museum complex at the park, although it is located in a peripheral neighborhood, near to the Chicago University. It is a museum which is destined to narrate the past and present history of African-Americans in the city. At the beginning of the permanent collection, the museum shows an image of a far away "Africa" which is divided in four regions: north, south, east and west. The exhibit starts with the glorified history of ancient Egypt and its emperors. We find royal objects and portraits of men and women of the empire. The museum shows "Africa" as a whole, as a continent, without establishing any kind of divisions between the countries or the cultures distinctive of each region. All of Africa is integrated into the exhibit, which serves as a reference for African-American immigrants.

In the contemporary section, the museum presents portraits of social and cultural leaders of Chicago. We found Margaaret Burroghs, a scholar of arts and humanities. Afterwards, a big corridor takes us into the history and transformation of barber shops. For example, we discover a reproduction of a barber shop of the 1940 with its hairbrushes, mirrors and beauty products. This part of the exhibit is accompanied by posters which illustrate the evolutive history of African head dressing, a very important element of the image of African identity and a symbol of a racial difference when compared to other identities and cultures. The core of the exhibit is located in the photographic and documentary archives. It is here that the history of domination and African slavery in the United States is shown. The museum shows evidence of the racism of "Whites" and the liberation struggles undertook by the "Black" community. We observe this part of the history with examples of ancient attestations of slave property as well as with announcements to buy and sell human beings. The document of the abolition of slavery, signed by Abraham Lincoln, is added to the exhibit beside these documents, thus marking the end of this cruel period in the life of African-Americans. The exhibit ends in a photographic room that narrates the history of the struggles won and lost, like those of Martin Luther King, Malcom X or the *Black Panthers*.

The narrative of this national American museum is not part of the national pride of the *Wasp* American history. It tells more about a sad episode in American history. Nevertheless, the existence of a museum of this type shows how the American state and its segregationist politics have changed. It stresses that the history of African-Americans is, today, part of the national American identity. If the national American imaginary appropriates the continental history of Africa this is because of Chicago's particular history. Anyway, it is the burden of African-American community to tell their own history.

V. THE CHINESE COMMUNITY

The Chinese immigrants arrived in the United States in the 19th century. During the 19th and the 20th centuries, 80 per cent of Chinese immigrants were male.[20] Today,

---

[19] See *Du Sable Museum on African American History*, Chicago. http://www.dusablemuseum.org/

[20] TOKARCZYK Michelle M. *Class definitions. On the lives and writings of Maxime Hong Kingston, Sandra Cisneros and Dorothy Allison*, Susquehanna University Press, USA, 2008, p. 58.

there are between 30 and 40 million Chinese immigrants dispersed in 136 countries outside China. The majority lives in south-east Asia, but it is in the United States where the largest population of Chinese has settled outside of Asia. At the beginning of the 19th century, in 1874 and after the anti-Chinese violence in San Francisco and Los Angeles, many immigrants of Chinese origin settled in Chicago.[21] The people of Chicago thought that this was a particular population and that they could live in peace with them. At that time, fires were common, so may Chinese became American citizens thanks to the loss of the offices which extended birth certificates.[22]

The cultural identity of Chinese immigrants is composed of many hybrid signs—because many Chinese became protestant and catholic. They did not remain Buddhist or Taoist. For a long time, the temples or monuments that represented their cultural or religious identity were not visible on the American territory. The only thing we find after 1940 is the "Mount Auburn Cemetery" which is the physical space to depose the dead of Chicago's Chinese community.[23]

Like the Mexicans who took the myth of *Aztlán* to give a sense of their new identity in American territory, the Chinese community of Chicago named itself: "The population of Tang street" in reference and honor to the Tang dynasty.[24] Around this neighborhood they created restaurants, boutiques, massage rooms, typical cloth stores as well as furniture and handmade crafts. The Chinese-American Museum, which is located in the Chinese neighborhood of Chicago, is one of the most recent community museums. It is made up by educated volunteers and academics of Asian background. This small museum has a temporary section to show the history, archaeology, utensils and cultural heritage of Chinese (silk, tofu, ancient papers), but also the photographic social history of the illegal immigrants at the beginning of the century. The museum bought the building in order to perform its activities without the state's aid. It is still not considered a national American museum, but rather a neighborhood museum made by and for the Chinese community, even if it is open for everybody.

VI. THE MEXICAN COMMUNITY

The Hispanic population represents 12.5 per cent of the United States, from which 60 per cent has a Mexican origin, which represents almost 21 million people.[25] 16 km away from the centre of Chicago, there are two neighborhoods identified as strictly Hispanic: *Little Village* and *Pilsen*. Long ago, Pilsen's population had mostly a "polish" origin, and the neighborhood remained with the name due to the popularity of the beer. The grand majority of the inhabitants of Pilsen today has a Mexican origin. The administrative organization of the neighborhood, its management and its urbanism are American, but the commerce, *boutiques*, coffee shops, recreation centers, libraries, schools and radio reflect the life of a small Mexico installed in the United States. The teachers of elementary schools, like for example in the Orozco primary school, have declared themselves proud of putting a Mexican flag at the heart of an American city.

The National Museum of Mexican Art[26] (NMMA) was created in 1987 by two teachers, Carlos Tortolero, the current

---

[21] HO, Chuimei. "Seeking a new World," in: *Chinese in Chicago (1870-1945)*, Chinatown Museum Foundation, Arcadia Publishing, GB, 2005.
[22] Ibid.
[23] Ibid.
[24] Ibid.

[25] ODGERS-ORTIZ Olga. *Problèmes d'Amérique Latine. Mexique. L'élan brisé*, "Flux Migratoire du Mexique vers les États-Unis: Changement et Continuité," PAL No. 50, Autonome 2003, p. 59.

director, and Helen Valdez. It is situated at the heart of Pilsen, Chicago, and considered the most important Latin museum in the American nation. The museum has a vast collection of Mexican and Chicano art. It is financed by the city, as it is a member of the Grant Park even though it is located far away of the city centre and of the monumental museal complex of *Loop*. The Museum of National Mexican Art receives part of its financing from the taxes destined to the American parks. According to Pete Rodríguez—a collector and resident of the Pilsen neighborhood—if the NMMA is a museum open to all Americans and not exclusive for Hispanic immigrants, it does not work enough for the community which it is supposed to represent: "The people of the museum are only there to keep their jobs. The museum pays one dollar by year and this cheap location is possible because the community pays taxes."[27] In fact, the museum's existence has been possible thanks to the taxes which community pays. The institution follows the instructions of American museums by consecrating its mission to the development and education of the society in general.

The National Museum of Mexican Art (NMMA), which wants to place "the Mexican beyond its national borders"[28] is divided according to different historical periods. The exhibits are usually organized in American territory with the support of specialists in art and in Mexican history. The exhibit's schedule is divided in four principal spheres: the day of the dead, contemporary art, traditional art and Mesoamerican hand-made crafts. In its permanent exhibit, the museum shows the topic of *La Mexicanidad*.[29] This exhibit shows paintings, models, pictures, sculptures and other art objects to explain, period by period, the national and official history of Mexico in different rooms. We find many moments in the exhibit. To begin with, we find the ethnic multiplicity of Pre-Hispanic cultures and, afterwards, the representation of the independence (1810), the *Reforma del Estado* (1857), the Mexican revolution (1910) and the political and artistic history of the Chicanos. In opposition of others Museums of the Grant Park of Chicago, the entry to the exhibits is free. In this way, the museum shows a different positioning toward the politics of cultural financing in the United States, because the act of guaranteeing the free entry represents a permanent struggle for the directory staff of this museum.[30]

In its museography, the museum takes the mystique out of art by stopping the exhibit's formalities and by going out beyond the "art status" which others American museums concede to art objects. For example, a piece of the famous photographer Alvarez Bravo is susceptible of being shown beside a hand-made object which does not have the status of an art work. The codes of the *mainstream* museum are contested by the Mexican museum, where "high" and "popular" culture come into contact. But it is not about anarchy in museography, as the rules of mediation exhibits are respected. For example, the support of texts and signals keep the same characteristics that those of Chicago's *Art Institute*; they just place them a little lower to make them accessible to children. Gener-

---

[26] Webpage of the National Museum of Mexican Art (NMMA) http://www.nationalmuseumofmexicanart.org/
[27] Conversation with Pete Rodríguez, art collector in Pilsen, 18 Street, Chicago, 20 April 2006.
[28] These are the words of Carlos Tortolero, director of the National Museum of Mexican Art. Chicago, interview, April 2006.

[29] "*La mexicanidad*" is all of that which belongs to the Mexican identity and which can be translated by the symbols which represents this national culture: the flag, the independence heroes, the revolution, the day of the dead, the virgin of Guadalupe, the Aztecs and the Mayas among others.
[30] Interview with Carlos Tortolero, director of the National Museum of Mexican Art. Chicago, April 2006.

ally, the museum follows the rules of national museums except in the choice of the colors for the walls[31] and in the way of valuing and showing its material and immaterial heritage.

The NMMA is a museum of the 80s, which implies that it was born after the New Yorker debates of the 70s, a period where the artists reclaimed the opening of the "museum–temple" toward more democratic forms, less elitist, less dogmatic and less religious.[32] It was about crossing the doors of the museum and "converting" it. This means making the museum a space for all, a "forum." The generalized petition of artists for the inclusion of their works in the museum/temples had been, since long time ago, a struggle for the artists coming from racial minorities in the United States. For this reason, the idea of the museum/forum was perfectly convenient to the social and political spirit of Chicago's NMMA. After its birth, the museum was known as a Museum & Centre. It developed a rich program which showed the arts of spectacle with the participation of music, dance and the literary encounters representative of Mexican culture. The Museum & Centre invited a considerable number of Mexican celebrities like the writers Octavio Paz or Carlos Fuentes, but also Mexican-Americans like the performance artist Guillermo Gomez-Peña or Sandra Cisneros. The idea of the Museum & Centre of Mexican art based its cultural politic on the idea of the museum made up by the community. It opened its doors to artists who come from Latin-American minorities and established bridges with the major figures of art and culture in both sides of the Mexican-American border.

---

[31] The walls of the exhibit in the museum are not white but purple, yellow or pink.
[32] CAMERON Duncan. "Le musée: un temple ou un forum,," dans *Vagues, une anthologie de la nouvelle muséologie*, Éditions W.M.E.S, France, 1992, pp. 77- 97.

VII. THE CONTRADICTION: FROM COMMUNITY MUSEUM TO NATIONAL MUSEUM

During almost 20 years and before being called the *National Museum of Mexican Art* (NMMA), this museum was the *Mexican Fine Arts Center Museum* of Chicago (MFACM). Under the subtle pressure of the administration and the assimilatory american politics, the Mexican museum had to change its name. The Museum & Center became the National American Museum. With the aim of guaranteeing free entry to its premises, the museum had to give up to nominal change. And it is here where the contradiction between community museums and national museums unfolds. The affirmation of Mexican national identity within the American territory could not continue to be subsidized by the American state, since this was incompatible with the national American culture and politics. The message for the community was simple. The Mexican museum could continue to offer its visitors a free entry, but only if it became part of the American nation, this means, by giving up its image of being a Mexican community museum.

Actually, what we are witnessing here is the symbolic struggle of two national imaginaries where the battle field is the museum. It is about two antagonist national traditions. This shows a contradiction, because it is impossible until the present day to narrate and show a national history following the perspective of another foreign and different nation. The history of the Mexican-American museum tells about a power struggle where signifying practices and the appropriation of objects of history are in dispute. The struggle about the nominal change of the museum was run by the American nationalism which has restituted the Mexican collection as a treasure of the American

Ray Arroyo Di Vicino explains "*El día de muertos*" to the children. Permanent Exhibition: "*La Mexicanidad.*"
© Cristina Castellano, 2006.

nation. This does not mean that the symbols of Mexican culture will completely integrate into the American imaginary. Frida Kahlo is not American and the Aztecs have not become one hundred per cent[33] heritage of American history. This does not mean that the *Día de muertos*,[34] traditional folklore or the national Mexican imaginary will become more popular than Halloween, today so typical of American folklore. Nevertheless, the rhetorical struggle for the name of the Mexican museum shows two neighboring imaginaries in tension, two different nations in territorial proximity.

VIII. Migration and Representation: A Comparison with France

The history of migration is normally somber when war, poverty or conflict have been the causes of territorial displacements. But the experience is a very different one when migration obeys a sort of voluntary impulse which makes individuals or communities displace themselves. In the museums where we did our study, the process of migration is complete. The immigrants live physically on American territory, they are more or less Americans, even if the symbols and the cultural practices of origin are incorporated and transformed in different ways. It is true that the immigrant artists and communities that belong to these museums demanded a new history of the United States. They contested

---

[33] I found this idea of one hundred per cent Americanization in the text of Denis Lacorne which states that: "The one hundred per cent American is an enthusiastic, loyal and productive immigrant. He learns English in the evening after work; he does everything he has to do to obtain a quick naturalization; he is respectful of the authorities in place, he avoids engaging with the "reds," revolutionaries and other suspects ; he endures all difficulties of industrial work without complaining; he does not go on strike due to feelings of national pride and he does not demand an increase of his salary; he forgets everything about his country of origin, his ancestors and his traditions with the aim of melting in and with the American nation. Briefly, he is a man of only one faith and only one slogan: America First." In Denis Lacorne. La crise de l'identité américaine. Du melting-pot au multiculturalisme, Fayard, France, 1997, p. 230 (my translation from the French).

[34] The "Day of the dead" in celebrated in Mexicans on the 1st and 2nd of November.

public museums and the representation that they made of communities. But this struggle is not only about ethnic communities, it is also a contestation of immigrants, women and all people who are not being treated like real citizens.[35]

The minorities in the United States do not challenge the idea of the museum, but the hegemonic representation that the national museum makes of themselves. Community museums have shown that an alternative to the official and authoritarian representational practices exists. The figure of the museum, which up to the present day legitimated the universal representations of nation and art, has given the voice to other forms of representation which have been formerly ignored. For African-Americans, their museum meant a moment to openly talk about the past, genocide, slavery and social injustice. Other communities like the Mexican or Chicano community opened up the doors toward cultural difference, popular traditions and to the possibility of belonging to a culture which would not only have to be "Anglo-Saxon," but also "Hispano-American,"

In France, the "community museum" does not exist. There are only the museums "in the" French community or museums "of the" French community. This means that the immigrants, or the French people who have also origins outside from the French Republic do not have the right of self-representation or the right to associate themselves in "communities" which seem separated from the national space. With the aim of ensuring equality, the national sovereignty of the State prohibits the demarcation of ethnic and racial differences. The first article of the French constitution explains that:

France is a secular, democratic and social Republic which ensures equality to all citizens before the law without distinction of origin, race or religion. It respects all beliefs. Its organization is decentralized. The law promotes equal access for men and women to all electoral mandates at elective functions, as well as to all professional and social responsibilities.[36]

The constitution looks for equality and universalism with the aim of favoring the access to all forms of civic representation. But, what happens when the French with a double cultural identity do not feel really completely represented in museums? How can this first article of the constitution grant to all the citizens the right to representation? Would a community museum really menace the sovereignty of the French state? Would it be pertinent to name the right to cultural representation and not only the citizen representation? This question is very difficult to answer and we cannot solve this dilemma here. But it is important to say that in France there are no community museums. The nearest category to this idea is the notion of *musées de la ville* (city museums):

[…] city museums constitute a complex type, wrongly identified since the beginning, between regional museums and ecomuseums (for example… In Saint-Quentin-en-Yvelines, the museum asserts itself as a "city museum" and shows interest in the heritage of the city from multiple perspectives: architecture, urbanism, history, geography, public art and ways of life; in Vitry, the MAC/VAL is a museum

---

[35] DAVALOS, Karen. "Exhibing mestizaje: the poetics and experience of Mexican Fine Arts Center Museum," in: *Museum Studies. An Anthology of Contexts*. Edited by Bettina Messias Carbonell, Blackwell Publishing, United States, UK, Australia, 2004, pp. 521-522.

[36] See 1st article of the Constitution of the French Republic. http://www.assemblee-nationale.fr/connaissance/constitution.asp (our translation from French).

of contemporary art which opens as the fruit of the long investment of the General Council, meanwhile the project of a museum of the suburbs (banlieue) in Seine-Saint-Denis has failed. In any case, when the museum becomes a social forum, it opens the question of its political legitimacy. The difficulty tends more and more toward the ambiguities of the definition of the city, in terms of social groups, multiculturalism, and the social relation with suburbs.[37]

To understand the major differences that exist between a city museum and a community museum, we have to think about the type of audience which museums want to address. The definition of city museums, in France, regards the museum as a place that addresses all inhabitants who are interested in discovering the environment or the heritage defined by the museum. The definition of the community museum in the United States is much more inspired by the culture of minorities, as these are the principal audience celebrating and sharing the symbols and the cultural practices exposed in community museums.

In France, the existence of a national minority museum is unimaginable because the concept of "minority" is not recognized by the state even if there are groups which reclaim this status.[38] A priori, the minorities in France do not exist and, if they exist, they are not represented as such in a national museum. The communities and social groups with hyphenated identities experiment their voices in music, art, journalism and other types of media and cultural manifestations, but not in national museums. Nevertheless, in the museum, it is the invention of universality which poses several problems—even if it looks to conciliate the conflict and cultural difference. The notion of universality would assume that the chosen and exposed objects in the national museums represent the heritage of all populations, even if many populations do not feel concerned by this approach of cultural identification.[39]

Contrary to this, in the United States, the museums administered by the minorities and for these minorities make believe that the problems of discrimination could be resolved. Paradoxically, the promotion of difference and self-representation of the communities at the museum has led to question other issues like the reproduction of clichés or folklore.[40] In the United States, the community museums built an "acceptable image of others," by exhibiting and affirming the cultural singularities of a community. Displaying difference and singular cultural identities make meaning in a positive way.[41] This kind of cultural contestation in the center of a nation also lead to the construction of prejudices (fixed identities) concerning a group. Finally, the real questions emerging from the analysis of community museums are: How to expose contemporary social history, different in the midst of a nation state which looks forward to negate or erase the differences? How to let cultural communities

---

[37] POULOT, D.. *Musée et muséologie*, Éditions La Découverte, Paris, 2009, pp.34-35 (our translation from French).

[38] BASTENIER, Albert. *Qu'est-ce qu'une société ethnique ?: ethnicité et racisme dans les sociétés européennes d'immigration*, Presses universitaires de France, Paris, 2004.

[39] This idea of national representation as a universal value is contested in the work of Mary Karen Davalos who made an original, brilliant academic work about the Mexican Museum of Chicago. See DAVALOS, Karen Mary. *Exhibing Mestizaje*, University of New Mexico Press, Albuquerque, 2001.

[40] DAVALOS, Karen. Exhibing mestizaje: the poetics and experience of Mexican Fine Arts Center Museum, in: Museum Studies. An Anthology of Contexts, edited par Bettina Messias Carbonell, Blackwell Publishing, United States, UK, Australia, 2004.

[41] Ibid.

represent themselves without falling into the *clichés*, and thus going beyond the national and identity discourses?

IX. Conclusion

Contradictions are evident and dissimulate something. A national museum of a specific nation cannot be, at the same time, a museum that exposes the cultural traits of a foreign sovereignty or another nation. A national American museum cannot be, at the same time, a national African, Chinese or Mexican museum. If a national American museum is at the same time a Mexican museum, this is due to the fact that the immigrant communities reclaim their own ancient cultural rights in a new territory and nation. The affirmation of identity is in contradiction with the idea of the sovereign nation because the connotation of the national is constructed by putting limits. The idea of nation is grounded in the installation of physical and symbolic borders, which would keep the autonomy and the singularity of each nation untouched.

Contrary to this idea, a national museum could "have" and also "exhibit" the treasures which are found in its national collection even if they comes from a foreign culture. If certain "community museums" in the United States are now "national museums," it is because there exists a "relation" or "connection" with the immigration history that built America. The fact of having a "National American Museum" which would be at the same time African-American or Mexican-American allows just to narrate another piece of the American history and justify the development of the pluralist rhetoric.

The existence of community museums in the United States shows a political practice of free representation in institutions. This allows the expression of different cultural identities and minorities, but this does not guarantee a real social change in the ways of seeing practiced by people in every day life; this does not change the racial prejudices. On the contrary, the fact of "rendering national" the histories, collections and narrations of minorities stressed the rhetorical national pluralism and hides a very radical politics of assimilation.

Nowadays, a central question is to know why nations which must find the pillars of their sovereignty in the political field would want to imagine their sovereignty based on culture. The question is to know if identities which call themselves nationals think themselves as a "fixed statement" living only in one specific territory. If this is the case, we must be careful with the nationalist speeches that could promote totalitarian discriminations against the communities or individual immigrants. It will be necessary to be attentive and avoid focusing on the national pride of cultural forms with the pretext of achieving sovereignty. At the end, the vital impulse that pushes people to go away from their homes, emigrate and reconstruct themselves again is part of the human condition. Migration, this desire to travel, to explore and to experience movement, is without doubt a human fact which has always existed, even before the birth of imagined nations.

References

ANDERSON, Benedict. *Imagined Communities. Reflections on the Origin and Spread of Nationalism*, 1st edition 1983, Verso, revised edition, London, NY, 2006.

BASTENIER, Albert. *Qu'est-ce qu'une société ethnique ?: ethnicité et racisme dans les sociétés européennes d'immigration*, Presses universitaires de France, Paris, 2004.

CAMERON, Duncan. "Le musée: un temple ou un forum," dans *Vagues, une anthologie de la nouvelle muséologie*, 1er édition 1971,

Volume 1, Éditions W.M.E.S, France, 1992.

DAVALOS, Karen Mary. *Exhibiting Mestizaje*, University of New Mexico Press, Albuquerque, 2001.

DAVALOS, Karen Mary. "Exhibing mestizaje: the poetics and experience of Mexican Fine Arts Center Museum," dans *Museum Studies. An Anthology of Contexts*. Edited by Bettina Messias Carbonell, Blackwell Publishing, USA, UK, Australia, 2004.

GIEBELHAUSEN, Michaela. "The architecture is the museum," dans *New Museum Theory and Practice, An Introduction*, Janet Marstine (éd.), Blackwell Publishing, USA, UK, 2006.

GUILBAUT, Serge. *Comment New York vola l'idée d'art moderne*, éditorial Jaqueline Chambon, Nîmes, France, 1996.

HALBWACHS, Maurice. *Chicago, expérience ethnique*, dans Annales d'histoire économique et sociale, 4e année, N. 13, 1932.

HALL, Stuart. *Identités et Cultures. Politiques des Cultural Studies*, édition établie par Maxime Cervulle, Tr. de l'anglais par Christophe Jaquet, Éditions Amsterdam, Paris, 2008.

HO, Chuimei. "Seeking a new World," dans *Chiness in Chicago (1870-1945)*, Chinatown Museum Fondation, Arcadia Publishing, UK, 2005.

ICOM. *Dictionarium Museologicum*, réalisé par le Groupe de Travail Terminologie du Comité International de l'ICOM pour la Documentation (CIDOC), Hungary, Budapest, 1986.

LACORNE, Denis. *La crise de l'identité américaine.* "Du melting-pot au multiculturalisme," Fayard, France, 1997.

MACDONALD, Sharon. *A companion to Museum Studies*, Blackwell Publishing, USA, UK, 2006.

ODGERS-ORTIZ, Olga. *Problèmes d'Amérique Latine. Mexique. L'élan brisé*, "Flux Migratoire du Mexique vers les États-Unis: Changement et Continuité," PAL No. 50, Autonome 2003.

POULOT, Dominique. *Une histoire des musées de France, XVIIIe – XXe siècle*, Éditions La Découverte, France, 2008.

POULOT, Dominique. *Musée et muséologie*, Éditions La Découverte, Paris, 2009

RIVIÈRE, George Henri. *Museum*, Vol.XXV, No. 1/2, revue trimestrielle de l'UNESCO, Presses Centrales, S.A., Lausanne, 1973.

TOKARCZYK, Michelle M. *Class definitions. On the lives and writings of Maxime Hong Kingston, Sandra Cisneros and Dorothy Allison*, Susquehanna University Press, USA, 2008.

WILLIAMS, Raymond. *Culture and materialism: selected essays*, Verso, New York, London, 1980, 2005.

The Challenge of Cultural Diversity in Europe
(Re)designing Cultural Heritages through Intercultural Dialogue

Estela Rodríguez García

Centro de Estudios Diálogo Global, Spain

stella_stellae@yahoo.es

Abstract: Western societies have constructed their collective imaginaries through the recuperation of objects and traditions that define them best. Europe mythically shaped its self-definition by "whitening" it, denying any recognition whatsoever of the cultural diversity of the people who inhabited the region for centuries. Since the 15th and 16th centuries, with the Renaissance, the invention of a common past involved emphasizing the Greek and Latin past, disconnected from any type of relationship with other cultures, religions or skin colors. The white marble of Roman sculptures, which many farmers found while tilling their land, became the desired color, the symbol of a Europe that nullified any presence of cultural and religious difference. Within this chosen definition, the chromatic spectrum of the others and their everyday objects were first defined as the war booty of dominant aristocracies, and later, as objects fit for ethnological museums. Today we have diversity in our streets and not just in our museums. When we walk through our cities, new strokes, colors and styles of clothing take us by surprise–those of foreigners from outside the European community, those who remain outside the Europe of their dreams and do not enjoy the citizenship rights of inhabitants of the European Union's member states.

I. Introduction: Multicultural Societies and Collective Imaginaries

"Ponte en su piel" ("Put Yourself in Her Skin") was part of a sensitivity campaign promoted by the city of Tarragona in 2006 that puts into context many elements of the debate we aim to expose in this article. At first glance, it speaks to us of the so-called "new immigration" of people from countries outside the European Union who have arrived in Catalonia in the past few decades and who now live in our cities, creating new realities and bringing to the fore new challenges and defining society's new needs in the early years of the 21st century (Pajares 2005; García y Barañano 2003). But it also speaks to us of our anxieties and obsessions, our fears and our way of perceiving "others." Western societies have constructed their collective imaginaries

---

Estela Rodriguez García is a Senior Researcher in the Communication Department at the Ramon Llull University (Barcelona, Spain). She is Director of the Center of Study and Investigation for Global Dialogues. And, in collaboration with Ramon Grosfoguel, she is Professor and coordinator of the International annual SUMMER SCHOOL "Interculturality, International Migration and the Dialogue between Civilizations Before and After 9/11" co-sponsored by the University of California at Berkeley and the Foundation of the Universidad Autonoma de Barcelona. She is also a member of the Sociedade Científica de Estudos da Arte, Universidade de Sao Paulo, Escola de Comunicaçoes e Artes.

through the recuperation of objects and traditions that define them best (Anderson 1993). At the time of the birth of nation-states, in the colonial and post-colonial eras, and in the current period of globalization, the icons and symbols that are a part of this community have been abstracted from their original locations and brought into those great storage areas we call museums. As a product of the era of the birth of nationalisms, museums clearly define, through the selection of cultural artifacts, who has belonged to a community and who has not, who "we" are and who are the "others."

Europe mythically shaped its self-definition by "whitening" it, denying any recognition whatsoever of the cultural diversity of the people who inhabited the region for centuries (Shohat and Stam 1994). Since the 15th and 16th centuries, with the Renaissance, the invention of a common past involved emphasizing the Greek and Latin past, disconnected from any type of relationship with other cultures, religions or skin colors (Mignolo 2003). The white marble of Roman sculptures, which many farmers found while tilling their land, became the *desired color*, the symbol of a Europe that nullified any presence of cultural and religious difference. Within this chosen definition, the chromatic spectrum of *the others* and their everyday objects were first defined as the war booty of dominant aristocracies, and later, as objects fit for ethnological museums (Chakrabarty 2000).

Today we have diversity in our streets and not just in our museums. When we walk through our cities, new strokes, colors and styles of clothing take us by surprise (Barkan and Denise 1998)—those of foreigners from outside the European community, those who remain outside the Europe of their dreams and do not enjoy the citizenship rights of inhabitants of the European Union's member states. As we have stressed in other studies, the definition of European identity has been linked with the idea of a cultural homogenization, but above all, as the philosopher Rosi Braidotti has written,[1] "this myth continues to be crucial for the legend of European nationalism." For this author, the reason European unification has taken 50 years to bring questions of culture and education to the agenda, above and beyond economic and military questions, has to do with the complexity of the definition of these concepts for each and every member country. Various identities—or *figurations* as Braidotti calls them—"remain outside this Europe: the migrant, the exile, the refugee or asylum-seeker, the undocumented foreigner, the homeless and the uprooted, the Filipina nanny who has replaced the more familiar figure of the *"chica canguro"* [babysitter] or *au pair* girl...." These immigrants, who have lived among us for decades, receive scant attention from the media, which often associate them with situations of criminality, underdevelopment or subalternity, reinforcing the cultural imaginaries that negatively affect our perception of other cultures (Rodríguez 2005). The same does not go for Euro-American globalized cultures, such as the Hollywood culture industry, consumer modes and products, music or fast food. These cultural products or products of consumption have become globalized to such an extent that it is difficult to know which country we are travelling in and this complicates our task of figuring out what to take pictures of in order to show to our friends after our trip. Néstor García Canclini, the Argentinian anthropologist living in Mexico, pays close attention to these new cultural mappings in his work

---

[1] Braidotti warns that the European Union's project may be subject to the "Fortress Europe" syndrome, that is, a Europe that protects itself against the "invasion" of foreigner and foreign customs and traditions. See Braidotti (1999: 27-46). These questions are also addressed by authors such as Floya Anthias, Philomena Essed, Helma Lutz, Nira Yuval Davis or Avtar Brah.

"Diferentes, desiguales y desconectados. Mapas de la interculturalidad" ["Different, Unequal and Unconnected: Maps of Interculturality"], noting that

> ...the identities of subjects are formed today in inter-ethnic and international processes, through flows produced by technologies and multinational corporations, globalized financial exchanges, repertoires of images and information created in order to be distributed throughout the planet by the cultural industries. Today we imagine what it means to be subjects not only from the standpoint of the culture into which we were born but also from the standpoint of an enormous variety of symbolic repertoires and models of behavior that we can cross-breed and combine. (García Canclini 2004:161)

A billboard slogan that greeted strollers along the Rambla Nova of Tarragona[2] carried the following warning: "May the color you desire for your skin not become your cross to bear." It made evident a new reality that went beyond the canons of beauty. Today we wish to have tanned skin by lying on the beaches of the Costa Dorada; we no longer need the hats and wide sunhats worn earlier by the women of the aristocracy and the bourgeoisie. In spite of this, the golden skin of the Muslim girl (with the icon of religious affiliation, the *hijab* or headscarf) is seen as a representation of her cultural difference and serves here as a reason to refuse discourses based on xenophobia and cultural racism (Martín Muñoz 2005).

The presence of immigration from outside Europe, and Muslim communities in particular, makes evident this symbolic negation that continues to operate in our collective imaginary, whether we define ourselves as coming from a certain religious culture or as being secular or agnostic. It provokes us to redefine our historiography in order to see others in order to know ourselves better. As García Canclini has written:

> In times of globalization, the most revealing object of study and the one which most questions ethnocentric or disciplinary pseudo-certainties, is interculturality. The social scientist, through empirical investigation of intercultural relations and the self-reflective critique of disciplinary fortresses, attempts to think from the position of exile. To study culture thus requires turning oneself into a specialist of intersections. (García Canclini 2004:101)

II. INTERCULTURAL DIALOGUE AND CULTURAL POLICIES IN EUROPE

As a reflection of this situation, and from a perspective of seeking new attitudes and confronting new challenges, UNESCO dedicated the year 2008 to the defense of cultural diversity and intercultural dialogue. Emphasis was placed on implementing the Convention on the Protection and Promotion of the Diversity of Cultural Expressions, which was approved in Paris on October 20, 2005, and came into effect on March 18, 2007. As the UNESCO website states:

---

[2] The "Rambla Nova" is the main street of the city of Tarragona. According to indices of the number of immigrants as of January 1, 2006 in the province of Tarragona, there were 105,211 persons of foreign nationality in the province of Tarragona, or roughly 14.3% of the total population. This percentage is higher than the overall percentage for Catalonia—13.1%—and for the province of Barcelona, 12.4%. See Gregorio Vizcaíno, *La población extranjera en Tarragona. Presente y evolución histórica*, Fundación Bofill, 2007.

the main objective of the convention consists of creating an ever more interconnected world, an environment that allows all cultural expressions to manifest themselves in their creative richness, to renovate themselves through exchange and cooperation, and to be accessible to all for the benefit of all humanity. (http://www.unesco.org)

Our interconnected world of the beginning of the 21st century is also a disconcerted world. Economic and cultural globalization requires us to face new challenges which make visible the fragility of certain societies in the face of the rapidity of communications. Among the studies that clarify these issues the most is the work by communication specialist Armand Mattelart, *Diversité culturelle et mondialisation*. Mattelart points out the difficulty of formulating stable definitions of terms in an era of globalization, especially in the area of culture (2006:93). He reminds us that the UNESCO convention is the fruit of a long process that began in 1982 with the World Conference on Cultural Policies in Mexico, during which the basic terms of a cultural policy based on the recognition of diversity were formulated:

> A policy which, by defining as its objective the development of creative faculties, both individual and collective, no longer limits itself to the area of the arts but is extended to other forms of invention (…). Nonetheless, 20 years had to go by before a new configuration of actors tried to convert this abstract principle into a practical juridical instrument capable of removing "cultural expressions" from the uniform logic of commodities.

Economic rules and cultural ones evolve at different rhythms. The rhythm of artistic and cultural expressions of minorities not included in the hegemonic forms of cultural production and reproduction is one that manifests itself outside these cultural circuits and creates others. Joost Smiers stresses this idea in his excellent and provocative study *Un mundo sin copyright. Artes y medios en la globalización* ["A world without copyrights: Art and media in a context of globalization"] (Smiers 2006:257), in which he speaks of a democracy that prospers when the viewpoints of minorities too are able to play a key role in social and cultural life. He writes: "Many artistic expressions are not taken into account in public debates over taste, language, design, musical genres, theatre, and the narrative structure of films or television programs. And this represents a loss for democracy."

The "European Year of Intercultural Dialogue" was proclaimed with the objective of calling attention to the dialogue among cultures as a matter of priority in Europe, given the challenges of globalization, and seeking the joint participation of governmental actors and civil society. In the aim of adapting this dialogue to the environment of the Spanish state, Royal Decree 367/2007 of March 16, 2007 created the "National Commission for the Encouragement and Promotion of Intercultural Dialogue," charged with reflecting on

> … the cultural diversity that derived from the successive enlargements of the European Union, the mobility resulting from the single market, migratory flows and exchanges with the rest of the world. Today it is a reality of our societies, which require adequate decision-making for Europe and for Spain. Since culture is a factor of social integration and the development of citizen identities, promoting and facilitating intercultural dialogue as a declared priority contributes

to social cohesion and the acceptance of different cultural identities and beliefs within European citizenship. From this perspective, intercultural dialogue is a factor of growth and quality of life and we must invite European citizens and all those who live in the European Union to take part in the management of this cultural diversity.[3]

In this spirit, many other authors advise us of the ever more important role of concept of culture and its necessary convergence with that of diversity. The French sociologist Alain Touraine stresses that the new century is defined by the rise of what he calls the new "cultural paradigm" (Touraine 2006). Other approaches, such as that of the anthropologist Arjun Appadurai, bring to light the fact that these new challenges require some profound changes in perception in order to allow for cultural pluralism that is sustainable over time, dynamic and without preconceived limits:

> The term cultural diversity speaks of the coexistence of groups of different cultural identities. This coexistence must have sufficient longevity, security and sustainability to allow the identities in question to produce themselves. For a cultural identity to be more than a slogan, it must evolve over time in a creative way and, given that the relations among groups are always evolving, the challenge is how to guide this evolution in a creative and sustainable way. (Appadurai and Stenou 2000:111-123)

With these words we enter discussions that are gaining more and more ground. In recent years terms such as "cultural rights" and "cultural citizenship" have gained more strength. From this perspective, a cultural right is defined as "the right to take part in the cultural life of a city."[4] Arjun Appadurai encourages us to reclaim the radical character of this concept (Appadurai y Stenou 2000:111-123):

> The very idea of *cultural rights* represents a radicalization of liberal social theory and goes significantly beyond the ideas of tolerance and recognition. It recognizes that the right to culture in daily life is fundamentally political and requires a significant level of autonomy, legal, juridical and spatial. It imposes on the states the obligation to provide spaces of cultural expression. The most radical form of this conception gives rise to *cultural citizenship*, which requires, in reality, the voluntary sharing of state power regarding law, language and territory.

To give autonomy to cultural and artistic expressions of immigrant communities and ethnic minorities of a given state would involve a great Copernican change in the new century: the creation of a cultural citizenship. I think this would cause cultural minorities and the state to be situated in a common cultural space, in which citizenship would have to be re-signified through the concept of difference. Other voices in Europe have echoed this

---

[3] Real Decreto [Royal Decree] 367/2007. See http://www.mcu.es

[4] Article 27 of the Universal Declaration of Human Rights. The Interarts Foundation, in collaboration with UNESCO and the AECI, organized the *Diálogo sobre Derechos Culturales y Desarrollo Humano* [Dialogue on Cultural Rights and Human Development] in the framework of the *Forum de las Culturas* of Barcelona in 2004. They developed an interesting questionnaire on the subject, with the aim of gaining a clearer vision of perceptions, at the regional, local and individual level, of cultural rights and the role of culture in development. See http://www.interarts.net

idea. Among them is the journal *Eurozine*,[5] whose web page contains a text that reads as follows:

> The concept of cultural citizenship responds to the development of the centrality of cultural production and consumption as necessary elements for benefiting from the rights of citizenship. Cultural citizenship is thus not assimilable to the concept of nationality, assimilation or tolerance but, rather, more closely related to the notions of recognition and empowerment. This concept is a vital instrument for the rethinking of identity and difference, and more specifically for conceptualising a Europe in which attention to political and social rights includes a full recognition of minority groups and cultural diversity.

This new Europe would not only recognize the cultural diversity that exists in its states (that is, their internal diversity and that which originates from immigration) but would also promote dialogue with the countries around it, in particular those of the Mediterranean. The attempt has been made to maintain such a climate of debate in Catalonia since the signature in 1995 of the so-called "Process of Barcelona," dedicated to developing different international discourses on these new attitudes toward the phenomena of immigration and cultural globalization.

The debates on cultural diversity in our societies will necessarily become a resource in the early part of this century, defined as it is by fragmentations, fissures and a sense of the ephemeral, and interested as it is in material and immaterial heritages—that which is fleeting and fragile and must be preserved and protected. The *cultural ecosystem* needs attention and spaces of expression, just as if it were a natural resource. As Smiers has stated (2006:17), cultural diversity and biodiversity will be two major social movements in the 21st century, since "economic globalization of the contemporary world does not guarantee the persistence of the cultural legacies to which we are heirs." The delicate balance of the cultural ecosystem needs a movement in which culture becomes conscious of its precarious state in the face of the laws of economics and consumption and develops networks that create alliances in local, regional and global settings.

III. CITIES THAT EDUCATE: BREAKING DOWN THE WALLS OF EDUCATIONAL POLICY AND CULTURAL AGENDAS

In the international context we have just described, cities take on a renewed importance in many cultural and educational discourses (Mascarell 2005). They take on a new role in nascent societies, in the midst of a full-scale crisis of hegemonic nation-states. The society emerging from the new social and technological transformations of globalization becomes volatile, permeable and changing—or, as Bauman says, "liquid" (Bauman 1999). García Canclini situates this phenomenon when he speaks of places and identities that change quickly in times of globalization:

> What is a *place* in globalization? Who speaks, and from where? What is the meaning of these contradictions between games and actors, military triumphs and political-cultural failures, worldwide dissemination and creative projects? The fascination of being in all places and the unease of not being with certainty in any, of be-

---

[5] *Eurozine* (http://www.eurozine.com), June 30, 2007.

ing many and none—all this changes the terms of the debate about the possibility of being subjects. (García Canclini 2005:25)

An example of this new role of municipal policies was the creation of the "Agenda 21 de la Cultura," promoted by the *Ayuntamiento* [city government] of Barcelona in the framework of the Forum Universal de las Culturas [Universal Forum of Cultures] of 2004, and approved on May 8, 2004, with the celebration of the IV Foro Autoridades Locales [4th Forum of Local Authorities]. The intention of this document was to promote the common efforts of cities and local governments on a world scale that were committed to human rights, cultural diversity, sustainability, participatory democracy and the creation of conditions for peace. It sought indeed to be the first document with a worldwide vocation seeking to establish the bases of a commitment of cities and local governments to cultural development. In order to assume this ambition, it proposed that May 21st of each year be celebrated as the *Worldwide Day of Cultural Diversity*. As it stressed on its website:

> In many parts of the world it may be observed that many problems of cities have to do with the relationship between culture and human development: linguistic and cultural rights of (so-called) minorities, struggles against poverty, migrations… In this context, many solutions call for giving cultural policy a more central role in local government (…). Concepts that belong to the world of cultural policy, such as memory, creativity, rituality or diversity, are now more essential than ever, in order to define local policies that are in the service of democracy and a freer form of citizenship. (http://www.agenda21culture.net)

The importance of local administration is also recognized in the area of education, shifting the outlook from the start toward ways of transmitting knowledge in a global world. The network of municipalities of the *Diputación* [provincial council] of Barcelona dedicated its most recent symposium on local educational policies to reaffirming the role of cities in all aspects and stages of knowledge. "*Ciudad.edu: nuevos retos, nuevos compromisos*" ["City.edu: new challenges, new commitments"], celebrated in October 2006, sought to concentrate on evaluating the adaptation of educational models to social change and making services adequate to emerging needs and realities—among them, making cultural diversity a serious and visible priority. The role of local administration in addressing this objective was underlined:

> Municipalities are one of the main actors in education policy, since it is on a territory that all agents of the educational system come into contact and that proximity takes on all its value (…). We begin with the strong conviction that territory is an actor of education which, when tightly enmeshed with the school system, causes the borders between formal and informal education to fade and fulfils its potential thereby. In this sense, the [local] environment must facilitate the carrying out of strategies and be endowed with resources for the fulfilling of its educational function, taking into account as well that community space is one of the elements that best helps to define their own identity.[6]

---

[6] Dossier of the convention "Ciudad.edu: nuevos retos, nuevos compromisos," World Trade Center, Barcelona, October 9-11, 2006. Special note should be taken of the session dedicated to the revision 10 years later of the Delors Report, at which Federico Mayor Zaragoza was present.

From now on, schools and cities must be permeable and must cooperate in developing the cognitive processes of pupils from the beginning and understand that contemporary knowledge society is preparing a world that is ever more interconnected, in which cultural and community referents take on more importance. The relationship between school and family comes into new relief in the context of this new attention paid to social cohesion and the relation between school and environment, between education in a given territorial space which is no longer simply a physical territory but also symbolic and expanded through connections with the media such as internet or television. Schools break down walls by recognizing that they are not the only way in which pupils form a consciousness of their identities. The old school walls are now painted with new graffiti which speak to us of the importance of youth and urban culture, and which claim their space for the construction of identities that are shaped in multiple ways, via a broad spectrum of symbolic, visual and virtual resources. They manifest themselves rapidly and in changing ways, since the hybridization of cultural identities is imperceptible or, as Appadurai has written:

> In an era when cultural groups may change their styles, when new groups arrive suddenly and disappear unpredictably, when young people revise their identities at dizzying speed, when cultural identities may change or realign, both externally and internally (…), the conception of cultural pluralism must be strictly directed toward the present. This will require the imagination of ordinary people to be agile and thus open to new regimes of diversity. (Appadurai and Stenou 2000:111-123)

The approach to cultural diversity and to the different cosmologies of the cultures that make up immigration from outside the European Community, present today in our classrooms, implies that we must take into account the inclusion of these practices as a tool of intercultural communication between immigrant pupils and native ones. The Basque educator Imanol Agirre mentions this idea in his work on "Teorías y prácticas en educación artística" [Theories and practices of artistic education]:

> The new times are characterized by a growing tendency toward a respect of difference, indeed a cult of difference, which should not constitute an obstacle to human relations. In education above all, attention to diversity (be it cultural, social or biological) is one of the main principles of politically correct and democratic education. Indeed, no one doubts that humanity, far from being a homogeneous whole, is a broad mosaic of ethos and world views, a plurality of manners of seeing the world that corresponds to a great variety of models of social configurations, systems of values, habits and customs and cultural productions (Agirre 2005:293).

IV. CLASSROOMS AND MUSEUMS FACING CULTURAL DIVERSITY: THE MUSEUM OF THE HISTORY OF IMMIGRATION OF CATALONIA

From the standpoint of the responsibility of informal education toward cultural diversity, museums too are raising questions about their collections, asking what version of history they are transmitting via their educational workshops which now include pupils from different cultural heritages and traditions (Calaf 2007). As we have seen, this discussion has little by little taken on more importance at the local, national and international level.[7] Reference is often made to an issue of the UNESCO journal *Museum International* dedicated to the cultural heritage of immigrants.[8] The issue speaks of the creation of new museums of immigration and the attention currently given to migratory processes. It introduces the debate on the necessity of deconstructing negative perceptions about the role of immigrants in contemporary societies and of implementing cultural and educational policies that interact constantly with society, aimed at promoting a non-stereotypical vision of their cultural resources in order to stake out the path of a common history in today's world. In its pages the issue further points out that attention to the cultural heritages of immigrants demonstrates the specific role of culture in processes of development—a key theme in UNESCO's work in recent decades. The ultimate goal would be to recreate a cultural heritage that includes the artistic practices of immigrant communities in order that these too may become cultural referents for the entire society.

For this very purpose we organized in 2006 the exhibit, commissioned by the Museum of Immigration of Catalonia[9] and the Museum of Hospitalet, a suburb of Barcelona, on the associations of immigrant women in Catalonia. In search of a title for the exhibit, we chose the following one: *"Viajando vidas, creando mundos. La experiencia y la obra de las mujeres migradas en Cataluña"* ["Traveling lives, creating worlds. The Experience and the Works of Immigrant Women in Catalonia"], which emphasized the agency of these women and the magnitude of their experiences.[10] The exhibit had the support of the *Diputación* of Barcelona and it travelled to various museums belonging to the network of local museums of the metropolitan area of Barcelona. The museographic project was centered on bringing out the historical aspect of the diasporic migrations and their geographical and cultural origins, but it stressed in particular the processes of construction of new identities in the destination cities and the agency and empowerment of these women through their management a diverse array of associations. In the effort to express the cultural questions that each woman carries with her when she travels, as if they were a suitcase, special importance was given to the practices of cultural and artistic production, to the symbolic production that becomes re-signified in the destination city. As we have emphasized in this article, the processes of creation in exile or in diaspora manifest themselves as a series of values of different character: the transit, the voyage, the diaspora, needs new forms of expression and new creative impulses—new works with new languages for new spaces with a different public, new contexts and new pretexts for artistic creation which does not stop because of these conditions. The artists invited to expose their work in the exhibit showed how this symbolic production becomes an enriching contribution that is hardly visible in the media and barely present in the city's museums of contempo-

---

[7] This debate is still incipient but ever more present in museological contexts. See, for example, the "IV Jornadas de Pedagogía del Arte y Museos" [Days of Art and Museum Pedagogy] organized by the Museo de Arte Moderno (Modern Art Museum) of Tarragona and dedicated to the theme of "museums and education for cultural diversity from the arts," April 18-25, 2007, Tarragona.
[8] *Museum International* no. 233-4, May 2007.
[9] This museum was founded in 2004 in Sant Adrián del Besós, Barcelona and is dedicated to the expression of the historical memory of internal migration (that is, originating from other regions of Spain) as well as extra-European migration. It seeks to contextualize discourses on migrations and what these represent in the construction of new common identities.

[10] The exhibit was commissioned by the Guinean Remei Sipi, president of the association E'waiso Ipola, an association of women of Equatorial Guinea.

rary art. Their works used the most varied mediums of expression—such as contemporary dance, theatre, audiovisual media, painting, sculpture, literature, photography—and turned themselves into surprising instruments of communication and social cohesion.[11] They constitute materials of great worth that open new and positive meanings, far from stereotyped images, and show us very compelling life stories and professional paths. They speak of the need to visualize one's cultural heritage, present in all societies although it is often unrecognized. But they further placed on the table the need to transform these collective imaginaries into a common and renewed heritage, in a Europe that recognizes both its internal diversity and that which comes from extra-European migration, providing it with places of expression in its cities, its classrooms and its museums.

V. In Conclusion: Brushstrokes for a Debate Without Limits

The cluster of concepts in circulation in this early part of the century mobilizes all our attention and capacity for understanding: diversity, citizenship, democracy, rights and law, tourism, cooperation, the ecosystem—all these need to be more *cultural* than ever. Cultural and liquid, in the sense of permeable and flexible, for the construction of a sustainable pluralism that goes beyond consensual discourse, pleasant words and images, which too often turn into sand that slips through our fingers. The consciousness of cultural diversity in our cities, regions and countries tells us as well, as we have seen, of our genealogies and heritages—cultural, social, family and personal. We always project a potential for utopia on the coming generations and that is why we attribute great importance to education, but the rapidity of the changes we are living through must now lead us to rethink these heritages starting from the present moment, from the very second we are consuming.

References

AGIRRE, Imanol. *Teorías y prácticas en Educación Artística*. Barcelona: Octaedro/EUB, 2005.

ANDERSON, B. *Comunidades imaginadas, Reflexiones sobre el origen y la difusión del nacionalismo*. México: Fondo de Cultura Económica, 1993 [original English version published in 1983].

APPADURAI, Arjun; STENOU, Katerina. "El pluralismo sostenible y el futuro de la pertenencia," in *Informe Mundial de la Cultura. Diversidad cultural, conflicto y pluralismo*, Madrid: Ediciones Mundi/Prensa/Ediciones UNESCO, 2000.

ARAYA, Mariel; RODRÍGUEZ, Estela. "Buscando habitar la ciudad. El reto de la vivienda para las mujeres inmigradas en Madrid y Barcelona," in *Scripta Nova. Revista electrónica de geografía y ciencias sociales*. Barcelona: Universidad de Barcelona, August 1, 2003, Vol. VII, no. 146(062). http://www.ub.es/geocrit/sn/sn-146(062).htm

BARKAN, Elazar; DENISE, Marie; *Borders, exiles, diasporas*. Stanford, California: Stanford University Press, 1998.

BAUMAN, Zygmunt. *Modernidad líquida*. Buenos Aires: Fondo de cultura económica, 1999.

BRAIDOTTI, Rosi. "Figuraciones de nomadismo. Identidad europea en una perspectiva crítica" in DE VILLOTA, Paloma (eds.). *Globalización y género*. Madrid: Síntesis, 1999.

CALAF, Roser; FONTAL, Olaia; VALLE, Rosa (coords.). *Museos de arte y educación. Construir patrimonios desde la diversidad*. Gijón : Trea, 2007.

CARBONELL, F i AJA, E., *Educació i immigració: els reptes educatius de la diversitat*. Barcelona: Ed. Mediterránea, 2000.

---

[11] Name of the immigrant women's artists in Catalonia: Margarita Pineda y Consuelo Bautista (Colombia); Samira Badrán (Palestine); Xia Hang (China); Motoko Araki (Japan); Niloufar Mirhadi (Iran); Jéssica Leung (United States); Natividad Oma, Montse Kondo, Paquita Belobe (Equatorial Guinea); Luz Cassino, Guigui Kohon, Paula Mariani (Argentina); Karel Mena (Venezuela).

CHAKRABARTY, Dipesh. *Provincializing Europe. Postcolonial Thought and Historical Difference.* Princeton and Oxford: Princeton University Press, 2000.

CHALMERS, F. G. *Arte, educación y diversidad cultural.* Barcelona: Paidós, 2003.

Colectivo IOE. *Inmigración, género y escuela. Exploración de los discursos del profesorado y el alumnado.* Madrid: CIDE Ministerio de Educación y Ciencia, 2007.

ESSOMBA, M.A. *SANDUK. Guia per a la formació dels educadors i educadores en interculturalitat i immigració. Programa Calidoscopi.* Barcelona: Secretaria General de Joventut-Fundació Jaume Bofill, 2001.

ESSOMBA, M.A. *Construir la escuela intercultural. Reflexiones y propuestas para trabajar la diversidad étnica y cultural.* Barcelona: Editorial Grao, 1999.

GARCÍA CANCLINI, Néstor. *Diferentes, desiguales, desconectados. Mapas de la interculturalidad.* Barcelona: Gedisa Editorial, 2004.

GARCIA, José Luis; BARAÑANO, Ascensión (coord.) *Culturas en contacto. Encuentros y desencuentros.* Madrid: Museo Nacional de Antropología-Universidad Complutense-Ministerio de Educación, Cultura y Deporte, 2003.

HERNÁNDEZ, Fernando. *Educación y cultura visual.* Barcelona: Octaedro-EUB, 2003.

MARTÍN MUÑOZ, Gema. "Mujeres musulmanas: entre el mito y la realidad" in CHECA, F. (eds.), *Mujeres en el camino. La presencia de la migración femenina en España.* Barcelona: Icaria, 2005.

MASCARELL, Ferran. *La Cultura en l'Era de la Incertesa. Societat, Cultura i Ciutat.* Barcelona: Roca Editorial, 2005.

MATTELART, Armand. *Diversidad cultural y mundialización.* Barcelona: Paidós Comunicación, 2006.

MIGNOLO, Walter. *Historias locales/diseños globales. Colonialidad, conocimientos subalternos y pensamiento fronterizo.* Madrid: Akal, 2003.

MUSEU D'ART MODERN DE TARRAGONA (MAMT). *El museu i l'educació per a la diversitat cultural de les arts.* Tarragona: Diputació de Tarragona, 2008.

PAJARES, Miguel. *La integración ciudadana. Una perspectiva para la inmigración.* Barcelona: Icaria, 2005.

RODRIGUEZ, Estela, "Ciudades interculturales: una ventana a la diversidad cultural a través de las artes y la cultura visual" in *Migraciones y mutaciones culturales en España. Sociedades, artes y literaturas.* Ed. MIAMPIKA, Landry-Wilfrid; VINUESA, Maya G.; LABRA, Ana & CAÑERO, Julio. Alcalá de Henares: Publicaciones de la UAH, 2007.

RODRÍGUEZ, Estela. "Mujeres inmigradas y medios de comunicación. Movimientos sociales en búsqueda de una representación propia" in CHECA, F. (eds.), *Mujeres en el camino. La presencia de la migración femenina en España.* Barcelona: Icaria, 2005

RODRÍGUEZ, Estela. "Políticas (inter)culturales en Barcelona. El teatro latinoamericano en la ciudad," pubished in *Revista de Arte y Cultura en América Latina*, CESA- Sociedade Científica de Estudos da Arte, Brasil (Volume XII, no. 1, 2004)

SHOHAT, Ella; STAM, Robert. *Unthinking Eurocentrism. Multiculturalism and the Media.* London: Routledge, 1994.

SMIERS, Joost. *Un mundo sin copyright. Artes y medios en la globalización.* Barcelona: Ed.Gedisa, 2006.

TOURAINE, Alain. *Un nuevo paradigma para el mundo de hoy.* Barcelona: Paidós, 2006.

VIZCAINO, Gregorio. *La població estrangera a Tarragona. Present i evolució històrica.* Fundació Bofill, 2007.

WALKER, John A.; CHAPLIN, Sarah. *Una introducción a la cultura visual.* Barcelona: Octaedro-EUB, 2002.

Immigrant Communities, Cultural Institutions and Political Space
The Success of the Immigration Museum in Melbourne, Australia

Ilham Boumankhar

University of Paris 1, Panthéon-Sorbonne, France

ilham.boumankhar@malix.univ-paris1.fr

Abstract: This article explores the concept of immigration as it is processed by the Immigration Museum in Melbourne, Australia, through the analysis of an investigation that was conducted on public museum, and the presentation of several interviews with the manager of Immigration museum, the senior curator and the manager of the Community Exhibitions. It examines how the relationship between the museum, immigrant communities and the political context establish the Australian immigration museum as a recognized social actor.

As a country, Australia is unique in that it is the smallest continent of the world. It involves a territory that is isolated in the Asia Pacific and belongs to the *Commonwealth*[1] as a former British settlement colony. This dual attribute, both geographical and political, has been consequential for the role played by immigration in Australia's social and cultural development with its specific colonial history. It is therefore not surprising that one of the oldest museums dedicated to immigration is the Immigration Museum in Melbourne, located in the State of Victoria. This museum was created with the initiative of the State Government of Victoria, who in the 1980s brought together actors to found

---

[1] *Commonwealth Secretariat*. 2004. The Commonwealth yearbook. June 2004, p.2: "The Commonwealth is an association of sovereign nations which support each other and work together towards international goals. It is also a 'family' of peoples with their common heritage in language, culture, law, education and democratic traditions, among other things. Commonwealth countries are able to work together in an atmosphere of greater trust and understanding than generally prevails among nations. By the end of 2003, there were 54 member countries in the Commonwealth."

Ilham Boumankhar is a PhD student in Cultural Studies at the University of Paris 1, Panthéon-Sorbonne. Beneficiary of research grant (allocataire de recherche) at CRICC Paris (Research Center of Images, Cultures and Cognitions), she started her research about Immigration and Museum since October 2007, with the opening of *la Cité Nationale de l'histoire de l'immigration* (the National Museum of Immigration History) in Paris. Her research focuses on Migration Studies, Cultural Theories, Ethno Cultural Relations, and Ethnomethodological approach from the perspective of the public reception. Her research thesis is a comparative study on the representation of immigration in the museum. Introducing her field research with the reception process of the everyday's life objects belonging to different immigrant communities or ethnic minorities, she made inquiries in the Immigration Museum in Melbourne (Australia) and the National Museum of Immigration History in Paris (France). She is particularly involved in questions of building identities, museum strategies, social and cultural issues, political influences, and the change in audience's beliefs about immigration.

a museum of immigration, and took the decision to set up a special section dedicated to immigration, one that remains attached to the National Museum of Victoria.[2]

The aim of this paper is to explore the social role of the museum of immigration in a context of multicultural policy and inter-community dialogue, and present the results of investigations carried out on the public museum between November 2009 and February 2010.

I. THE AUSTRALIAN MUSEUM CONTEXT

The Immigration Museum in Melbourne opened in 1998 in the former customs office[3], a symbolic place of immigration control and registration of new arrivals. This inauguration endorsed a significant socio-cultural dimension in a state that is

> one of the most culturally diverse in Australia. Almost a quarter of its population is foreign born, and 43.5% of the people, when they do not themselves come from abroad, have at least one parent who was not born in the Australian soil.

Population comes from more than 200 different countries, speaks over 180 languages or dialects and joins more than 110 religious faiths.[4]

Australia, therefore, brings together in the same area a group of multiethnic and multicultural communities, making migration a situation of great complexity.

Yet, even though Australia now practices a multicultural policy, it has been in place only since 1972[5] when it came about as a result of repealing an immigration policy based on criteria of racial discrimination and exclusion. Indeed, *Terra Australis*[6], which was primarily a penitentiary

---

[2] The Museum of Victoria includes the Melbourne Museum, the Immigration Museum, the Scienceworks and the Royal Exhibition Building. Further information is available on the official website of the museum. URL: http://museumvictoria.com.au/ (Visited on November 8th, 2009)

[3] "The Customs House building is one of Melbourne's most important 19th century public buildings. In this building customs officers recorded all goods entering or leaving Victoria; the customs duties they collected formed the backbone of government revenue. Customs officers also controlled immigration, recording every arrival, and administering a White Australia Policy that excluded immigrants on the basis of their race. Customs officers were also in charge of censorship, determining what material might offend mainstream social values." Source: http://museumvictoria.com.au/customshouse/ (Visited on september 6th, 2010)

[4] SEBASTIAN, P. 2007. *Mobiliser les communautés et transmettre leurs histoires: le rôle du musée de l'Immigration dans l'une des villes les plus multiculturelles du monde.* In *Museum International*, N°233/234, vol.59. N°1/2, UNESCO, p.157. (Translation: SEBASTIAN, P. 2007. *Mobilizing Communities and Sharing Stories: the role of the Immigration Museum in one of the most multicultural cities in the world.* In *Museum International*, No. 233/234, vol.59. No. 1 / 2, UNESCO).

[5] DUTTON, D. 2002. *One of us: a century of Australian citizenship.* Sydney, UNSW Press, p.75: "The end of the White Australia policy eventually came from the Labor Party and its group of anti-racism reformers when Whitlam won government in December 1972. The Party's platform called for a non-racial immigration programme and ratification of *the International Convention for the Elimination of All Forms of Racial Discrimination (1966)*. This had become party policy in mid-1971 at the biennial National Conference, culminating a long crusade to reform Labor policy from within."

[6] BALBI, Adrien. 1833. *Abrégé de géographie*. Paris, éditions Jules Renouard, p.38: Dans cet ouvrage l'auteur explique comment dès le seizième siècle, toutes les terres connues sont partagées en trois monde: "le *Monde ancien (orbis vetus)* qui embrassait l'Europe, l'Asie et l'Afrique; le *Monde nouveau (orbis novus)* qui comprenait l'Amérique; et la *Terre australe* ou *magellanique (terra australis* ou *magellanica)*." (Translation: BALBI, A. 1833. *Abridged of geography*. Paris: Editions Jules Renouard, p.38: In this book the author explains how in the sixteenth century all the known lands are divided into three worlds: "the *Former World (Orbis vetus)* that embracing Europe, Asia and Africa and the *New World (novus orbis)*, which included America, and *South Land* or *Magellanic Land (terra australis* or *magellanica)*").

destination[7], quickly became an extra British colony in the French and British conquest. Great Britain and Ireland were the two main sources of settlement for over a century and a half, immigration policy having then focused on creating an ideal society homogeneous and white[8]. Subsequently, other European countries have fueled settlement migration, the criteria for entry to the territory being still based on the ethnicity of immigrants, according to White Policy[9]. "Practiced today, such a policy would lead to disapproval and certainly even indignation."[10]

It is precisely international opinion, new university exchanges, and the geographical reality that led Australia to revise its immigration policy in a progressive manner. When the Labor Party[11] won the elections in 1972, it repealed the White Policy and implemented a policy modeled on social diversity[12], but mostly and implicitly allowed the recognition of the rights for Aboriginal people[13]. Multiculturalism is a policy that applies not only to immigration but also to all Australians. Beyond the cultural and ethnic diversity of Australia, it is a set of policy measures that respond to the cultural variety of Australian society.[14]

The creation of the Immigration Museum contributes to the implementation of a multicultural policy[15]. The musealization of immigration allows the identification of new areas of discussion of immigration issues, and presents the diversity of items offered or loaned by immigrants to tell their stories. The museum becomes a "social actor embedded in a territory with legitimacy and guaranteeing

---

[7] VERNAY, J-F., BEN-MESSAHEL, S. 2009. *Des frontières de l'interculturalité: Etude pluridisciplinaire de la représentation culturelle: Identité et Altérité*. Villeneuve-d'Ascq, Presses Universitaires du Septentrion, p.18 : « L'Australie avait été la dernière colonie britannique à accepter des bagnards entre 1850 et 1868). (Translation: VERNAY, J-F., BEN-MESSAHEL, S. 2009. *Borders of interculturalism: Multidisciplinary study of cultural representation: Identity and Otherness*. Villeneuve d'Ascq, Presses Universitaires du Septentrion, p.18: "Australia was the last British colony to accept convicts between 1850 and 1868").

[8] PONS, X. 1996. *Multiculturalism in Australia*. Paris, L'Harmattan, p.32: "Especially, for nearly two centuries, Australia was desperately trying to preserve a "pure" racial society which is a fantasy rather than reality" (Original version in French: PONS, X. 1996. *Le multiculturalisme en Australie*. Paris, L'Harmattan).

[9] Ibid, p.63 : « the White Australia Policy would be for more than half a century, an article of faith for the vast majority of Australians (…) to prevent the entry of Asian immigrants but mostly to expel some ethnic minorities. " See reference: *Press Release, Immigration*, William McMahon Prime Minister, 4 May 1972, in series A1838, item 1531/1 part 10, NAA. Cité par DUTTON, D. 2002. *One of us: a century of Australian citizenship*. Sydney, UNSW Press, p.77: « The aim of immigration policy remains the preservation in Australia of an essentially homogenous society».

[10] PONS, X. 1996. *Multiculturalism in Australia*. Op. cit., p32.

[11] Ibid, p.98: "As a convinced anti-racist and anticolonialist, Whitlam believed that the Conservative policy on immigration was harmful to the country, partly because it was filled with intolerance; 'it should not be discrimination based on race, color or nationality,' he declared in 1971. It remained for him to gain power in order to pass his noble ideas into reality. In December 1972 the Labour Party won the parliamentary elections and Whitlam became Prime Minister. He would soon launch the entry of Australia into the era of multiculturalism."

[12] JUPP, J. 2007. *From White Australia to Woomera. The story of Australian immigration*. Cambridge, Cambridge University Press, Second Edition, p.23: "Even before multiculturalism had been effectively entrenched as official policy, there were already very large language communities in Australia."

[13] PONS, X. 1996. *Multiculturalism in Australia*. Op. cit., p.99: « During the postwar, The Aborigenes's integration in the Australian society always encountered many difficulties. (…) We did not any longer considered their imminent extinction, but we did not resigned to the extent for them and their culture, a place that is dignified and equitable in a country that was theirs yet."

[14] Hawke, B. 1990. Foreword. In *National Agenda for a Multicultural Australia – The Year in Review August 1989-July 1990*. Canberra, AGPS, p.69. Quoted by PONS, X. 1996. *Multiculturalism in Australia*. Op. cit., p.125 : « It is a policy that manages the consequences of cultural diversity in the interests of the individual and society as a whole».

the broadcast content and a spatial-temporal framework of citizenship."[16] The Australian case shows clearly that the museum is a political tool in charge of defending the government's multicultural policy and maintains an ongoing dialogue with communities in the State of Victoria. The policy is "intended to encourage the development of cultural minorities in the majority so as to create an atmosphere of mutual tolerance, a social body that knows how to combine diversity and homogeneity, which is not a simple mosaic of race or religion, where ethnic groups coexisted without actually meet and even fewer understand."[17] The museum exhibits embraced both the collective and political histories that shaped the Australian immigration while integrating the individual experience of each Australian, through ongoing collaboration between the actors of the museum and immigrant communities.

II. THE IMMIGRATION MUSEUM IN MELBOURNE

The Immigration Museum in Melbourne aims to introduce and explore the history of immigrants in the state of Victoria.[18] Featuring also a Discovery Center[19], it allows visitors to share their stories, but also access a database on immigrant communities in the state. As for the permanent exhibition, it presents the history of immigration since the arrival of settlers, the fate of Aboriginal people, the different immigration policies, the major historical waves of immigrants, and the integration of newcomers into the host society, with the desire to embody every story.[20] There are various objects that illustrate the permanent exhibition, as tools of work, family memories, cultural products, traditional handicrafts, decorative items or everyday objects such as clothing, shoes, accessories, etc. Each object is placed under a window that marks the different waves of migration and the diversity of newcomers and introduces visitors to what is immigration.[21]

---

[15] SAUVAGE, A. 2008. *Between law and science: Australian museums dealing with aboriginal critique*. In LAGAYETTE, P. (dir.). 2008. *Rencontres australiennes. Regards croisés sur l'identité d'un peuple et d'une nation*. Paris, Presses de l'Université Paris-Sorbonne, p.58: "Museums have always proved to be closely linked to the politics of the day, both reflecting their society and providing them which cultural and scientific justifications so as to legitimate economic and social policies. Their recent restructure, both through renovating and building new museums, testify to the wind of change that is operating under the auspices of a globalised reflection on colonial heritage and its racial classification of people." (Translation: In LAGAYETTE, P. 2008. *Meeting Australia: crossing perspectives on the identity of a people and a nation*. Paris, Presses de l'Université Paris-Sorbonne).

[16] VIDAL, G. 2006. *Contribution à l'étude de l'interactivité: Les usages du multimédia de musée*. Bordeaux, Presses Universitaires de Bordeaux, Collection L@byrinthes, p.52. (Translation : VIDAL, G. 2006. *Contribution to the study of interactivity: The uses of multimedia in museum*. Universitaires de Bordeaux, Collection L@byrinthes).

[17] PONS, X. 1996. *Multiculturalism in Australia*. Op. cit, p.24.

[18] Presentation text of museum available in the official website: "The Immigration Museum explores the stories of real people from all over the world who have migrated to Victoria." URL: http://museumvictoria.com.au/immigrationmuseum/about-us/ (Visited in September 18th, 2010)

[19] Ibid: The Discovery Centre allows "delving into our rare collection of books in the reference library and exploring our online and multimedia resources to learn more about migrant communities and your own migration history. You can also read migration stories, or write your own, on the Share A Story database." URL: http://museumvictoria.com.au/immigrationmuseum/discoverycentre/visit-our-onsite-centre/ (Visited in September 18th, 2010)

[20] "From the reasons for making the journey, to the moment of arrival in a new country, and the impact on indigenous communities, these stories are sometimes sad, sometimes funny, but always engaging." Presentation text of museum available in the official website. URL: http://museumvictoria.com.au/immigrationmuseum/about-us/ (Visited in September 18th, 2010)

The first theme of the permanent exhibition is entitled "Leaving Home"[22] and introduces visitors to the different reasons why men and women, sometimes whole families, are leaving their country of origin to settle in the State of Victoria. This exhibition consists of both sounds, objects, moving images and video projected to explore both the motivations causing people to immigrate, but what these people have brought with them.[23] The sounds recreate the atmosphere of marine ports that receive thousands of immigrants. The objects are those that immigrants brought with them, starting with their suitcases. The moving images are a series of photographs projected rapidly (20 frames per second) so as to create a movement. It shows men, women and children of all ages who are getting on with a suitcase. The videos are also projected showing the reality of migration routes and testimonies of the different life stories of immigrants, ranging from forced migration (due to war) and selective immigration (to have a better life) (see Photo 1). The texts that accompany each and every part of the permanent exhibition highlight the diverse origins of Australian immigration.[24]

Other theme make up the permanent exhibition[25] and thus has various tools that demonstrate the skills of newcomers, as well as clothing and costume traditions from their countries of origin, and various administrative documents tracing their travels since leaving until they arrived in Victoria.[26]

---

[21] Introductory text to the first permanent exhibition of immigration from Melbourne, Victoria, entitled "Leaving Home": "Luggage lies at the heart of the migration experience. It is a symbol of both what is brought and what is left behind. It contains people's hopes and fears, as they leave one life and begin another." ©*Immigration Museum*, Melbourne, Victoria. (November 2009- February 2010)

[22] Presentation text of the exhibition available in URL: http://museumvictoria.com.au/leaving-home (Visited in January 7th, 2010): Event Type: Permanent Exhibition: "What would it take to make you leave your homeland and travel thousands of miles to another country? People have migrated to Australia for many reasons. Some flee from the ravages of war, hunger, religious persecution or political repressions. Others have been lured by a sense of adventure, by the prospect of a new beginning, of owning land, of making a fortune, or to be reunited with love ones. Many arrive with keepsakes, precious reminders of loved ones or special places. The experiences of arriving in a new country vary from person to person. Using sound, objects, still and moving images we explore the reasons why people left their countries to come to Australia and what they brought with them." ©*Immigration Museum*, Melbourne, Victoria. (November 2009- February 2010)

[23] Ibid.

[24] Presentation text of the exhibition "Crossing the globe" in the Immigration Museum in Melbourne, Victoria: "World events have resulted in significant waves of migration, drawing many people to Australia for more than 200 years." ©*Immigration Museum*, Melbourne, Victoria. (November 2009- February 2010)

[25] These themes are: "Leaving Home, Immigrant stories and timeline, Journeys of a Lifetime, Customs Gallery, Getting in, Station Pier: gateway to a new life, Ancient Hampi." URL: http://museumvictoria.com.au/immigrationmuseum/whatson/current-exhibitions/ (Visited in January 7th, 2010)

[26] Presentation text of the exhibition "Immigrant stories and timeline" available in URL: http://museumvictoria.com.au/immigrationmuseum/whatson/current-exhibitions/immigrant-stories/ (Visited in January 7th, 2010): Event Type: Permanent Exhibition: "Immigration is about us all—those who were here and those who came. Settling into a new country is not easy. Immigrants have to adapt to an unfamiliar environment and lifestyle, while maintaining aspects of their previous culture and way of life. Many newcomers spent their new lives in limbo, spending months in temporary migrant accommodation, committed to two year labour contracts. For others, settlement has been far easier because they spoke English, or government had offered assistant land or home scheme. Generations of immigrants have had to adapt to a new climate, new landscape, new language, new currency, and new lifestyle, especially those who have settled in rural areas. Each immigrant has their own unique story to tell. Whilst for many it was difficult, the vast majority eventually found their feet. This gallery explores why they came, where they settled and how they started a new life in Victoria. Around the walls of the gallery is an immigration timeline that highlights key events in the history of immigration."

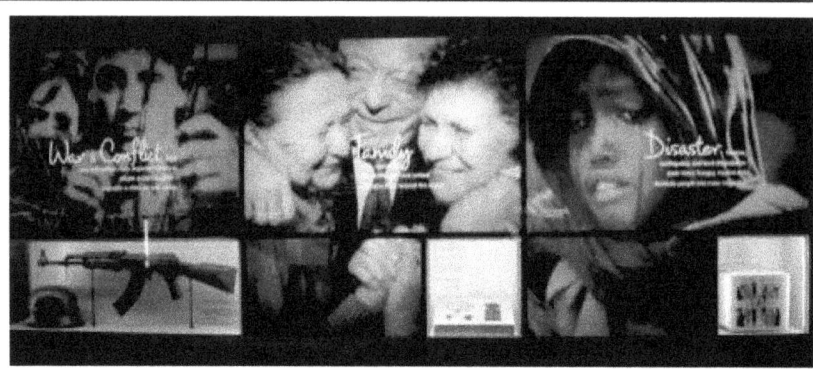

Photo 1: Thematic Presentation at the Entrance to the Immigration Museum in Melbourne (©Ilham Boumankhar 2010)

The various reasons[27] leading people to immigrate to Australia are surveyed upon entry to the museum, and are accompanied by different types of objects to illustrate each historical period, such as a box of the Red Cross[28] on display to illustrate the International conflict or a gun of World War II[29] to illustrate the war. An entire floor of the museum is devoted to the Victoria harbour "Station Pier,"[30] which is a symbolic place of the passage of all immigrants. An important part of the exhibition is devoted to immigration policy in Australia; the various tests of passage were subjected to immigrants, and the paperwork provided by the customs office (see Photo 2).[31]

A history of government measures related to immigration policy is presented,

Photo 2: Administrative Documents Exposed in the Immigration Museum in Melbourne (©Ilham Boumankhar 2010)

---

[27] Presentation text of the permanent exhibition: "Why did you or your family come to Australia? People have migrated to Australia for many different reasons, from many different places. Freedom, A better life, Disaster, Family, War, Conflict..., etc." ©*Immigration Museum*, Melbourne, Victoria. (November 2009- February 2010)

[28] Information listed on cartels: "*International Red Cross First aid container*, used during the conflict in Bosnia, 1992-95. The box originally contained beans, sugar, oil, corned beef, cheese, yeast, soap, detergent and toothpaste. (On loan from Australian Red Cross)." ©*Immigration Museum*, Melbourne, Victoria. (November 2009- February 2010)

[29] Information listed on cartels: "*World War Two German helmet. Chinese Type 56 rifle* commonly used in conflicts such as Vietnam, Cambodia and Korea during the 1950s-1970s. (©*Museum Victoria collection*)."

[30] Presentation text of the exhibition "Station Pier: gateway to a new life" available in URL: http://museumvictoria.com.au/immigrationmuseum/whatson/current-exhibitions/station-pier/ (Visited in January 7th, 2010) Event Type: Permanent Exhibition: "The exhibition provides an historical overview of Station Pier, including its early days as Railway Pier in the 1850s, and its upgrade in the 1920s in response to the growing needs of the city and port of Melbourne."

through various administrative documents that reflect the different periods of the measures (such as passports, identity papers and travel documents).

Four sections share the history of immigration policy in Australia: first is the period between 1840 and 1900[32], representing Australia as the second British Empire, since the settlers came mainly from Great Britain. The second period was between 1901 and 1945[33] and corresponds to the application of the Immigration Restriction Act (or White Policy), which is the law implementing the access to Australian territory through ethnic criteria. The objective of this policy is the preservation of a white society. The third period is between 1946 and 1972[34], which corresponds to the relaxation of immigration policy after the Second World War, and allows trade with neighboring countries that are mainly Asia and the Middle East. And the fourth period is more recent and is between 1973 and 2006[35], and is the policy of multicultural Australia, where the question of national identity is still ongoing. This last part emphasizes the policy of opening cultural and ethnic diversity of Australian society, which does not solidify the concept of identity in a definition, but adapts to the diversity of individuals in the Australian multicultural society.

Thus in the section "Immigration and National Identity," migration history experienced by Australia raises various issues

---

[31] Presentation text of the exhibition "Getting In" available in URL: http://museumvictoria.com.au/immigrationmuseum/whatson/current-exhibitions/getting-in/ (Visited in January 7th, 2010): Event Type: Permanent Exhibition: "More than 9 million people have migrated to Australia since 1788. Countless others have tried and failed. Find out why… This permanent exhibition documents the immigration policies that have shaped Victoria and Australia since the 1800s and how these policies have been a significant factor in forming a national identity. This confronting exhibition utilises images, historical objects, a computer interactive and personal stories to explore the impact of these policies and the resulting cultural diversity in Victoria. Getting In was developed in response to market research conducted at the Immigration Museum that found visitors wanted to know more about the process of getting in to Australia, what people went through, who was accepted and who wasn't, and the effect this had on society. The exhibition does this by exploring the history of immigration policy and how it has changed dramatically over the past two hundred years. Four timeframes outline the main threads in immigration policy: the gold rush days of the 1840s to 1900, Federation to the end of the Second World War (1901 to 1945), then post-war to the early seventies (1946 to 1972) and finally 1973 to the present day."

[32] Presentation text: "1840-1900: Old England and the New." "During the nineteenth century most immigrants came from Great Britain. (…) Immigration policy was governed by Great Britain, although the Australian colonies began to introduce their own immigration acts in the mid-nineteenth century, following the end of convict transportation. These acts aimed to control the massive influx of people during the gold rushes." © Immigration Museum de Melbourne. (October 2009- March 2010)

[33] Presentation text: "1901-1945: One nation, one people, one destiny." "(…) The newly federated Australian Government quickly introduced national legislation to protect its security and asserts its identity as a member of the British Empire. One of the first acts passed was the Immigration Restriction Act—known as the White Australia policy." © Immigration Museum de Melbourne. (October 2009- March 2010)

[34] Presentation text: "1946-1972: Encouraging immigration." "Extending the invitation: many immigration assistance schemes were established in the post-war period. (…)The 1950 Colombo Plan allowed students from developing countries to study in Australia, some of whom were later accepted as permanent residents." © Immigration Museum de Melbourne. (October 2009- March 2010)

[35] Presentation text: "1973-today. 'Australia for tomorrow'": "Since the early 1970s Australia's immigration levels have been dramatically reduced and the composition of the intake has changed. The proposition of European immigrants has declined while immigration from Asia and the Middle East has increased. Despite this, in 1999-2000 the largest number of immigrants came from New Zealand; the second largest number came from Great Britain. Australia today accepts immigrants from any country, based on their ability to meet criteria determined by the Government according to Australia's economic, social political needs. In 2001, nearly one in four Australians was born overseas ." © Immigration Museum de Melbourne. (October 2009- March 2010)

related to the societal definition of national identity: "For over two centuries immigration has raised questions about national identity. What kind of society do we want? Is Australia a southern outpost of British culture? Or is its identity bound to Asia and the Pacific? Is there a 'typical' Australian? Or does the very idea of 'typical' deny the diversity of our society? How does Aboriginal identity fit into the idea of Australia as an immigrant nation? Can different cultures maintain their identities while participating in a 'national identity'?"[36] And the museum to clarify that the immigration policy is fluctuating according to "the increasing population, developing a work force, responses to global humanitarian needs that have been tempered by the preferences of particular nationalities and cultures."[37] The museum takes a constructivist position focusing on openness to diversity and invites visitors to question concepts such as identity, nation, immigration, culture, race or ethnicity.

Stories of individual immigrants, administrative difficulties they went through to settle in Australia, obstacles they encountered in integrating into Australian society, and different modes of adaptation, whether on the professional, social and cultural level, are explored. With the desire to immerse visitors in the experiences of immigrants, many facilities are also introduced, such as dictation test[38], which was part of the systems used to select immigrants based on their ethnic origins. Thus, the entrant must write a dictated text in a European language and was denied access to the territory in case of failure.

Similarly, an interview room equipped with interactive screens allows the simulation of an interview between an officer of the Immigration Control and various applicants to entry visa (see Photos 3). The viewer is positioned in place of the screening officer, and has a detailed sheet that must be completed, while at the screen, an immigrant presents the reasons why he wants to stay in Australia. The visitor is instructed to decide, through a touch screen, if the candidate is authorized to obtain an entry visa to Australia.

The ambition for the museum is to explain to visitors the various evaluation criteria for immigration agents over several periods that marked major changes in immigration policy in Australia. The exhibition is set based on an inclusive approach, allowing each visitor to feel involved in the issue of immigration. The "Community Gallery"[39] allows visitors to participate in exhibitions, sharing content objects, photographs, memorabilia and personal stories. Maria Tence[40], manager of the National Museum of Victoria, responsible for community exhibitions, works with community representatives, associations or families belonging to the community presented. If there are on average three communities that are exposed in the year, very often the choice of communities is related to comprehension difficulties

---

[36] Presentation text: "Immigration and national identity." "(…) The selection of immigrants over time has always been influenced by the sort of nation that governments and special interest groups have wanted to create. Issues such as increasing the population, developing a workforce and responding to global humanitarian needs have been tempered by preferences for particular nationalities and cultures." © Immigration Museum de Melbourne. (October 2009- March 2010)
[37] Ibid.

[38] Exposition "1901-1945 The closed door." Presentation text: "The dictation test was intended to conceal the fact that Australia had a policy of outright racial discrimination, which would have been diplomatically unpopular. It aimed to stop non-European immigration in an indirect way—by refusing admission to those who failed to pass a test given in a foreign language. Dictation tests were intentionally confusing, even when read in English. About 50 words long, they had to be written down in a prescribed language. If an applicant did manage to pass the test, it could be conducted again in other languages until the applicant failed." © Immigration Museum de Melbourne. (October 2009-March 2010).

Photos 3: Screens in Place in the Interview Room. (Note: Photo A is a touch screen available to the visitor and with whom he chooses the applicant's file that he wishes to question. Photo B is a video screen, where you can see the applicant submit the reasons why he wants to stay in Australia) (©Ilham Boumankhar 2010)

encountered in relation to their stories and their cultural practices. The year 2009-2010 was devoted to the communities in which developments in their country remains tense and sometimes hopeless, such as Palestinian communities, Kurdish and Timorese. The role of the gallery community is to maintain dialogue with communities in the State of Victoria but also to establish exchanges between communities. There are also cultural festivals communities[41] that aim to promote these exchanges.

III. INVESTIGATIONS CONDUCTED AT MELBOURNE MUSEUM

Between November 2009 and February 2010, I conducted a series of investigation on both audiences at the Melbourne Museum and during the reception of the exhibits under the theme of immigration and management of the museum about the organization exhibitions related to the diversity of migratory origins.[42]

In this section, I study firstly the results

---

[39] Presentation text: "Community Gallery." "Community Gallery exhibitions are developed by Victoria's culturally, linguistically and religiously diverse communities in collaboration with the Immigration Museum. These exhibitions are community generated and represent stories, photographs and objects of significance to them. These exhibitions allow Victorians communities to share their culture and heritage through their immigration stories. In sharing the stories of Victoria's multicultural communities we contribute to the understanding of modern Australian society. The museum's collections are enriched with artefacts and stories from these exhibitions, for future generations to learn from and be inspired by." © Immigration Museum de Melbourne. (October 2009- March 2010)
[40] Maria Tence, *Manager, Community Exhibitions*, was among those interviewed in the fourth part of this article.

[41] Presentation text about the "Community Cultural Festivals" available in the museum official website: "The Immigration Museum presents three community cultural festivals per year. The festivals celebrate and promote Victoria's rich cultural diversity. Festivals are developed and presented in partnership with representatives from a particular culturally diverse community and include contributions from organizations and individuals." URL: http://museumvictoria.com.au/immigrationmuseum/about-us/community-engagement/cultural-festivals/ (Visited in September 19th, 2010)
[42] This work is part of a research thesis [by?] in Cultural Studies at the University of Paris 1 Panthéon-Sorbonne, under the provisional title: "Receipt process of material object in society's museum: comparative study between the Immigration Museum in Melbourne and the National Museum of the History of Immigration in Paris."

of a questionnaire distributed to the public to analyze quantitative data that informs us about the profile of visitors and reception of exhibitions. And secondly, I present the summary of the three interviews conducted with Padmini Sebastian, Manager of the Immigration Museum in Melbourne, Maria Tence Manager of the Community Exhibition Gallery, and Moya McFadzean, Curator Senior of the Immigration Museum in Melbourne.

A. Presentation and analysis of questionnaire results

The questionnaire consists of 20 questions that aim to investigate the profile of visitors, their circumstances and goals of their visits and their "impressions" on the treatment of immigration by the Melbourne Museum. It consists mainly of closed questions[43], which gives the possibility of completing the answer when the frame of predetermined response is inadequate, but also some open questions[44]. This survey, mainly quantitative, contributes also, thanks to the open questions, to refine knowledge on the profile of visitors, to assess their relationship with immigration, to understand the circumstances of visits, and to clarify the extent of their interest in the museum of immigration and expectations regarding the information disseminated. I collected 247 questionnaires completed by visitors between December 2009 and February 2010. Prior to the analysis of questionnaire results, I inserted a question allowing the visitor to check the age to which he belongs. 26% of visitors, who completed the questionnaire, are in the age group 25-30 years, 23% of visitors 50 years and older, 19% are between 15 and 25 years, 17% are between 30 and 40 years and 15% are between 40 and 50years. Thus we can see a good distribution of the age group of visitors who completed the questionnaire.

The content of the questionnaire is divided into four parts. The first part gives us information about the visitor: "Is he an immigrant? What is his country of origin? Did any members of his family immigrate to Australia? Who? Did they find it difficult to integrate into Australian society? Why did they decide to immigrate in the first place? Did they intend to return to their country of birth?"

The second part informs about the motivations for visiting the museum: "What is the main reason you have decided to come to the museum of immigration? (Your own history; family history; genealogical research; or curiosity, etc.) Did you find the immigration museum interesting? If not, why? Is this your first visit?"

The third part brings us into direct relationship with the visitor experience with exhibitions: "What was most memorable for you? (Explanatory Materials and Talks, The Artifacts, Your general experience of the Museum, Other lasting impressions.) Did you find objects related to your own history? Or did you find information linked to your story? Did you keep cultural practices in relation to your home country?"

The fourth part is more about the opinions of visitors on the immigration issue: "Do you believe in a multicultural society where immigrants retain their native culture, traditions and speak the language they want? If yes, do you think this society is Australia? Generally speaking, has immigration had a harmful or a beneficial effect

---

[43] LANGENDORFF, F. 2007. *Individu, culture et société: Sensibilisation aux sciences humaines*. Paris, Publibook, p.141: « Une question fermée propose un cadre de réponse prédéterminé, que ce soit: oui/non ou des catégories de réponses parmi lesquelles la personne interrogée fait son choix ». (Translation: LANGENDORFF, F. 2007. *Individual, Culture and Society: Awareness of social sciences*. Paris, Publibook, p.141: "A closed question offers a predetermined answer, either yes / no or different response categories of which the respondent makes his choice.")

[44] Ibid, p.141: "An open question "opens" a lot of freedom in the response, it often starts with "what do you think of"...."

on your way of life? Do you think that the Museum deals well the immigration question? If not, can you explain?"

This survey provides us, with both quantitative data that are numbered, but also qualitative data that shed light on connections between the visitor and his relationship with immigration. Therefore, to the question "Are you an immigrant in Australia?" responses are shared with 105 visitors who answered "yes" and 142 who answered "no." It is a sharing, almost equal, that is yet not visible in the responses to the question that follows. Indeed, if the visitor answered "yes," he should complete the following question No. 2, which is "what is your country?" And if he answered "no" skip to question No. 3. But over 247 questionnaires collected, there are 238 visitors who responded to the question about country of origin (No. 2) while logically, only 105 visitors were asked. This reflects the fact that the term "immigrant" means every person in Australia with immigrant history. If in France a "settler" or "immigrant" is clearly someone who was born in a foreign country, which makes the "quality of immigrants as permanent[45]," in Australia, immigrants, formerly designated by the word "settler" which means "founder of a colony" means all those with an immigrant story. It is also a concept that is intergenerational, because a person born in Australia considers himself as an immigrant if his parents or even his grandparents were not born in Australia. This may be related to the fact that one of the peculiarities of the Multiculturalism Act is to encourage immigrants to live in Australian society by importing their own culture.[46] Australians with immigrant backgrounds are always connected to their country of origin, and define themselves as Australian with another origin. This explains that 96% of visitors answer the second question about the country of origin. This is an issue that highlights the diversity of countries of origin of visitors, and emphasizes the multicultural nature of Australian society, and Melbourne in particular. And the countries of origin that are predominantly present in the diverse origins of the visitors encountered, are Italy, New Zealand, Greece or England and Wales. Beyond these mentioned countries, countries of origin are divided between other European countries and also Asian countries. Question No. 3 is about the family migration route[47]: "Is that one or more members of your family who immigrated to Australia?" A large majority of visitors answered "yes," confirming that the term "immigrant" is part of a family trajectory. Question No. 4 focuses on members of the family visitors who immigrated to Australia.

98 visitors say it is their parents who immigrated to Australia and 111 visitors answered that it was their grandparents. Therefore, a large majority of visitors are the second or third generation immigrant

---

[45] "According to the definition adopted by the French High Council for Integration, an immigrant is a person who is born abroad and who resides in France. French people who were born abroad and living in France are therefore not counted. Conversely, some immigrants have become French, the other remaining foreigners. People who are foreign and immigrant, do not fully coincide: an immigrant is not necessarily foreign and conversely, some foreigners were born in France (mainly minors). The quality of an immigrant is permanent: a person continues to belong to the immigrant population even if he is French by acquisition. It is the country of birth, not nationality at birth, which defines the origin geography of an immigrant." URL: http://www.insee.fr/fr/methodes/default.asp?page=definitions/immigre.htm (Visited in September 26th, 2010)

[46] JUPP, J. 1997. *Immigration and National Identity: Multiculturalism*. In G. Stokes ed. *The Politics of Identity in Australia*, Cambridge: Cambridge University Press, pp. 132-144. The author outlines the objectives that are contradictory to the law about multiculturalism, which is that for every individual to preserve its own identity already established, and adding a multicultural identity that emphasizes adherence to the values, institutions and forms of behavior rather than to belong to one culture (British-Australian white) uniform.

in Australia. Question No. 5 addresses the difficulties of integrating immigrants into Australian society (including visitors and their families). To the question "Did they find it difficult to integrate into Australian society?" more than half of the visitors viewed answered "no." This demonstrates an ease in integration, whatever is the country of origin of immigrants in Australian society[48]. In Question No.6, "why did they decide to immigrate?" two responses to the four choices dominate; "economic reasons" and that "to join another family member." The "political reasons" came in third place and "discovering a new country" in last place with little variation. This is an indicator of the health of the Australian economy that "is experiencing certain prosperity. (...) It is the service sector, not agriculture, which is driving the Australian economy. Tourism and education in particular are an important source of revenue for the country."[49] Adding that "to join another family member" is a motivation that may go hand in hand with the "economic reasons." Question No. 7 deals with the intentions of these immigrants (including the visitor and his family): "Did they intend to return to their country of origin?" This question is deliberately vague about the nature of return: temporary or permanent. However, a large majority of visitors (235) said they did not intend to return to their countries of origin. Immigration concerned is permanent.

This first part of the questionnaire shows the personals and subsidiaries relations that visitors have with the concept of immigration. In this case, in the Melbourne Museum, most visitors are immigrants or descendants of immigrants who have no difficulty integrating into Australian society and also to designate themselves as immigrant.

The second part of the questionnaire informs us about the motivations that led the visitors to come to the Immigration Museum in Melbourne. To the question No. 8: "What is the main reason you have decided to come to the museum of immigration?" many visitors replied for "family history" and for "genealogy." Indeed, the Immigration Museum in Melbourne has a genealogical center[50] allowing visitors to conduct genealogical research from administrative records or patronymic information. Other responses of visitors are for "their own history," or "curiosity" or "other." In the questionnaire, if the visitor replied "other," he has the opportunity to complete the nature of his response. Over 9 visitors who checked "other," 4 did not complete the answer. But 5 visitors

---

[47] FORLOT, G. 2008. *With his language in his pocket: trajectory of French emigrants in Canada (1945-2000)*. Louvain-La-Neuve, Louvain University Press, p.77:"The migration trajectory is more a synonym for "path." It includes four phases. The first phase, the pre-migration, is not necessarily generating a migration plan, even if it is intrinsically linked subsequently. It is first coined by the collective and individual history of everyone, it contains events related to the country of origin or destination (war, economic recession, the socio-political crises ...) and to migrants themselves (for example, family tensions (...) meeting ...). (...) In addition to these events, which is found throughout the trajectory, everyone is subject to representations of what is possible with migration and what can be the country of destination. (...) This first phase is composed of two basic components: the substrate and the contact. (...) The second phase, the migration project, comes both from this personal and collective story pre-migratory and a will power—or obligation—to live a different experience. (...) The path or trajectory is the third phase (...) it precedes a fourth phase, the migration experience, where migrants become immigrants—but still emigrating as he arrives with his references and his history, lives a strong personal development of many events and an adaptation process that takes several forms."(Original version in French: FORLOT, G. 2008. *Avec sa langue en poche: parcours de français émigrés au Canada (1945-2000)*. Louvain-La-Neuve, Presses universitaires de Louvain).

[48] That we relate to the policy of selective immigration based on professionals, students, linguistic, and financial criteria.

[49] PONS, X. 2005. *Words of Australia*. Toulouse, PU Mirail, p.38 (Original version in French: PONS, X. 2005. *Les mots de l'Australie*. Toulouse, PU Mirail).

mentioned "tourist map," "random," "on the advice of someone," and 2 others have written "research school." 206 visitors said they came for personal reasons related to their own history, their family and genealogical research. This question highlights the success of the main mission of the Melbourne Museum which is to "create a strong relationship with the various communities in the State of Victoria."[51] The next issue (No. 9) is about the visitor's interest at the end of their guided tour. "Did he find the immigration museum interesting?" 229 visitors answered "yes." The question (No. 10) allows the visitor if he answers "no" to give his reasons. Over 18 visitors who answered "no," 12 gave a reason: 6 visitors responded that "there was too much information, too much text to read." 2 visitors responded that the "museum is sad. The stories and testimonies do not give a happy feeling." A visitor noted on his questionnaire that he had "migrated for love." 2 others said: "thousands of objects without interest" or "useless objects." 1 visitor said: "The Chinese community is not represented in a positive way" and another visitor said, "Immigration is not enough update." The nature of negative responses is a criticism from visitors to the museum, about the exhibition content and the overall impression (atmosphere, feeling) that they retain during their visit experience.[52] It is interesting that some criticism about handling of immigration is based on family history or individual origin, seeking to position their own story from the global content broadcast by the museum. Question No. 11 is about the number of visits, "Is it your first visit?" 220 visitors answered "yes" and 27 responded "no." For the vast majority of visitors, it was their first visit to the Immigration Museum in Melbourne.

This second part of the questionnaire helps to define the framework of motivations for visiting. The result is that for 89% of visitors, it was the first visit to the museum, with 84% of visitors who came for personal reasons (their own history, their family history and genealogy research). And 7% of visitors expressed opinions about the museum. This confirms, in a sense, both the attractive informative and social function of Immigration Museum in Melbourne.

The third part of the questionnaire focuses on the visitor's interest related to the content of the exhibitions at the museum. So the question No. 12, focuses on what marked the visitor and is a multiple choice question. These choices are: "explanatory materials and talks, the artifacts, your general experience of the museum, other lasting impressions." The visitor could complete his answer if he checked off

---

[50] "The Genealogy Centre. The Helen Mcpherson Smith Genealogy Centre is the home of the Library's Genealogy Collection. The centre holds a wide cariety of material on microfilm, microfiche, CD-ROM and online, and a number of genealogy-related books and journals. It has computers providing access to the Library's catalogue, databases and the internet, as well as printing and downloading facilities." Information collectée sur le dépliant de la *State Library of Victorua*. 328 Swanston Street. Melbourne 3000. URL: http://slv.vic.gov.au/ (Visited in February 3rd, 2010)

[51] Text available in the official website of the Immigration museum: "Developing strong relationships with Victoria's culturally diverse communities." URL: http://museumvictoria.com.au/immigrationmuseum/ (Visited in February 3rd, 2010)

[52] The visitor experience is a set of cognitive and affective activities of the museum-goers when visiting exhibition. We speak of museum experience to consolidate these activities in the museum. See reference: FALK, J.H., DIERKING, L. D., 2009 (1992). *The museum experience*. Michigan, Mellen Candage (ed.), p.67: "As they move through museum spaces, visitors selectively look at and examine objects and labels in exhibits. They asks questions about what they see, hold discussions with each other, and attempts to personalize and make sense of what they see. The important aspect of their activity is that it is selective. Visitors choose, sometimes apparently randomly, what to focus on. The things they choose to examine are woven into their own museum experience."

"other." Just over half of visitors (55%) said they had been marked by the explanatory materials and talks. They constitute a large part of the permanent exhibition, as each theme of the exhibition is accompanied by evidence (video, audio) of immigrants. 29% of visitors checked "artifacts," 8% indicated "the overall experience of the museum" and 8% indicated "other." The 21 visitors who answered "other" had the opportunity to complete their choice: 10 visitors were marked by the "mood of music," 7 visitors about "Ancient Hampi,"[53] which corresponds to a temporary exhibition about India integrated into the museum route. This exhibition features photographs of the ancient temple of Hampi (see Photo 4) and give the opportunity for visitors to test a mobile platform to discover it, equipped with 3D glasses, photographs of India in full size. 2 visitors wrote: "Discovery Centre" which includes the library and genealogy center of the museum[54], allowing visitors to do more research, and 2 visitors answered "availability of the museum staff." The following questions (No. 13 and No. 14) examined the relationship of visitors to objects that are exposed and the information disseminated at the museum. More than half of visitors found the exhibits in relation to their own history. This constitutes 60% against 40% of visitors. 72% of visitors found "information" that are related to their own history. Visitors are more sensitive to the historical information that is disseminated by the museum and in which they manage to locate their own history. Question No. 15 deals with the safeguarding of cultural practices in the country of origin. This question also assumes that these practices are still applicable in the daily life of the visitor. 60% of visitors said they had retained cultural practices against 40%. We can establish a link between the varieties of country of origin of visitors, established in the first part of the questionnaire, which underlines the cultural diversity of visitors, with the majority percentage of cultural practices.

This part of the questionnaire provides information on the quality of the relation between the visitor and the museum's content, and emphasizes the reality of interaction with the museum exhibitions, the theme of immigration and the different profiles of visitors.

The last part of the questionnaire aims to interrogate visitors about the concept of immigration. To question No. 16 which is: "Do you believe in a multicultural society where immigrants retain their native culture, traditions and speak the language they want?" 96% of the visitors answered "yes." The next question is: "If yes, do you think this society is Australia?" 96% of the visitors answered "yes." These results show that "the current demographic landscape of Australia (…) has nothing to do with the one it showed at the end of the Second World War, now showing a large ethno-cultural diversity"[55] combined with a social cohesion, where everyone is free to express his or her own culture. A large percentage shows that the ethno-cultural diversity is constitutive to Australian society. 96% of visitors believe the Australian

---

[53] Exhibition: *"Ancient Hampi: The Hindu Kingdom Brought to Life.* Immerse yourself in the ancient world of Hampi. This international exhibition offers visitors the opportunity to immerse themselves in the stunning World Heritage site of Hampi in southern India. Using state of the art digital technologies, this ground breaking experience presents 3D stereographic panoramas of an extraordinary site with all its mythological, archaeological, artistic and historic significance. Ancient Hampi includes animations of Hindu myths and stories, an immersive digital interactive space showing panoramic images of the site and its landscape, as well as captivating photography." URL: http://museumvictoria.com.au/immigrationmuseum/whatson/current-exhibitions/ancient-hampi/ (Visited in January 12th, 2010)

[54] Discovery Centre's presentation text: "Browse our extensive range of resources, including topical websites and infosheets based on Museum Victoria's collections and research." URL: http://museumvictoria.com.au/immigrationmuseum/discoverycentre/ (Visited in February 3rd, 2010)

the same question concerns the contribution (positive or negative) of the migration paths in the daily lives of visitors involved. 171 visitors (69% of visitors) said that immigration has had a beneficial effect on their lifestyle. 42 visitors answered that it had no effect, while 34 visitors answered that this had a detrimental effect. The results of this question outweigh the positive results that were obtained on the perception of immigration by visitors. This implies that for some visitors, having an immigrant background cannot be well in everyday life, which may refer to certain forms of cultural and racial discrimination, or to a migratory journey difficulties, or a daily disagreement with an immigrant population. The possibilities remain in large numbers. Question No. 19 deals with the visitor's impressions about the treatment of immigration by the museum. When asked: "Do you think that the Museum deals well the immigration question?" 95% of the visitors answered "yes." For those who answered "no" who were 12 visitors, they could give their reason after the last question No. 20: "If not, can you explain?" The explanations were very different: 2 visitors think that "the museum gives a sad version of immigration history." One of the two wrote, "between the nostalgic music, video testimonies of war, the old objects, this makes the museum looks like a sanctuary." 2 other visitors wrote that "China is represented only to say it has long been discriminated by the White Policy, not for its culture, while Japan is presented in relation to some know-how from Japan." One of the two visitors wrote about the lack of representation by referring to South Korea, as opposed to a showcase about Japan. 2 visitors noted that "there is nothing about the Greek community" and two others noted "an imbalance between the first floor and second floor." One of the two wrote that "the first floor is especially nice to visit with the boat[56] (see Photo 5) that enables to understand the

Photo 4: Photographic Exhibition about India*
at the Immigration Museum in Melbourne
(©Ilham Boumankhar 2010)

* Note: Presentation text in the cartel: "*John Gollings, Colour and Black and white photographs, 1980-2005*: A selection from over 15,000 images of Hampi taken in a period of 25 years. John Gollongs' work is a major contribution to the study of Vijayanagara."
©*Immigration Museum*, Melbourne, Victoria.
(November 2009- February 2010)

community as a "multicultural society" where several cultures, different practices (customs and religions) and where a multitude of different languages are spoken in

---

[55] LAGAYETTE, P. 2008. *Meeting Australia: crossing perspectives on the identity of a people and a nation*. Paris, Presses de l'Université Paris-Sorbonne, p.12: "The current demographic landscape of Australia (...) has nothing to do with the one she showed at the end of the Second World War, showing now a large ethno-cultural diversity." (Original version in French: LAGAYETTE, P. 2008. *Rencontres australiennes: regards croisés sur l'identité d'un peuple et d'une nation*. Paris, Presses de l'Université Paris-Sorbonne, p.12 : "le paysage démographique actuel de l'Australie n'a (...) plus rien à voir avec celui qu'elle affichait au sortir de la Deuxième guerre mondiale, montrant dorénavant une grande diversité ethno-culturelle").

Photo 5: Exhibition "Journeys of a Lifetime." Showing the Reconstruction of a Boat on Which the First Immigrants Arrived in Australia
(©Ilham Boumankhar 2010)

crossing of the first immigrants, but the second floor, apart from the two models of boats[57], the rest is not interesting." One visitor wrote "I expected more, I'm bored" and one other visitor highlighted a "big imbalance in the quality of the exhibits between the two floors."

These results demonstrate the various visitors' expectations about the museum and the issue of immigration. It is interesting to note that some visitors expect a "good representation" of their affiliated country in the immigration museum, which emphasizes that they "assumed that [the museum] is [a] social, political and cultural actor which is important in our society,"[58] and expect that all countries' immigrants are mentioned. These various remarks about the treatment of the theme

---

[56] Presentation text : "*The journey*. All immigrants, no matter when they arrived in Victoria, are linked by the common experience of a journey. Over the past two centuries changing forms of transport have meant that this voyage has varied in both duration and degree of comfort. The journey remains one of the moist memorable aspects of any immigration experience. You are invited to explore these spaces and immerse yourself in the experiences of previous generations of immigrants. Feel free to use any of the furniture and to touch anything you like." © Immigration Museum, Melbourne, Victoria. (November 2009- February 2010)

[57] This is the model of the East which was the ship carrying immigrants in the 19th century from Britain to Australia. Text cartel presentation of the model: "Orient—Queen of the seas. The Orient was one of the most famous ships to carry migrants between Britain and Australia in the nineteenth century. Built in 1879 as the flagship for the newly formed Orient Steam Navigation Company, it was the largest steamship launched worldwide since Brunel's colossal Great Eastern of 1858. The Orient was an immediate success carrying 735 passengers to Melbourne on its maiden voyage in record time." ©*Immigration Museum,* Melbourne, Victoria. (November 2009- February 2010)

of immigration in the museum also highlight that "the exhibition of objects already contains a certain vision, but do not tell everything [about] how visitors will appropriate this vision. The gaze of visitors, in fact reflects the ambivalence of the principles of exposure, but in an unbalanced manner"[59] through "the gap between different logics of representation."[60]

Analysis of the results of the questionnaire provides an interesting perspective on the profile of visitors and how they define themselves through the museum, and with the concept of immigration and Australian society. We maintain, however, that to be defined as an "immigrant"[61] in Australia is relative, both in the spoken language, or the family lineage or affiliation to a country; this makes the museum management a more complex exercise.

B. Meeting with Padmini Sebastian, Manager of the Immigration Museum in Melbourne

The interview I conducted with Padimini Sebastian, Manager of the Immigration Museum in Melbourne, was held in her office, in February 9th, 2010[62]. This interview aimed to present my research[63] findings to discuss and ask some general questions about the museum.

Relations with the Victorian Government

The Museum of Victoria was founded by the State Government of Victoria. In this

---

[58] DUBE, P. LAPOINTE, A. 1997. *The museum as a symbolic territory of the nation.* In TURGEON, L., LETOURNEAU, J., FALL, K. 1999. *Spaces of identity.* Quebec, Les Presses de l'Université de Laval, p.149: "assume that [the museum] is an agent for social, political and cultural that is important in our society." (Original version in French: DUBE, P. LAPOINTE, A. 1997. *Le musée en tant que territoire symbolique de la nation.* In TURGEON, L., LETOURNEAU, J., FALL, K. 1999. *Les espaces de l'identité.* Québec, Les Presses de l'Université de Laval, p.149 : "acquis que [le musée] est un agent social, politique et culturel d'importance dans notre société").

[59] CHRISTIAN, M. 1999. *The visitor's gaze in le Louvre.* In LARDELLIER, P. 1999. *The visitor's gaze in the museum.* In Public Museum and No. 16, Presses Universitaires de Lyon, July-December 1999, p.28: "The exhibition contains objects that have a certain way of look, but does not tell how visitors will appropriate it. The gaze of visitors reflects the ambivalence indeed of exhibition principles, but in an unbalanced way." (Original version in French: CHRISTIAN, M. 1999. *Le regard au Louvre.* In LARDELLIER, P. 1999. *Le regard du musée.* Publics et Musée n°16, éditions Presses Universitaires de Lyon, Juillet-décembre 1999).

[60] BLANCHET, A., GOTMAN, A. 1992. *The investigation and its methods: the interview.* Paris, Nathan, p.52. (Original version inn French: BLANCHET, A., GOTMAN, A. 1992. *L'enquête et ses méthodes: l'entretien.* Paris, Nathan)

[61] *Australian Bureau of Statistics. Queensland Office.* 1994. *The social Characteristics of immigrants in Australia.* Canberra, Australian Government Publishing Service, p.3: "The first term which needs to be clearly defined is the word 'immigrant'. This is not as straightforward as it might seem. There is a tendency to refer to a person as an immigrant for only a short period of time after his or her arrival. Once resident in the new country for sufficient time, the word immigrant no longer seems appropriate as a description. Term sus as "of Italian origin," "Turkish descent" or "Spanish-speaking" may be more appropriate (DILGEA 1988, p.5). For example, not many people would refer to an 80-year-old man who was born in England and has resided in Australia since arriving at the age of twenty as an immigrant. There are a number of other ways the word immigrant is interpreted by government departments, the media and the general public. Often it is used to refer only to people of non-English-speaking background, whether borne in Australia or not. The word is also often linked with the concept of disadvantage and only applied to those of low economic status emigrating under assistance schemes or of refugee status. The debate can be further confused by including those Australia-born people with foreign ancestral or cultural affiliation as immigrants."

[62] Interview with Ms Padmini Sebastian at the Immigration Museum offices, at level 4, 22 William St, Melbourne (on the corner of William St and Flinders Lane) Melbourne, February 9th, 2010.

[63] Investigations conducted at the museum that consists of questionnaires to visitors, and focus groups conducted with visitors, and were conducted as part of a PhD in Cultural Studies at the University of Paris 1 Panthéon-Sorbonne.

Photo 6: Padmini Sebastian, Manager of the Immigration Museum in Melbourne (©Ilham Boumankhar 2010)

sense, the museum has a civic role which aims to represent and reflect the state of Victoria under the light of immigration. The museum is open for a little over 10 years and no interference from the government so far has been noted, unlike the Australian National Museum[64] which was the subject of government intervention in relation to the establishment of a gallery devoted to Aboriginal art[65]. The Immigration museum, however, must comply with the policies and procedures of the government in its management of financial resources, while respecting the code of ethics for museums. In terms of content, the museum is free to act as it sees the issues related to immigration. The content is oriented to the theme of the museum and visitor experience that the museum wants to show. Sometimes the content is distributed in correspondence with government issues and may be subject to litigation, but the aim of the museum remains to pacify the issues of migration and provide an area of exchange of the issues. The fact that the Australian Government, through its immigration policy, will always be able to conduct the line of how to identify, differentiate, or to shape an identity linked to the Australian nation is unavoidable. But, the museum's role is not to judge this conductive line but to provide a space for dialogue.

---

[64] Presentation text: "Opened in March 2001, the National Museum is the first museum dedicated to the history of Australia and Australians, exploring issues, events and key figures who have shaped and influenced the nation. Exhibition design and technology presents the stories of Australia an exciting and inventive manner, including use of multimedia, live performances and hands-on activities to appeal to a wide audience." URL: http://www.nma.gov.au/visit/overseas_visitors/french/ (Visited in February 11th, 2010)

[65] WINDSCHUTTLE, K. 2001. *How not to run a museum? People's history at the postmodern museum.* In *The Sydney Line*, September 2001. URL: http://www.sydneyline.com/National%20Museum.htm (Visited in February 11th, 2010). In this article, the author explains the various discussions that took place in different areas on the National Museum of Australia. He explains how some authors report including all Australian government interference in the management of museum exhibits: "The content of the museum's displays has attracted less public discussion but has been the source of considerable acrimony within its governing council." The author refers in particular to several statements by government officials, academics and historians, including Graeme Davison, Professor of History at Monash University, which is the largest university in Australia. He states that: "David (Barnette—journaliste) gives the impression—which I am sure he does not really hold -- that the museum should follow the historical views of the government of the day. I am sure that this is not your view, or that of the council. The objective must be to ensure that whatever historical interpretations are expressed by the museum can survive changes of government and councils." Il cite aussi l'article publié dans le *National Museum*, intitulé *National Museums: Negotiating Histories* (2001) de Darryl McIntyre et Kirsten Wehner, qui écrivent: "Histories of colonialism and imperialism led to the formation of many national museum collections and the discourses of racial and social hierarchy and exclusion through which these were displayed. An increasing awareness of these discourses has meant that many museums often find their own collections something of a problem... Many museums are now concerned with the reinterpretation of colonial pasts, seeking to educate visitors about the complex and often unjust social relations which are part of their national history."

The Management of the Museum about the Diversity of Countries that Make up the History of Australian Immigration

All socio-ethno-cultural stories that are part of the history of Australian immigration cannot be represented at the same time in the museum. This is an exercise in representation that is realized over time. To manage this, Sebastian Padmini had created "a framework for establish emerging communities." It is a specific database created by the museum, which is useful to identify and list the emerging communities. It exists through the consultative relationship that the museum has with these communities during the preparation of exhibitions that deal with migration reports of these communities. The construction of an exhibition is realized in cooperation with immigrant communities, who share their experiences of their everyday life, between culture of origin and culture of the host society. This experience ranges from the journey and the installation to the hope of building a new life, but sometimes the experience of migration is also a disenchantment with a former life that the migrant will never see again, because of war or ecological disaster. Through the collection, the online programs, cultural festivals, the community exhibition, and a long term galleries, the challenge is "to represent as many people as possible." The permanent exhibition has not so far been completed. Partnership work done with these communities is not intended to collect only those representative objects and witnesses of community cultures but to share and delegate their story so that the museum can transmit them. It is very difficult to represent all communities to provide a perspective that is fair and equitable; it requires considerable work and commitment within the communities but also and especially from the museum.

Each year six community projects are set up in the form of exhibition or festival. There are 80 different communities with which the museum is working. The collections are completed and are posted on the museum site[66]. The museum's manager understands that the immigration museum visitors will always expect a representation of their cultural origin within the museum. But she says that this representation is not always present because the diversity of communities in Australia is too important. The objective of the Immigration Museum is tender, however, towards a comprehensive representation of Australian immigration.

Collaboration with the Museum's Diverse Communities

The community displays and the festival program require a full commitment from the museum in relation to the different communities. Two museum curators have the charge, in full time, to maintain a contact with these communities. It is not for the museum to just express some interest for these communities but to forge a real bond of cooperation in the preparation of these events with these communities.

For this, the museum has a matrix or a database that enables it to consider the community exhibitions to come, over the next thirty years. The ambition of the museum is to create a place for the emergence and visibility of new communities in the State of Victoria. Once the identification of communities is integrated into a real museum project, the involvement of curators and researchers is integral, since the process of finding representations of communities and objects that bring this representation is not regarded as fixed but as an interactional dynamics between the

---

[66] Each object in the collection of the Museum of Victoria is listed and featured on the official site of the museum. Available in URL: http://museumvictoria.com.au/collections-research/our-collections/ (consulté le 11 février 2011)

museum, the society and communities. This is a collaborative work, which lasts more than twelve months and which allows communities to express themselves and bring the necessary materials to museum work. A real exchange takes place between the museum and communities to work not only on a given time for a specific event but for future exhibitions. The contact is also maintained over time to maintain a relationship of trust between community groups and immigration museum. Building a relationship of partnership is one of the missions of the museum that also allows him to set new goals. Indeed, each community exhibition gives rise to heated discussion between community representatives and members of the museum, allowing the seizure of representations of different perspectives and issues of a community exhibition. The interest of these discussions is to converge the knowledge of the various parties involved in assembling the museum project.

Issues Relating to the Permanent Exhibition

The permanent exhibition covers the period of the history of Australian immigration since 1830 until 2000. The reason the immigration museum has not updated its permanent exhibition is linked to the financial prospects allocated by the Australian government and the lack of staff that can be engaged in this type of project. Moreover, the past ten years have seen the configuration of ethno-cultural Australian immigration to diversify and the immigration policy to change. The technical means to establish an exhibition can also affect a varied range of museum representation of this diversity. The challenge for the museum focuses on ease of understanding for these new migration patterns that are coupled with new technical implementation exposure. In addition, the museum is currently working on a project that will be accessible to the public in March 2011, which is oriented around the concepts of identity, race, culture, etc. This kind of project, in conjunction with the daily activities of the museum maintained, requires careful planning and organization that is played in time. The purpose is to propose a real-time interaction between the visitor and the museum in order to raise issues about the representation of immigration.

Paralleling the Point of View of Visitors with the Permanent Exhibition

We pointed out in this part of the interview with Padmini Sebastian, the influence of multimedia (background music and documentaries) on some visitors who have given their opinion. The answer is that the aim of the museum in this area is to reflect as much experience as possible about immigration. The documentary's images refer to images of destruction, war, famine but also construction, installation and love. It is paradoxical that many images are juxtaposed. But immigration is a multifaceted experience of contradictions. The museum's goal is to give to visitors an overview of immersive experience. The documentaries are composed of short sequences dealing with various immigration issues. Music, on the other hand, was treated so as to remain close to neutral. is interesting that some visitors find it sad or nostalgic. This is part of the diversity of visitor experiences that is aspired to by the museum, which seeks to reflect the visitors, and at the same time, make them project the migration patterns of immigrants. Immigration status is not a phenomenon of the 20th or the 21st centuries only. Some are refugees fleeing famine, environmental disasters, and war. Immigration may also reflect dramatic stories, and it is a fact that the museum has to show.

Future projects of the museum

The exhibition, which will take place in March 2011 on the theme of contemporary identity, is an important exhibition as it will allow visitors to reflect on what immigration means in all aspects of travel and mobility that implies. It will examine also how it continues to shape the identity of immigrants, generations and societies. We live in a globalized world where movements of people are international. In this sense, the museum is also interested in Australians who have left their country to settle elsewhere, and return to Australia with their rich cultural experience. Immigration also concern Australians who have left their country to settle elsewhere, and return to Australia with their rich cultural experience. Change on the national level is fast, and the museum explores the technological possibilities for the treatment of these concepts. The goal is to find visitors but also residents to regard the museum not as a cultural institution but also as a social division of immigration issues. This exhibition will benefit both to present a new interactive and immersive experience for visitors, but also have an online program where visitors can get involved, complete and share in an abiding respect for each difference.

C. Meeting with Maria Tence, Manager of the Community Exhibitions Gallery in the Immigration Museum in Melbourne

The interview with Maria Tence, head of the Gallery of Exhibition Community, the Immigration Museum in Melbourne, was held in the museum's research library, February 17th, 2010[67]. This interview was

---

[67] Interview with Ms Maria Tence, Manager, Community Exhibitions, at the Library Research of the Immigration Museum, 400 Flinders Street, Melbourne, February 17th, 2010

Photo 7: Maria Tence, Manager of the Community Exhibitions Gallery in the Immigration Museum in Melbourne (©Ilham Boumankhar 2010)

intended both to present my results of investigations but also to gather information about the management of the Community Exhibitions organized by the museum and also the museum's interactions with communities in the process of collecting objects.

Presentation of the Community Gallery[68]

Maria Tence began working with communities as part of a museum exhibition project more than 12 years ago, along with Padmini Sebastian and Moya McFadzean[69] even though the project of an Immigration Museum in Melbourne was just starting. Since then, her work has evolved considerably. While initially it was to establish a communication link with the various communities and explain the opportunity for a partnership with a civic museum, then it was more to negotiate the different modes of representation and dissemination of individual and collective histories with the communities in question. Immigration to Australia has an interesting diversity of communities. These are more or less ancient, and if today the collection of objects is simpler, it was not the same at the opening of the museum. In fact, immigrants who came to Australia after the Second World War had never come into contact with a cultural institution since most came from rural areas of Europe. For these early immigrants, the museum was more a place where the antiquities were stored. It is therefore an educational understanding of the role of museums in representing the communities that initiated the communication between museums and communities. A gallery of communities has been developed for the purpose of exclusive collaborative work with communities. Indeed, for the museum to acquire validity in the eyes of communities, it was both to integrate them into the social history and contemporary Australian immigration, and to reserve a specific space for them. Initially this gallery was called "nexus gallery." The word "nexus" means "the link between members of a group"[70] in relation to sharing the same language. Indeed, sharing the same language within a community, it was seen by the museum as a cultural partnership rather than a factor of social integration it facilitated. The name was changed in 2004 at the request of several artists who wanted to make this space an entry, access, and artistic discovery. However, the immigration museum wanted an exhibition space reserved for collective voice and social history. In this sense, it became the "Community Exhibition Gallery."

The working methods for organizing these exhibitions are very different from the methods usually practiced in museums. Indeed, the museum allows communities to propose an exhibition by completing an application form. From this starting point, a specific group is formed to offer, from the observation of past exhibitions, suggestions based on a scoring system. The highest score is retained in the final decision. The project started being built via an interaction between a group of 5 individuals from a specific community and the team in charge of the museum project, under the direction of Maria Tence. The value of group work helps prevent the individualization of the project. Indeed, in the early days some community representatives took the project too much to heart, offering screenings of representation too personal. However, the project's objective is to provide a collective view from individual stories. There are different perspectives that are offered, and various negotiations that take place during the process of realization of the exhibition project community. The role of Maria Tence evolved, moving

---

[68] Presentation text: *Community Exhibitions:* "Tell your community's experiences and stories of migration and diversity… The Immigration Museum's *Community Gallery* hosts three exhibitions annually. Each exhibition is presented for a period of between 14 and 16 weeks. The program is flexible so as to accommodate the cultural needs of as many groups as possible. Community exhibitions are created by communities themselves with support from the Museum. The museum provides financial, marketing and promotional support so that communities can create quality exhibitions. Communities must be able to demonstrate community support and endorsement for exhibitions so that they are inclusive and representative of the community. Where possible community exhibitions are scheduled to coincide with important milestones or celebrations in the participating community's calendar? What are the aims of the Community Gallery? To provide a forum for community groups, organizations and special interest groups to tell stories and investigate themes relating to immigration, cultural diversity and identity. To encourage community collaboration, participation and ownership. To document and promote the diverse community stories and experiences that are an important part of Australian history. To contribute to the history collections of Museum Victoria and the State of Victoria. There is an application and selection process if you wish to present your Community's exhibition at the Immigration Museum." URL: http://museumvictoria.com.au/immigrationmuseum/about-us/community-engagement/community-exhibitions/

[69] Moya McFadzean is the chief curator of the Immigration Museum in Melbourne. The next section is devoted to the interview we conducted with her in February 23rd, 2010 at the Swan House Immigration Museum.

[70] *Nexus* …n. pl. nexus. Definition: 1. *A means of connection between members of a group or things in a series; link; bond* 2. *A connected group or series.* Source URL: http://www.thefreedictionary.com/nexus

from "someone who negotiates" to one who "works as a custodian" of the immigration museum. The aim is both to strengthen dialogue with communities to reassure them about the mission of the museum and the fair representation through the transmission of their material witnesses. It is a constant and permanent work which requires a management of current issues that also existed 10 years ago. Indeed, there are communities that have not yet been exhibited in the museum, and those who struggle to communicate their collective history or who have not yet reached a consensus about their own history because they are recent communities. As Maria Tence says: "my role is to let them understand how we are here to preserve their story and that they are also part of their communities' culture and history."

The role of Maria Tence is to make clear what is the benefit for communities to work with the Immigration Museum. The goal is to keep a record of their arrival in Australia as immigrants but also to convey their origins, history and cultural traditions. It is urging them to tell their stories, that every individual belonging to a community participates in the collective history of the community. These stories are not about their social success as a newcomer in Australian society, but the choices that led them to come to Australia, their cultural background and their contribution to the Australian society. Australian society has changed with their arrival; it changed its legislative framework. So there is an interesting balance that the community gallery exhibition attempts to address and reflect. The aim is to provide an overview of the history of these communities both old and new.

Management of community diversity

The working methods of the museum vary depending on whether it is a project for a permanent exhibition or a temporary exhibition.

The permanent exhibition is to reflect the complexity and diversity of individual stories while recontextualizing in a global trajectory of immigration to Australia. These compose micro-themes that fit and explain a macro-theme. For this, the museum has a matrix methodology that consists of different parts, which themselves constitute a tree that make up the history of immigration in terms of geographical origins. The operation of this matrix is both rational and objective. To better manage the contents of the permanent exhibition, the museum must ensure that each part is checked and then processed. Not everything can be treated, but the museum must ensure that the broad themes that make up the history of immigration are present. The objective is to enrich gradually and proportionately, the permanent exhibition through the temporary exhibition gallery that represents the community exhibitions.

Temporary exhibitions are preparing for several years because it is a process that requires going out to meet the communities who want to work with the museum and put on an exhibition project. But the starting point of these exhibitions is initiated by communities. The museum policy is very clear: to let the communities decide what they want to convey. The community has both the history of a member of this community, the contribution of the person arriving in Australia, the type of contribution (economic or social) and the relationship to the collective history of the community. The profile of the stories must meet two criteria: the singularity and the collectivity. The stories must be original, unique, and fit into the overall history of the community by contributing to its enrichment and visual explanations. The museum's role is to avoid stereotypes to get closer to the truth of the stories. That's why there are several projects taking place simultaneously. Sometimes projects are reinterpreted in two or three years later because some interesting stories have emerged, or new objects have been collected. The exhibition is therefore more flexible than the permanent exhibition, but requires a significant investment in terms of verification, processing and updating sources and objects.

The Issue of Intercultural Communities

Communication is carried around the ability for communities to be exposed in the Immigration Museum, to tell their arrival in Australian society. The fact that individuals belonging to this community feel 100% immigrant or even 1% immigrant is not important; the key is to tell their migration routes. The existence of the gallery of Community Exhibition tends to value those communities; whether they arrived in Australia in 1830 or 2010, they are all immigrants. So they all have their place in the museum.

The influence of Australian society in these communities is inevitable. Australian society has an egalitarian approach to immigrants, due to the fact that Irish immigrants arriving in Australia have struggled at the outset to establish Catholic schools, and establish a Catholic Church. Parliament has legislated that each individual has the right to practice religion he wants, and live as he wishes. Australian society was thus built on this cultural pluralism, and has a philosophy of respect for differences. Certainly there was a time it had to go beyond racial politics between the white and the arrival of early immigrants and ethnic culture. But once this step crossed, it allowed Australian society to impose its model of multiculturalism and equality. And because Australia suffered "the tyranny of distance," because it is a Commonwealth country isolated in Oceania, it practices an immigration policy that allows new immigrants to preserve and maintain their cultural heritage and religious.

The impact on Australian communities comes from that distance. Because some foods can be imported, there are the culinary traditions that have been rehabilitated. For example, the curry a few years ago was not found in Australia, cannot be produced by Australia and cannot be imported for reasons of border security; for this reason the basics of curry dishes cooked in some communities have changed. The immigration process is an inevitable process of change. Individuals who decide to immigrate to a country which is different from their country of origin must accept this change and adjust their lifestyle. However, they also try to maintain links with their countries of origin, a link to both memorial and comfort. In this sense, they form communities. The growing diversity of communities encourages the museum to represent with the target to create a cross-community interaction in a historic approach that is intra- and inter-societal. Because many immigrants came to Australia to escape situations of political and cultural tension, environmental catastrophe but also of war in their own countries, they are looking for peace and harmony. That is why they try to preserve this state at all costs, avoiding attacks and intercultural violence. According to Maria Tence, "Even if, in many ways, we are recognized as a 'lucky country' because we have a lot of land, a lot of sunshine, and a lot of beach, now we can use the same words 'lucky country' in a way that means we have a social harmony and an egalitarian society compared to other countries in the world."

The Intercommunity Recognition Process

For Maria Tence, what differentiates the intercommunity recognition process between France and Australia is how each community is addressed at a macro level (society and community) and at a micro level (individual) and at a meso level (social organization). Indeed, in France every community forms enclaves. A specific community will find themselves located in the same urban areas, working in the same streets and gathering in the same places. In Australia, it's different because communities are dispersed or mixed. For example, Lygon Street in Melbourne is considered the Italian neighborhood because there are many businesses that are run by Italians, but they live in different places and mingle more in Australian society. This mixture allows children to mix with other children belonging to other communities and become familiar with these communities. Intercommunity dialogue begins early and often this affects the parents. In addition, the curriculum includes multicultural learning of the Australian history, and each student can learn in school his history and language of origin to preserve his cultural heritage. Distribution patterns and location of communities differ between France and Australia.

The Next Community Exhibitions

The community Gallery exhibitions presented an exhibition devoted to the Kurdish[71] community in Australia, and later, in October 2010, the Timorese[72] community. The year 2009-2010 was devoted to the communities in which developments in their country remains tense, sometimes hopeless as Palestinian communities, Kurdish and Timorese. Sometimes these tensions are reflected in the discussions between museums and communities. Sharing one of her discussions with the community, Maria Tence said: "The Kurdish community I worked with, told me: "you know, be prepared, 'cause Kurdish community might force you to close the exhibition, if it is not suitable." And I said: "In Australia, no community can force the closure of an exhibition." So, it is a permanent work of dialogue with communities to ensure that the beneficial intentions of the museum are maintained. The museum must also establish and promote intercommunity interactions and sometimes pacify them. The gallery exhibits community is an area of community representation but also a forum for discussion between the different actors involved in the project design museum and an intercommunal meeting place. The existence of the gallery is to overcome the various sub-themes that are not covered by the permanent exhibition but also to provide a voice for communities, a chance to speak, to tell their story and leave a trace.

D. Meeting with Moya McFadzean, Senior Curator of the Immigration Museum in Melbourne

The interview with Ms. Moya McFadzean, senior curator of the Immigra-

---

[71] Presentation text: "Survival of a Culture: Kurds in Australia. 16 Mar—25 Sep 2010. Explore the culture of Australia's Kurdish community.This exhibition explores how the Kurdish culture has survived through adversity, invasion, and division of the Kurds' traditional lands. Survival of a Culture: Kurds in Australia examines the traditions at the core of the Kurdish culture that have enabled it to survive, and which Kurds proudly maintain in Australia today. A variety of objects will be on display, including traditional costumes, instruments, hand-made carpets, hand-woven crafts and pewter ware." URL: http://museumvictoria.com.au/immigrationmuseum/whatson/upcoming-exhbitions/survival-of-a-culture-kurds-in-australia/ (Visited on February 20th, 2010)

[72] The Timorese community hails from the island of Timor, which is an island in the Indonesian archipelago. This island has two types of settlement, an eastern half which is the Republic of East Timor (to which the exhibition is dedicated) and the western half is part of the Indonesian province of East Nusa Tenggara. The population of East Timor suffered abuses by anti-independence militias and flee the island to seek refuge in Australia.

Photo 8: Moya McFadzean, Senior Curator of the Immigration Museum in Melbourne (©Ilham Boumankhar 2010)

tion Museum in Melbourne, was held at the Swann House which is the building where her office is located, in February 23rd, 2010[73]. This interview was intended to discuss my survey results and gather information on her work as a senior curator, responsible for both the museum's collections but also as one in charge of the exhibition process objects.

Presentation of the Work of Chief Curator of the Immigration Museum

As a senior curator of the Immigration Museum in Melbourne, Moya McFadzean first worked for the National Museum of Victoria in 1995 as a curator for the Australian Society and Technology Department. Because she has specialized in studying the history of Australian immigration and immigration history of the State of Victoria in particular, she has been appointed senior curator of the Immigration museum collections. If the collection of the Museum of Victoria was established since 1854, that of the Museum of Immigration is a contemporary collection.[74] This collection started by the Department of Social History Museum in Victoria since 1990 and has served as a launching base for the proposed immigration museum opened in 1998. As a curator appointed to a museum collection recently, her work has been to initiate first communication links with community networks to develop a collection plan for the museum of immigration. Subsequently, it was targeted to produce collections for exhibitions and to determine the audience profile of the museum in terms of migration-related cultural activities[75].

She defines her work on the collection of objects as a proactive work, since the museum is responsible to create and complete his own collection in partnership with communities in the State of Victoria. The objective of this collection of objects was to cover a wide range of cultures and historical periods to reflect the history of migration in Victoria. Emphasis was placed on documentation of individual stories and family migration through personal items and stories. These are the many individual and family histories that make up the overall history of the Victorian and Australian immigration. From objects collected from communities, the curator's job begins. Domestic objects, objects in relation to immigrant labor, photographs and lots of luggage. The bags are a symbol of immigrant mobility. As a conservative, it is not simply to dispose of these objects but also to inform, to tell their stories. During the collection process, it often receives immigrants who decide to share their stories and

---

[73] *Interview with Ms Moya McFadzean*, at the Swann House of the Immigration Museum, 22 William Street, Melbourne, February 23rd, 2010

[74] Complementary document prepared by Moya McFadzean. Collection plan at the Immigration Museum: "The Migration Collection documents the migration experiences of Victorians since the 1830s and, consequently, the long history of the cultural diversity of the Victorian population. The collection officially commenced in 1990, with collecting and programming activity increasing dramatically after the establishment of the Immigration Museum in 1998, one of Museum Victoria's three campuses."

[75] Ibid: "This has resulted in the broadening of community networks, focused collecting for exhibitions and the raising of the museum's public profile in terms of migration-related cultural activities."

donate or loan their objects, to ask them specific questions about objects. The collection process therefore involves a collaborative effort between the owner of the object and the curator who collects the history of objects. This support is necessary because often the banality of the objects, or the fact that they blend into the everyday life of the owner, has the consequence that they are not explicit on the details of stories they carry or their past practice. The museum curator is present to complete the story with maximum detail, to create conditions for exhibitions that aim to engender a sense of empathy in the viewer. To do this, Moya McFadzean considers ways and basic techniques that can help to effectively tell the personal stories attached to objects while integrating them into the general history of immigration.

Objects collected are those accumulated by immigrants during their migratory journey, but also they include objects made or acquired after their settlement in Australia. They must be integrated with personal stories and family and with the broader themes of political and immigration process, method of settlement of immigrants, of different generations of immigrants, of the relationship between marriage and migration, of health and migration, and of nation and identity. These sensitive issues have arisen following the exhibition "The Human Body"[76] on which Moya McFadzean worked, as a curator of the museum's Australia Gallery of Victoria in Melbourne in 2002. The exhibition raised the question of morphological differences, racial, cultural, social contact among individuals.

In addition, since Australia had previously based its policy of immigration on a racist basis favoring White immigration, it was especially important to recognize that past but also to update the questions of immigration identity and multicultural policy in Australia. What are the resonances of these policies on individuals, and how people were affected by the policy? The growing collection of documents relating to Australian immigration policy and the process, by which people are selected, redirected or returned, providing a vital bridge between the personal stories and narratives of nations, either Australia or other countries to which immigrants originate. The local community activities about migration are also represented, including cultural organizations who maintain cultural traditions. Government policies to support communities who wish to preserve and practice their cultural heritage are discussed. Administrative groups created to facilitate community dialogue such as the "Council of good neighbors"[77] are processed by the museum but also are

---

[76] Reference to the exhibition "The Human Body" as part of wider exposure on "Body Odyssey," which took place from August 3rd, 2002 to January 27th, 2003 at the Museum Victoria in Melbourne. Text of the presentation is: *"Individual identity: really you:* The questions: How am I structurally the same as other humans? How am I unique? Recur in many of the themes throughout The Human Body exhibition. The techniques used to uncover the macro and micro structure of the human body have revealed our relationship with other living things. We share the same basic body structure with all vertebrates, the same cellular structure with all animals, and the same genetic coding material as all living things. What then makes each of us unique? The obvious external characteristics are the most notable. Are you male or female? What color is your skin, hair, eyes? There are many other less obvious structural features. Are your ear lobes fixed or free? What is your blood type? What is the sequence of your DNA? You may argue that what makes you 'you' is not only your structure but your unique set of memories and experiences. However, you may want to then ask the question, Can individual consciousness and memory also be explained or mapped to brain biochemistry and physiology? Or how much of me is nature and how much is nurture?" URL: http://museumvictoria.com.au/body-odyssey Text available in .pdf format on URL: http://museumvictoria.com.au/search/?q=Individual%20identity:%20really%20you (Visited on February 24th, 2010)

[77] Document complémentaire rédigé par Moya McFadzean. Plan de collecte des objets de l'*Immigration Museum:*" the Good Neighbour Council."

protest groups and political movements, for and against immigration, multiculturalism and diversity. The physical collection consists of so many objects as documents that mark the stages of the migration process of individuals as objects of material culture in relation to social events related to the history of immigration[78]—such as historical events and protests which are illustrated in an exhibition by the posters or badges used then.

The issue of immigration is strongly linked to personal identities. The task of collecting objects, documentation and exhibition implementation is even more important that it can be positioned in a contemporary context. How from household objects, tools of work, family heirlooms and community artifacts, do we get to deal with social issues, culture, race, and identity that are all concepts that are closely related to the immigration questions? Moya McFadzean admits that it is a difficult work of constant questioning, but also a job that is rewarding with a systematic collaboration with the owners of objects in order to help them interpret and represent their personal history. If the work of Maria Tence, manager of community exhibition, begins with communities, the work of Moya McFadzean, senior curator, starts from the objects. Her mission is to operate within this framework, a collection of reactive objects, sometimes from contexts and personal histories controversial, but with the constant objective of clarifying the issues of immigration and innovating the exhibition process objects.

The Adjustments in the Practice of Museum Curator

Before the Immigration Museum in Melbourne was created by the State Government of Victoria, there was a museum of migration in Adelaide since 1986. The Migration Museum of South Australia is a museum that deals with migration issues in the State of South Australia with the main purpose of fighting against racism and discrimination in this state.[79] The objective of this museum is to give voice to diversity and therefore community to claim their rightful place in the state. Because the majority of Australians were English, Scottish, or originating in Wales, there was a strong dominance of British communities which left only little room for other communities growing. So, this Migration Museum was intended to hear other voices. Contrary to the State of South Australia, Victoria State showed instead a significant diversity and the role of immigration museum was to know the history of immigration but also to establish an intercommunity dialogue, with the assumption that everyone in Australia is an immigrant. In this sense, as a museum curator, Moya McFadzean needed early in the project, to adjust her way of working

---

[78] Ibid: "The Migration Collection is a relatively recent one, and has had three curators since the collection was formed in 1990. Items relevant to the collection had also been collected via the earlier Technology and Social History collections (for example, shipping material, Australian Natives Association certificates, and medals). However, as migration was not the primary motivation for collection, such items tend to be poorly provenance in terms of their migration histories. Much of the collection documents (to varying degrees) the material culture relating to the migration experiences of individuals and families; consequently, objects tend to be personal, domestic and work-related in nature."

[79] Presentation text in the official website of the *South Australia Migration Museum*: "Preservation, interpretation and celebration of our heritage and culture underpin the work of the Migration Museum. Among the core values of the Museum are social inclusion, countering racism, and lifelong learning. Here history can be explored in ways that connect with contemporary issues. Since opening in 1986 the Museum staffs have collaborated with representatives from over 100 different cultural and community groups to develop exhibitions and special programs that tell the story of multicultural life in South Australia." URL: http://www.history.sa.gov.au/migration/migration.htm (Visited on February 24th,2010)

because of the topic of immigration. It was no longer only to display objects and personal and collective histories, but also to promote all communities living in Australia and give them a fair vote. Put the story of an Irishman, a Scottish or English at the same level as that of an Iraqi, an Afghan or Turkish[80] or from a country in Africa.[81] Dealing with immigration properly also involves democratic use of museum resources.

But this is not always obvious, because immigration is a subject that varies depending on its degree of impact on a daily basis for individuals. Those whose great great grandparents were immigrants, no longer consider themselves immigrants, while for others, the comparison of different model of society and culture is everywhere. For the work of a museum curator, it is a complex factor to be taken into account while relativizing the objectives of exposure that are to make understandable the multicultural nature of Australian society, the history of various migrations, impacts of this immigration in today's society, all in relation to the contributions of immigrants to society but also to cultural and social changes of these immigrants into society. These are all moving parameters that the curator must keep in mind when working with a museum of immigration, a work that must constantly update and cope with modern and contemporary issues.

The Process of Exhibition Objects

At the museum, there is always a senior curator who is a kind of coordinator of the development team for an exhibition which is the function of Moya McFadzean. The curators' work is done in close collaboration with the designer who tries to articulate the message to be broadcast and representation through objects, texts and sometimes videos. The dialogue is not always easy between conservative and designer. It is established in a productive negotiation, which can both give rise to new ideas to put on display, but also remain on status quo of conventional exposure setting.

The gallery "Leaving Home" presents several objects that are not objects intended to tell a personal story, but symbolic objects of different reasons that led to immigration. There are also controversial items like a rifle, symbolizing the war, and for that purpose, the designer had the idea of positioning the profile such that it does not face the visitor giving the impression that they are facing the barrel of a gun, thereby awakening, for some, bad memories. The aim was to put on a display, both neutral and symbolic, while following the main theme. It is important to work with the designers of the exhibition, because sometimes they do not measure the extent that an exposure setting can have on certain objects. The last discussion Moya McFadzean had with a designer concerned the exposure setting of the Koran, the sacred book of Islam, in the gallery "Spirituality and Identity" in the upcoming exhibition, where the designer wanted to expose it suspended in a showcase. But as a religious text, it is important to put on a pedestal, to show the respect that is brought to the object from the museum. The designer does not seem to perceive the nuances in the understanding, or how the meaning of each item is perceived as a whole by the public. Those are many issues related to the understanding and interpretation of objects, which also depend on how the objects are exhibited.

---

[80] Document complémentaire rédigé par Moya McFadzean. Plan de collecte des objets de l'*Immigration Museum*: "Key items and stories include: Stories represented by one or two 'iconic' objects which powerfully capture the experience and/or which symbolize 'large' migration moments. Stories from Asia, Africa and Latin and South America, post 1970 stories and 19th-century stories."
[81] *Interview with Ms Moya McFadzean*, at the Swann House of the Immigration Museum, 22 William Street, Melbourne, February 23rd, 2010

Issues Related to the Next Exhibition Linking 'Identity' and 'Race'

The following exhibition, held in March 2010, connected the concepts of 'identity' and 'race'[82]. This exhibition was developed and led by Moya McFadzean. The aim was to focus on what makes up the identity of an individual in a contemporary perspective, and according to different themes related to immigration, to define the issue of race. This was to establish connections between the components of identity: ethnicity, religion, spirituality, citizenship, and contemporary social history, while implicitly including issues relating to class age, gender, social status etc. Starting with the visible identity, which is on the surface, this is to ask the following questions: how do we identify ourselves? How do we identify the others? Then it is to introduce topics related to race: how do we build the images we have of others? How do we make assumptions about others? How do we make our prejudices or our stereotypes? How do we discriminate? How do we perceive it and how do we live with it? Developing the relationship between identity and race is to ask questions based on the perception that an individual has of himself and how he composes his identity from his social status, personal interests, his spiritual beliefs, cultural heritage, but also how society perceives it, or how other people perceive it, based on ethno-racial characteristics, clothing practices that fall into a ethno-religious or ethnic–cultural category, etc. On the other hand, it is also to understand how an individual constructs his identity when the family inheritance or cultural transmission is absent, as this may be the case for a Holocaust survivor, a refugee, or an orphan. The exhibition is developed around an immersion process, to make the visitor experience issues of racism, discrimination, even when they are more insidious. The different forms of ownership are consulted, depending on the language, community, spirituality. It may also be transmitted by routine activities such as sport. Indeed, whether you are an athlete or a spectator, it is an important part of social and cultural life in Australia. The different types of popular culture practices or cultural affiliation are consulted, which is everything involved in building the identity of an individual beyond the racial characteristics that usually come first. It is also about creating an intergenerational dialogue related to these issues which are not lived in the same way at different times.

The purpose is to understand how identity is created from a personal point of view, and how it is affected by the collective (whether it is social, spiritual, cultural, etc.) to finally explore differences and what forms social diversity. All this was integrated within a broader context of Australian immigration policy, theories of difference, theories of race[83] as well as eugenics[84], Darwin and historical context with the issue of Australian aborigines and its "stolen generation"[85]. Through the exploration of material and popular culture, this exhibition explores the representations of identity and race in the contemporary context in order to promote the right to difference and diversity in Australia, which are also current international issues.

---

[82] "Identity and Race in Contemporary Australia at the Immigration Museum, an exhibition that will engage visitors in thinking about the complex issue of what it means to be an Australian in the 21st century." URL: http://museumvictoria.com.au/immigrationmuseum/search/?q=race%20identity (Visited on February 24th, 2010)

[83] BANTON, M. 1998. *Racial theories*. Cambridge, Cambridge University Press, p.7: "Racial theories have been superseded by more powerful explanations which do not need any concept of race. Where the typologists regarded racial characteristics as the properties of species, population genetics in the 1930s demonstrated that the unit of selection was not the species but the gene."

IV. Conclusion

My investigations at the Immigration Museum in Melbourne, whether involving questionnaires or interviews conducted with managers of various sections of the museum, highlight issues of representation and the question of immigration in the Australian context. While it is the place of diversity and multiculturalism, the social and political history of Australia has both paradoxes but also exceptions that demonstrate how the phenomenon of migration can both inspire the change, power relations, new economic patterns and social structures. The effects relate to the self-understanding of the country and result in social cohesion that is consolidated with contradictions.

If the Immigration Museum in Melbourne has the mission to "save and interpret the experience of people who immigrated to the State of Victoria and Australia, as well as promote and celebrate cultural diversity and Australian identity that result,"[86] it requires an ongoing collaboration with communities and social actor that are involved in maintaining social cohesion in Australia, while moderating political events. Even if immigration is constitutive of Australian history, it remains a social dynamic in constant motion, seeking from the museum to be engaged in a work of adjustment and continuous communication to foster intercultural exchange. My study has shown that immigration produces a multiplicity schema of the identity of individuals, and diversity of social realities. The migration routes are equally diverse between immigrants who fled wars, genocide, famine, and those attracted by the economic reality of Australia and seeking a new life.[87] They reflect experiences of immigration through the generations, ethnic differences (in a nation that was governed by a white policy for over a century) and cultural practices which are transmitted through the languages, religions, community belonging, etc., in a nation whose founding principle of multiculturalism policy is the preservation of the origins and cultural practices. "What we are talking about in terms of immigration and ethnicity is actually a set of processes related to globalization of economic activity, cultural activity, of identity formation. Immigration and ethnicity are constituted as otherness."[88] Even if the social landscape of Australia makes the migratory common, the political

---

[84] RUELLAND, J. G. 2004. *The empire of genes, history of sociobiology*. Lyon, ENS éditions, p.210: « The theory of eugenics, Francis Galton, which is, historically has experienced limited success. The close relationship between eugenics and sociobiology are made at two levels: first sociobiology takes on its own the main theses of eugenics Galton, then it takes any action taken by the theory of eugenics in his attempts to institutionalization. Eugenics may claim to Darwin, who remarked that man is not for himself, what he does for horses, dogs and cattle, and relies on random mating , and secondly that the abstention of artificial selection is coupled with a decrease of natural selection through the development of technological civilization and humanitarian ideas».(Translated from the original version in French: RUELLAND, J. G. 2004. *L'empire des gènes, histoire de la sociobiologie*. Lyon, ENS editions)

[85] *Interview with Ms Moya McFadzean*, at the Swann House of the Immigration Museum, 22 William Street, Melbourne, February 23rd, 2010

[86] HORN, B. 2006. Obstacles et éléments moteurs : pour la constitution d'un public au musée de l'Immigration à Melbourne en Australie. In MUSEUM International N°231. Septembre 2006, p.87. (Translation: HORN, B. 2006. Obstacles and driving elements: building an audience at the Immigration Museum in Melbourne, Australia. In MUSEUM International N°231. September 2006)

[87] RICHARDS, E. 2008. *Destination Australia*. Opus cité, p.xi: "Behind the transitions, Australia has remained one the greatest immigrant nations. Its immigrants have been conduits for changing currents from the rest of the world including war, genocide, famine and population displacement; their individual stories brought vibrations of these distant worlds directly into an otherwise insulated Australia. What Australia made of them and their alien baggage is a central issue in the story, as also is the fate of the immigrants themselves."

and social history of Australia requires the museum to deal with immigration issues very carefully, in order "to facilitate transmission between generations as well as encounters between migrants and host populations, through telling their story.[89]

BIBLIOGRAPHY

BALBI, Adrien. 1833. *Abrégé de géographie*. Paris, éditions Jules Renouard.

BANTON, M. 1998. *Racial theories*. Cambridge, Cambridge University Press.

BLANCHET, A., GOTMAN, A. 1992. *L'enquête et ses méthodes: l'entretien*. Paris, Nathan.

CHRISTIAN, M. 1999. *Le regard au Louvre*. In LARDELLIER, P. 1999. *Le regard du musée*. Publics et Musée n°16, éditions Presses Universitaires de Lyon, Juillet-décembre 1999.

DUBE, P. LAPOINTE, A. 1997. *Le musée en tant que territoire symbolique de la nation*. In TURGEON, L., LETOURNEAU, J., FALL, K. 1999. *Les espaces de l'identité*. Québec, Les Presses de l'Université de Laval.

DUTTON, D. 2002. *One of us: a century of Australian citizenship*. Sydney, UNSW Press.

FORLOT, G. 2008. *Avec sa langue en poche: parcours de français émigrés au Canada (1945-2000)*. Louvain-La-Neuve, Presses universitaires de Louvain

HAWKE, B. 1990. Foreword. In *National Agenda for a Multicultural Australia – The Year in Review August 1989-July 1990*. Canberra, AGPS.

HORN, B. 2006. *Obstacles et éléments moteurs : pour la constitution d'un public au musée de l'Immigration à Melbourne en Australie*. In MUSEUM International N°231. Septembre 2006.

---

[88] PERALDI, M., PERRIN, E. 1996. *Réseaux productifs et territoires urbains*. Toulouse, Presses Universitaires du Mirail, pp.42-43. (Translation : PERALDI, M., PERRIN, E. 1996. *Productive networks and urban areas*. . Toulouse, Presses Universitaires du Mirail).
[89] Official website containing all the museums of immigration from all over the world: "The international network of institutions for migration includes museums and other institutions promoting the public understanding of migration." URL : http://www.migrationmuseums.org/web/index.php?page=l-initiative (Visited on February 26th, 2010)

JUPP, J. 1997. *Immigration and National Identity: Multiculturalism*. In G. STOKES ed. *The Politics of Identity in Australia*. Cambridge, Cambridge University Press, pp. 132-144.

JUPP, J. 2007. *From White Australia to Woomera. The story of Australian immigration*. Cambridge, Cambridge University Press, Second Edition.

LAGAYETTE, P. 2008. *Rencontres australiennes: regards croisés sur l'identité d'un peuple et d'une nation*. Paris, Presses de l'Université Paris-Sorbonne.

LANGENDORFF, F. 2007. *Individu, culture et société: Sensibilisation aux sciences humaines*. Paris, Publibook.

PERALDI, M., PERRIN, E. 1996. *Réseaux productifs et territoires urbains*. Toulouse, Presses Universitaires du Mirail.

PONS, X. 1996. *Le multiculturalisme en Australie*. Paris, L'Harmattan.

PONS, X. 2005. *Les mots de l'Australie*. Toulouse, PU Mirail.

RICHARDS, E. 2008. *Destination Australia*. Sydney, University of New South Wales Press.

RUELLAND, J. G. 2004. *L'empire des gènes, histoire de la sociobiologie*. Lyon, ENS éditions.

SAUVAGE, A. 2008. *Between law and science: Australian museums dealing with aboriginal critique*. In LAGAYETTE, P. (dir.). 2008. *Rencontres australiennes. Regards croisés sur l'identité d'un peuple et d'une nation*. Paris, Presses de l'Université Paris-Sorbonne.

SEBASTIAN, P. 2007. *Mobiliser les communautés et transmettre leurs histoires: le rôle du musée de l'Immigration dans l'une des villes les plus multiculturelles du monde*. In Museum International, N°233/234, vol.59. N°1/2, UNESCO.

VERNAY, J-F., BEN-MESSAHEL, S. 2009. *Des frontières de l'interculturalité: Etude pluridisciplinaire de la représentation culturelle : Identité et Altérité*. Villeneuve-d'Ascq, Presses Universitaires du Septentrion.

VIDAL, G. 2006. *Contribution à l'étude de l'interactivité: Les usages du multimédia de musée*. Bordeaux, Presses Universitaires de Bordeaux, Collection L@byrinthes.

WINDSCHUTTLE, K. 2001. *How not to run a museum? People's history at the postmodern museum*. In The Sydney Line, September 2001.

Websites:

URL: http://museumvictoria.com.au/immigrationmuseum/about-us/

"Indépendance!": The Belgo-Congolese Dispute in the Tervuren Museum

Véronique Bragard

Université catholique de Louvain, Belgium

veronique.bragard@uclouvain.be

Abstract: 50 years after Congolese Independence was declared on June 30th 1960 with Joseph Kasa-Vubu as President and Patrice Lumumba as Prime Minister, the Tervuren Museum of Central Africa (Brussels), originally built as the "Musée du Congo" by Léopold II, inaugurated the exhibition "Indépendance! Congolese Tell Their Stories of 50 Years of Independence." This article examines how this event offers a sharp contrast to many Belgian museographic approaches to Belgium's colonial past and emerges as a groundbreaking step for Belgium in recognizing the devastating effects of its colonial past. The study first analyzes the past of denial experienced by the Congolese community of Belgium to contextualize the Belgo-Congolese dispute and then further analyzes the "Indépendance!" exhibition as a response to the need of museums to embrace non-fixed and creative memory. The exhibit accordingly becomes this contact site in Clifford's sense, i.e., a place where Belgians, Congolese and Belgo-Congolese people and memories are brought together, and where new meanings can be imaginatively shaped.

I. INTRODUCTION

As I was writing this article, Belgium was celebrating the 50th anniversary of Congolese independence but the country of "Tintin au Congo" is far from having fully entered a postcolonial era of self-criticism, being still trapped in a national myth of glory and civilizing colonialism. Its former Foreign Minister Louis Michel's words that Leopold II was not such an inhuman exploiter ("*Léopold II ne mérite pas de tels reproches*" ["Leopold II does not deserve such criticism"] *Le Soir* 22.06.2010), or the fact that communities are faced with difficulties when organizing a screening of the film *Lumumba* for independence celebrations, testify to the country's palpable reluctance to face its colonial past. And yet, the many (post)colonial settings of recent graphic novels or the covering in July 2010 of the statue of Leopold II with a necklace of crocheted chopped hands expose a colonial past that haunts and reaches into the present in strange forms. Contesting the content of Belgium's community-centered debates (Belgium is divided into three linguist communities about to separate), the social anthropologist Bambi Ceuppens is not the first person to notice that "many Belgians pay more attention to Leopold's

---

Véronique Bragard is Associate Professor in Comparative Literature and Literatures in English at the Université catholique de Louvain, Belgium. She has published and edited widely on Indo-Caribbean, Indian Ocean and postcolonial Literatures. She is the author of *Transoceanic Dialogues: Coolitude in Caribbean and Indian Ocean Literatures* (Peter Lang, 2008). Her current projects include postcolonial literatures, the Belgian colonial past and Congolese Literatures, and the representation of trauma and hospitality in post 9/11 literary texts/graphic novels.

statues than to the Congolese people living in Belgium" (2007, my translation). If, as we will see, this anniversary has been an opportunity to organize a number of exhibitions and activities around Congolese history and culture, it has remained mostly a cultural/artistic phenomenon that has not raised any significant political debate on how the Congolese community of Belgium is perceived, helped, stereotyped or acknowledged. The king's silence when he attended Congo's official ceremonies is indicative of this lack of engagement with the realities that Congolese people have to face. In the event of such a silence, one must note the growing interest in discussing the Congolese diaspora within the Belgian academia and social spheres.

In an analysis of the presence of Belgium's colonial past in museums, Stéphanie Planche and I (2009) have demonstrated how the representation of the colonial past of Belgium revolves around two polarized versions: between imperial nostalgia and incrimination, between politically orientated representations and bric-à-brac accumulation of objects brought back by colonials, and between traditional structures/buildings and innovative creative presentations. As emphasized in our analysis, the main debate focuses on the image of Leopold II, a king whose ghost[1] still oscillates between shame and genius.[2] Adopting a comparative approach to specific museographic representations of Belgium's colonial past, our article argues that confronting and assessing the colonial past of the country reveals the specificity of the postcolonial Belgian context, in which this problematic history has been debated within a broader national identity crisis that is taking overwhelming proportions. Attempting to scrutinize the history of the Congolese diaspora in Belgium, the exhibition "Black Paris—Black Brussels" tackled the question of Congolese migration to Belgium, mostly in a creative fashion. Recent commemoration exhibitions have adopted a similar approach: "Independence" (Tervuren) explores the memory of independence via testimonies and popular culture, *Lisolo Na Bisu (notre histoire): le soldat congolais de la force publique* focuses on the Congolese soldier in the civil service between 1885 and 1960, *Kinshasa Bruxelles: de Matonge à Matonge* (Tervuren) exposes the photographs of Jean-Dominique Burton to establish echoes and dialogues between the two neighborhoods (Brussels's and Kinshasa's Matonge situated 6000 km from each other), *Ligablo* presents popular and symbolic objects that have marked the Congolese imagination since the 1960s, *Paul Panda Farnana* (by Antoine Tshitungu Kongolo) explores the emblematic figure of Farnana who migrated to Belgium, fought with the Belgian army during WWI, and founded the *Union Congolaise de Belgique*.

This article focuses on the exhibition "Indépendance! 50 ans d'indépendance racontés par des Congolais" ("Independence! Congolese tell their stories of 50 years of independence") as a groundbreaking step for Belgium in recognizing the devastating effects of its colonial past as well as the Belgo-Congolese dispute, the effects of which are still felt by the Congolese community of Belgium.

II. CONGOLESE MIGRANTS IN BELGIUM

As Belgium is preparing the opening of a museum of emigration, the *Red Star Line*

---

[1] I am alluding here to the title *L'Ombre du roi*, the first volume of a collection of graphic novels *Africa Dreams* about the colonial past of Belgium that has recently appeared with Casterman 2010. Of course, this title also refers to Hochschild's famous work *King Leopold's Ghost*, New York, 1999.
[2] See the volume Dujardin (V.), Rosoux (V.), de Wilde d'Estmael (T.), Planche (S.) et Plasman (P.-L.) (dir.), *Leopold II : génie ou gêne*. Racines, 2009.

Museum of Antwerp, one must remember the country's migration and colonial history. Belgium has evidently been shaped by several migratory movements that started with massive internal migrations. Flemish peasants in the north were attracted by the industrialization of the southern region of Wallonia, followed by Italians who were 'invited' to work in the mines in 1946 when Belgium signed a protocol with Italy. Continuing with Spain (1956), Greece (1957), Morocco (1964), Turkey (1964), Tunisia (1969), Algeria (1970), and Yugoslavia (1970), the Belgian government pursued several bilateral agreements.[3] This was followed by stricter policies and even in 1974 an official ban on recruiting new unqualified foreign workers. References to the Italian migrants are now to be found at the Bois du Cazier museum in Charleroi, a museum that addresses the industrialization and mining periods at the same time as it commemorates the Bois du Cazier catastrophe that killed 262 coal miners, among whom many Italians.

One might be surprised by the fact that Congo, Belgium's former colony, is not mentioned in the list above. Although Congo is absent from these references, in the first phase of the migrants' legalization campaign of 2000, as Marco Martiniello and Andrea Rea point out, "two nationalities stood out: Congolese, with 17.6 percent of the applications, and Moroccans, with 12.4 percent." The question I wish to raise here is: What is the status of the Congolese diaspora in Belgium? How have Congolese migrants (not) been accepted in a country that has for decades held colonial power in the Congo, and how are they represented in the exhibition "Indépendance"?

---

[3] http://www.migrationinformation.org/feature/display.cfm?ID=164

III. THE CONGOLESE COMMUNITY IN BELGIUM: A PAST OF DENIAL

The starting point of my reflections is the temporary exhibition *Be.welcome* hosted by the Atomium in Brussels in 2010. Central to this exhibit organized jointly between the Atomium and the Musée de l'Europe is the idea that we need to make the problem of migration "less alarming" by showing how people have been migrating since the dawn of times and how, culturally, immigrants and their descendants have both adapted to the local culture they have fruitfully reshaped. Statistics show that migrants in Belgium come essentially from the European union. An interactive and most creative exhibit, it attempts to create a response in the viewer. One example is Aime Ntakiyioca's now famous photographs of a Black man in European folkloric costumes, which ironically questions the idea of a national and fixed identity. Another one, which foregrounds the creativity of the famous Congolese writer and performer Pie Tshibanda, imagines three telephone conversations between migrants and their loved ones back home. Other installations provide the point of view of the immigrant but also those who belong to the host country. Although general, it also depicts the history of migration in Belgium and foregrounds its cosmopolitan cities. Several works, like the photographs of restaurants, point to how immigrants and their offspring have contributed to the diversification of Belgian society—at the popular level at least.

As far as the representation of Congolese people is concerned, the following panel—translated here from the French—is worth scrutiny (see panel, next page).

The second sentence of the panel, although it seems to point to a large community—the third largest non-European group of migrants in Belgium—is somewhat contradicted by the last sentence

> *How did our former colony participate in this migration process?*
>
> *On January 2008, one estimated that the population that is born Congolese reaches a little more than 45,000 people. They are the third group of migrants, after Moroccans and Turks, having a nationality that does not belong to one of the European Union countries. Unlike Moroccan and Turkish migration, the Congolese presence did not meet a process of labor recruitment.*

recognizing that Belgium has not privileged Congolese laborers. In the permanent museum of Le Bois du Cazier, another analogous panel declares "Historical reasons account for the considerable presence of Congolese people" (my translation). This argument contrasts heavily with the observation of the historian Guy Vanthemsche, for instance, that in the present context "Congolese people living in Belgium only constitute a small fraction of the immigrant population" (290; my translation). What the term "non-négligeable" considerable means and alludes to is quite confusing. One needs to highlight the fact that the number of Congolese people is very small compared to the two other large non-European communities in Belgium: migrants of Moroccan and Turkish descent. If we compare the figures of Congolese (17,451) and Algerian (12,431) migrants in 1991, we can observe that the number of Congolese migrants was almost equivalent. What a comparison of those figures highlights is that the Congolese community in Belgium is extremely small although the Congo DR was a Belgian colony. However, in 2006, the Congolese community counted 40,000 members, twice the size of the Algerian community in Belgium. This rise obviously testifies to a change in attitude either from the Belgian government or/and from the Congolese population. Last but not least, in terms of figures, the fact that the Congolese community is larger in France than in Belgium is also worth noting. As Demart rightfully remarks "Those figures which one has observed since the 1990s break away from dominant trends in international migration: the ones of the ancient metropolis as first destination for migratory flux. In 1997, 52% of the Congolese of Europe lived in France and 29% in Belgium"[4] (my translation). The panels mentioned above indirectly reveal through their silences that, as Sarah Demart pursues,

> If asylum-seekers are registered in France from the 1970s onwards, in Belgium the status of refugee is associated with shame until the 1980s. It is because of the increasing decline of the economy and of the social conditions in Congo-Zaïre that this reality will become obvious (my translation).

Belgium's relation to its former colony and migrants more generally is imbued with shame, a state that shows through the awkward and opaque references found in the exhibitions above in which the Congolese community is represented with obvious detachment.

The current Belgian public debate on migrants, in particular Moroccans and Turks, has been largely inspired by the electoral success of Vlaams Blok from 1989

---

[4] LUTUTALA Bernard, 1997, "L'élargissement de l'espace de vie des Africains: comment le pays des 'oncles' européens devient aussi celui des 'neveux' africains," / "The expansion of the living space of Africans: how the country of European 'uncles' also becomes the one of African 'nephews" (my translation) *Revue Tiers-Monde*, 150, pp. 333-346. Cited in Demart.

onwards. At the time, Congolese hardly featured in these debates. Congolese came to Belgium in the aftermath of independence as students; as the political situation in their country of origin deteriorated from the end of the 1980s onwards, they started applying for political asylum. At the time, however, public debates were dominated by Muslims and Congolese remained an absent category. This situation continued when, from the 1990s onwards, following the two Congo-wars, more and more Congolese arrived in Belgium, claiming political asylum. The Congolese diaspora is now one of the largest in the world, with major communities in other African countries like South-Africa, but also Canada, the United States, France, Belgium, China, Japan, Germany, and the UK.

What the panels analyzed above indirectly but certainly point out is that Belgium has been particularly reluctant to welcome Congolese migrants. The first Congolese people who came to Belgium arrived in 1884. Some are also remembered because they were the famous village natives exhibited for Leopold II's world exhibition of 1897 and associated with the panels "Do not feed the blacks" (my translation). Later, some Congolese soldiers, like Panda Farnana, fought in WWI with 31 Congolese in Belgium and, as the "Indépendance!" exhibition highlights, Congolese people strongly contributed to the war effort from Congo as they were forced to participate in the "effort de guerre" (see Verhaegen) that led to massive migrational movements to the Congolese cities.

If Congolese migrants numbered 10 at the end of the Second World War, in 1961 there were 2,585 Congolese in Belgium. This number increased except in "two stagnation periods in 1985 and 1995," which probably confirms the fact that "Belgium turned its back on Mobutu's Zaïre" (Coolsaet 53, my translation). What other figures also obliquely point out is that the Congolese migration to Belgium has shifted from a student migration to an asylum seeker and family regrouping form of migration.

The idea that Congolese people did not participate in the labor force migrations of the 1950s is of note. Contrary to France or the United Kingdom—countries that welcomed a great number of migrants in the 1950s, such as the Windrush generation—the Belgian attitude reveals itself to many as atypical and even shocking. Reading beyond these panels forces us to consider the attitude of Belgium towards the invisible immigrant community of Congolese migrants. As confirmed by Vantemsche (2007), Congolese migration to Belgium was not at all encouraged by Belgian authorities. Several critics have attempted to explain this "Congolese exception." According to Lusanda Ndamina-Maduka, demographic, political and economic reasons explain the fact that "Belgium did not use colonial labour on its territory" (Ndamina-Maduka: 14). Demographically speaking, Congo had a very small population density and it was already difficult for colonizers to find laborers to exploit natural resources. Politically, Belgian colonials were afraid of losing their prestige and determined to prevent Congolese people from discovering "the taste of affluence" (Ndamina-Maduka: 16). Many also wanted to prevent them from entering into contact with anticolonial communist or progressive ideas. In this context, Cornet observes that the strict color bar and segregationist system imposed on the Congolese population was a system close to Apartheid (Cornet). Within that context, the inclusion of Congolese workers in the Belgian society was conceived as impossible. As Ceuppens adds, "their presence in Belgium was an anomaly which disturbed the colonial order" (2008).

Last but not least, economically, Congo needed its Congolese laborers. Only the servants of former colonials as well as mariners managed to progressively enter Belgian society as they were the only ones to reach the old continent. Many of the sailors stayed and became *carabouyas* (candy) sellers because the colonial lobby did not want them to take higher positions. Bambi Ceuppens further argues that until the 1960s, Congolese people were not allowed to come to Belgium. From 1917 onwards, they could only come to Belgium with the explicit permission of the Governor General; this condition was obviously lifted once Congo gained independence on 30 June 1960. In other words, in the mid-sixties Belgian authorities were forced to deal with the migratory movement from Congo. At that moment, Congolese came as students, with the perspective to go back. Nowadays, Congolese people in Belgium are the migrant group with the highest level of education in Belgian society. The paradox is that this level of education is what one would expect of that particular group of 'foreigners' called 'expatriates,' while in actual fact Congolese have the "the highest rate of unemployment"[5] in Belgian society. Demart (2010) concludes her observations with the question whether those figures should be considered as the markers of a form of post-colonialism, a question that seems to pervade in the new Tervuren exhibition presented below.

IV. "CONGOLESE TELL THEIR STORIES" TO BELGIAN VISITORS

Scheduled by the Tervuren Museum of Central Africa (Brussels) on the occasion of the 50th anniversary of the independence of Belgium's former colony and inaugurated in June 2010, the exhibition "Indépendance! Congolese Tell Their Stories of 50 Years of Independence" explores the independence of Congo but also its history and its contemporary agony. The fact that it is presented in the Royal Tervuren museum is extremely symbolic as the RMCA is a controversial site first designed as a colonial propaganda tool by King Leopold II and then turned into an ethnographic museum of Central Africa. As many have observed and Rahier pinned down, the conservatism of the museum "reflects and reinforces a certain denial of responsibility for the colonial past in Belgian civil society" (Rahier 77). The "Indépendance!" exhibition, which is dedicated to all the victims of the violence in Congo, is the result of a collaboration between the Royal Museum for Central Africa, the Institut des Musées nationaux du Congo and the Université de Kinshasa and part of a new reactualization of the museum. One of the curators of this exhibition, Bambi Ceuppens, worked for months with Congolese people to record their experiences of the independence period. The exhibition is based on interviews of very different people who "speak only for themselves, providing subjective and thus sometimes diverging points of view" on a period and past that alight conflicting memories whether in Belgium or Congo. The diversified content of the exhibition made of testimonies, memories, symbolic objects and creative art foregrounds an immaterial heritage. What I underscore in my examination of the exhibition is how this event interweaves a traditional historical approach with a creative appropriation of memory.

Held in a small part of the Royal Museum for Central Africa (Tervuren/Brussels), the exhibition, which records only Congolese voices, starts and ends within the Belgian context, thereby reminding one of the roles Belgium played in Congo's development. This Congolese voice is immediately heard with a reading of Yoka's "Letter from a man from Kinshasa to the village uncle" (1995; my translation) by Congolese writer In Koli Jean Bofane.

---

[5] According to Sarah Demart: "the unemployement rate of Congolese people in Belgium is above all the other populations in Belgium: foreign as well as native" (my translation).

The first room opens with "Indépendance cha-cha" (whose first lines express "independence we acquired it[6]"), the famous Kabasele and African Jazz independence song, and plunges visitors into the independence round table discussions that took place in February 1960 in the Palais des Congrès in Brussels. The organization of this first room epitomizes in many ways a strongly critical approach to Congolese history and memory as the room is divided into the political negotiations, on the left, and the economic ones on the right. This division makes clear that Congolese authorities were invited to both Round Tables but as the major leaders were busy with the electoral campaign at the time of the Economic Round Table, they sent young and inexperienced representatives. In many ways in this second Round Table, "the Belgians fulfil(led) their wish for a politically decolonized, economically subservient Congo" (Booklet of the exhibition, 6).

What is more, in the middle of this room filled with the pictures of male participants stands a brightly colored female shoe made out of 'African' fabrics and designed by Anglo-Nigerian artist Yinka Shonibare. This shoe, which reminds the audience of women's role in the independence movement, is one example of the many objects displayed in the exhibition to convey how collectivity and women in particular participated in the independence days. The lyrics of the famous "Indépendance Cha Cha" song printed on the wall are foregrounded as an instrument of communication that contained the names of the Congolese delegates and became "the independence anthem of other African Countries" (Booklet, 8).

The second room opens with the "Colour Bar," the unfair system upon which the whole history of the country has been built. The power issue central to the past of the Congo Democratic Republic goes back to the colonial segregation system. Within the Congolese heterogeneous society, racial categories separated Congolese "évolués," as they were called, from the Belgian subjects, who were the only ones to attain citizenship. The exhibition emphasizes the segregation in trains, for instance, in which "indigenous and Asians" were separated from the colonials. The next section, which is devoted to the Congolese war effort, presents photographs of Congolese soldiers sent to fight in Burma, Egypt or Madagascar. More relevant still is the way the exhibition emphasizes that the whole Congolese population was involved in the war, forcibly producing uranium and rubber.

Central to this exhibition, which highlights how the Congolese population anticipated and experienced independence, is the question of resistance. The section devoted to "Resistance" shows important Congolese figures like Simon Kimbangu, with a recent graphic novel devoted to this Congolese martyr now considered one of the first to have foreseen the liberation of the country. A Protestant Catechist, he advocated the social message that "whites will become blacks and vice versa" and died a martyr in prison after a sentence of 30 years. Newspaper clips from the Congo-

---

[6] Rewritten by Congolese-Belgian rapper Baloji in a song entitled "le jour d'après" with the musicians of deceased Wendo Kolosoy. Baloji's words:

j'ai repris cette chanson fédératrice (I have rewritten this unifying song)
symbole de la crédulité de nos prémisses (symbol of the incredulity of our premises)
entre indépendance et armistice (between independence and armistice)
mais pour que nos démocraties progressent (but for our democracies to progress)
faut qu'elle apprennent de leurs erreurs de jeunesse (they need to learn from their youthful mistakes)
mon pays est un continent émergent (my country is an emergent continent)
bâti en moins de 50 ans (built in less than 50 years)

lese press reveal the social demands of workers for equal salaries. Expanding on the topic of resistance but of another kind, the "Bills" showcase exposes pictures of the marginal counterculture created in 1950s by some indigenous youths who aspired to modernity.

The core of the exhibition is obviously the independence showcase, which presents the act of independence itself and the events that surrounded it. Films and a map of Matonge (Kinshasa) show that two 1959 events led to the independence round table. In January 1959, riots rocked Leopoldville following the colonial government's decision to forbid a meeting of ABAKO (cultural-political association of the Bakongo). At the same time, the result of a football game in King Baudouin stadium was being contested. The encounter of those two groups in the streets of Kinshasa embodied the coming together of both a political elite and a working-class group. These events culminated in the elections, followed by the Round Tables and the signing of the golden book by two leading figures: Prime Ministers Eyskens and Lumumba. Next to the photograph of the two men signing the convention is a painting representing Belgian King Baudouin and Lumumba signing the Golden Book. The discrepancy created by the juxtaposition of the two images shows how the imaginary memories of that period put emphasis on the role of the monarchy.

The juxtaposition of history and memory is central to this exhibition. The independence days were followed by the Katanga and South Kasai secession, Lumumba's assassination, violent rebellions and the Mobutu dictatorship. The dates of these historical moments are recorded in a long timeline that, unlike the rest of the exhibition but in a complementary manner, is extremely factual. One showcase presents Mobutu's Zaïranization that advocated a return to authenticity and nationalized companies such as the Union Minière (which became the Gécamines, the famous company that exploited the copper, symbol of colonial Belgian enterprise). The showcase juxtaposes images of the Mobutu years that marked postcolonial Congo with images of decline and a painting of a Gulliveresque Mobutu brought down by Congolese people.

The second part of the exhibition, more thematic than chronological, concentrates on the violence and the destructive years that followed independence. The question this section raises mainly with creative art is why the situation in Congo deteriorated after independence, leading this young nation to become one of the poorest nations in the world despite its many natural resources. Many of the paintings, sculptures, and photographs presented in this section emphasize the continuity between the colonial and postcolonial Congolese periods characterized by submission and exploitation. From a Congolese perspective, the image of Boula Matari—the stone crusher but also the name given to sculptures depicting colonial agents—is represented with several statues: the explorer Stanley, King Albert I, King Baudouin I and Joseph Kasa-Vubu. The display of these statuettes points to how Boula Matari has come to embody the numerous forms of invasion and exploitation, from the white colonizer to the oppressive postcolonial state.

The room that follows expands on the theme of violence exercised by Europeans through Congolese assistants. Next to some drawings of whipping which evoke the continuity between the slave trade, Leopoldian colonial years and the chains of dictatorship, is Sammy Baloji's work "Travailleurs à la Gécamine." This photomontage superimposes old photographs of chained minors in colonial times and contemporary images of abandoned mining sites to evoke rap-singer Baloji's words that Congo development is like the Gecamines, its growth has stopped like the

Dula-Nkulu "Air Congo – Arrestation de Lumumba" – huile sur toile – 37.2 x 47.5 cm. Reproduced with permission from the MRAC.

Gecamine Company. The shackles of the miners denounce the past as well as the contemporary massive exploitation of Congolese miners and resources of this *Katanga business*[7]. Reminiscent of these exploitative acts and Leopold's taking the best pieces of the Cake at the 1885 Berlin conference (illustrated in the caricature of "Le réveillon des souverains"), Bosoku Ekunde's "The UN and Africa" depicts foreign nations cutting out the best parts of a large piece of meat from which Congolese people only get the leftovers. Faustin Tshobo-i-Ngana's (2009) words presented on the wall that Congo gave the world slaves, latex, copper, uranium, coltan and soon water but has received nothing in return raises the question whether Belgium is not liable to repay.

The central feature of the exhibition is its creative approach to memory present in the display of fables and paintings from the beginning to the end. These metaphorical approaches to politics and memory have a twofold purpose: they are an indirect way of criticizing political authority in Congo and, within this exhibition, an indirect way of engaging with the Belgian version of Congolese history. The paintings of Chéri Samba, Moke, and Trésor Cherin, among others, illustrate the hopes of the population at the time of Lumumba for example.

One small room is devoted to paintings of Lumumba where the assassinated leader is portrayed as a Christ figure while other paintings like Dula Nkulu's "Air Congo" depict him without his suit, captured and chained. Of course, images such as this one point to the fact that Lumumba made several enemies but also remind one of the

---

[7] Title of the 2009 Thierry Michel film that shows the devastating crisis in Katanga where Congolese people and resources are exploited.

> *Congolese Diaspora: representing by its number the third group of non-European migrants. Congolese living in Belgium say they often regret that Belgium recognizes neither their presence nor the ties that have united both countries for so long.*

fact that his violent assassination was the object of a Belgian parliamentary commission which concluded that the Belgian government was morally responsible for the assassination. The 2011 "Truth, Justice, and Reparation" demonstration supporting the lawsuit filed by Patrice Lumumba's family against twelve Belgian citizens suspected of having participated in the transfer, torture and assassination of Patrice Lumumba confirm Lumumba's "assassination's Long Shadow" (Hochschild 2011).

Many of these creative works establish a contrast between the emerging nationalism of a population and its political/economic failure. It foregrounds resistances and repressions in strikes—revolts that led to the independence riots in 1959. Creative approaches like those paintings question the discrepancy between the image/dreams of independence and the realities of a country that has suffered a great deal throughout the centuries because it has been coveted by imperial powers. Several other pieces, among them "Belly," the sculpture of a female body with bullets, call to mind and denounce the sexual violence perpetrated on Congolese women, who we are reminded, were allowed to vote for the first time in 1977 but mostly participated in the elections of 2006, the first that can be considered democratic. Despite democratic improvements, fighting continues in the DRC.

V. THE UNWELCOMED CONGOLESE COMMUNITY IN BELGIUM

The very last section of the exhibition is devoted to the Congolese diaspora in Belgium and the dreams of Congolese migrants trying to reach Belgium which they call Lola (paradise). Illustrated by paintings of the Atomium, the site of dreams *par excellence* for Congolese people who attempt to migrate to Belgium or be accepted in Belgium, it evokes a long history of "I love you, me neither," a love/hate feeling that characterizes the relationship between Belgium and its former colony and Congo and its former colonial invader. The end of the exhibit points an accusing finger at how Congolese people have been (un)welcomed by a colonial power that has exploited their country for decades. This last panel—translated from the French—needs to be examined in depth (see panel above).

If the panel uses similar demographic figures as the tables analyzed at the beginning of this article to point to the significance of the Congolese community in Belgium, it equally denounces that Congolese migrants have never really been welcomed by Belgium since the colonization of their country.

The exhibit closes the way it has begun, with music, one of the most important forms of expression within the third-space of creativity between Congo and Belgium. Short filmed interviews of musicians participating in the Project Heritage Congo (among whom the grandchildren of famous political figures—Banza M'Poyo Kasavuvu and Teddy Lumumba) present how they wish to change the situation with committed urban music. They express how disturbed they feel by the picture they see. They regret that they are not recognized. In view of the colonial past, many of them express the wish to be a privileged community. Some like Senso express they do not feel at home in Belgium and yet Belgium is their home. They want to be welcome and not treated as foreigners.

VI. Conclusion

The very last element on the way out of the exhibition is the independence anniversary wax cloth that, again, reminds the visitor of women's participation in Congolese economy and history. More symbolic is the fact that the fabric, originally introduced by the Dutch for African markets, the import of which was forbidden by Mobutu, is still preferred by Congolese women. Now produced in Africa, some cloth is imported from neighboring countries like Tanzania, but the market is controlled by Chinese companies who, among other things, sell cheap imitations of "authentic Dutch wax cloth" (my translation). A symbol of possible but failed economic independence, the wax cloth reaffirms the main message of the exhibition: "indépendance!."

Held in the (in)famous Tervuren museum, the "Indépendance!" exhibition offers a sharp contrast to the Royal Museum built by Leopold II and originally called the "Musée du Congo." The Congolese people who, a century earlier, were displayed in Leopold II's monumental gardens (which for some of them resulted in death), are eventually replacing the stuffed animals and pre-colonial artifacts the museum has been presenting for decades. One can only regret that the contrast between the content presented above and the room where it is held is not itself foregrounded within the framework of the exhibition. A critical comment on the giant 1910 map of the "Congo Belge" on the wall of the room of the exhibition could have constituted an obvious critical response to the colonial presence, reminiscent of the destructive colonial enterprise and point to how the building is nowadays a contested site as it evokes the glorification of the colonial past of Belgium.

If Congolese voices in museums seem to slowly emerge in temporary exhibitions such as "Indépendance!"—something one can only encourage—their history as well as the assessment of their relationship with Belgium are still to be acknowledged. When the Belgian King attended Independence celebrations in June 2010, some activists in Belgium, like Pauline Imbach, demanded apologies:

> The most important thing would be the acknowledgment of this past, which remains taboo. Belgium refuses to acknowledge its historical responsibilities as illustrated in the fifty anniversary celebrations from which the historical question was simply removed (my translation).

If some will disagree with this, most Congolese people believe Belgium still has a role to play in Congo. What Pauline Imbach's comment unveils is probably how this exhibition has been to some extent marginalized and has avoided a number of explicit critical comments. Among the statues of the Boula Matari, Leopold II has obviously been avoided! What is more, the absence of a Belgian government when the event took place did not encourage the way it was received. And yet, the "Indépendance!" exhibition, as this article emphasizes, constitutes a groundbreaking milestone towards an acknowledgement of the Belgo-Congolese dispute which points to Belgium's responsibility in the chaotic situation of the country.

As Adam Hochschild observed in a lecture held in Liège in 2010, there is in Belgium no Congolese population politically strong enough to lobby so that Congolese history is presented in a different light. Nevertheless, as Lusanda Ndamnia-Maduka already asserted in 1994 "despite Belgium's refusal to import Congolese laborers during the colonial period, Belgium will not avoid the problems metropolises are encountering with their former colonies they will continue to attract as long as the gaps between North and South will not be reduced" (1994:19). What most critics point out is that the Congolese community in Belgium—though somewhat fragmented in a bewildering number of associations (political, cultural, for development aid, etc.) and churches and not devoid of problems—is stable. Of note is the fact that the Congolese neighborhood of Brussels is called Matonge (which is also a district of Kinshasa), probably the only European neighborhood to have an African name.[8] The fact that some (although very few) Congolese people have recently gained some political visibility is a hopeful sign for the future.

With plural, nuanced and open representations of the past, the "Indépendance!" exhibition testifies to the need of museums to embrace non-fixed memory. By redefining the relations between Congo and Belgium as well as addressing plural colonial and postcolonial memories by means of creative and popular culture, it materializes James Clifford's idea of museums as "contact zones," i.e., of museums' structures becoming "an ongoing historical, political, moral *relationship*—a power-charged set of exchanges, of push and pull" (Clifford 1997:192). The exhibit accordingly becomes this contact site where Belgians, Congolese and Belgo-Congolese people and memories are brought together, and where new meanings can be imaginatively created.

REFERENCES

Bragard, Véronique & Planche, Stéphanie. "Museum Practices and the Belgian Colonial Past: Questioning the Memories of an Ambivalent Metropole," *African and Black Diaspora: An International Journal* 2:2 (July 2009): 181-191.

---

[8] Strictly speaking it's not an African neighbourhood since very few Africans live there. Most inhabitants are European. It's a meeting place and shopping area for Africans from Belgium and abroad.

Clifford, James. *Routes: Travel and Translation in the Late Twentieth Century*, Harvard University Press: Cambridge, 1997.

Coolsaet, Rik. *Chronique d'une politique étrangère. Les relations extérieures de la Belgique*. Vie ouvrière: 1992.

Cornet, Anne. "Migrations subsahariennes en Belgique: approche historique" *Migrations Subsahariennes Colloquium* (unpublished paper presented in Louvain-la-Neuve in October 2010).

Ceuppens, Bambi. "Can the Subaltern remember?" Contestations publiques du patrimoine colonial belge Katholieke Universiteit Leuven, 2007.

Ceuppens, Bambi. "Histoire de la diaspora congolaise en Belgique." Formation des guides (Juin 2008).

Demart, Sarah. "Derrière la délinquance juvénile associée au quartier Matonge : la transformation de la présence congolaise en Belgique." Journée d'études « Belgique- RD Congo, 50 années de migration" (June 2010).

http://www.diversiteit.be/?action=onderdeel&onderdeel=263&titel=Belgi%C3%AB+%E2%80%93+DR+Congo%3A+50+jaar+migratie

Desert, Christian. "Belgique. Reconnaître ses responsabilités historiques : interview avec Pauline Imbach." Mrax (September-October 2010). http://www.cadtm.org/Belgique-Reconnaitre-ses

Hochschild, Adam. "An Assasination's Long Shadow," *The New York Times* (January 16th, 2011).

Martiniello, Marco and Andrea Rea. "Belgium's Immigration Policy Brings Renewal and Challenges." Migration Information Source. Accessed September 2010. http://www.migrationinformation.org/feature/display.cfm?ID=164

Ndamina-Makuda, Lusanda. "Pourquoi la Belgique n'a pas employé de main-d'oeuvre coloniale sur son territoire?" *Migrance* 4-5 (1994): 14-19.

Rahier, Jean Muteba. "The Ghost of Leopold II: The Belgian Royal Museum of Central Africa and Its Dusty Colonialist Exhibition." *Research in African Literatures* 34:1 (2003): 58-83.

Vanthemsche, Guy. *La Belgique et le Congo. Nouvelle Histoire de Belgique*. Volume 4. Editions Complexe: 2007.

Verhagen, Benoît. dans *Le Congo belge durant la seconde guerre mondiale. Receuil d'études*. Académie Royale des Sciences d'Outre-Mer, 1983.

Representation of Africa and the African Diaspora in European Museums

Artwell Cain

National Institute of Dutch Slavery Past and Legacy, The Netherlands

---

a.cain@ninsee.nl

Abstract: Museums in Europe have a tradition of marginalizing the image and narrative of persons from the African Diaspora. This is often evident in the frequency of appearances and the quality of these scarce productions. Another point of interest is the manner in which these productions are presented. On the one hand, several questions arise regarding the representation of the African after the abolishment of chattel slavery right up to this present age of emancipation. Who gathers and presents these cultural artifacts? Which criteria are applied during the gathering and production of these presentations? Which sorts of museums are inclined to present the African Diaspora in their productions? On the other hand, the participation of persons from the African Diaspora in museums in Europe is problematic. Persons of African Diaspora are not by definition employed as administrators, curators and other stakeholders in these museums. Interest in Europe about Africa and the African Diaspora has always been partial, distorted or deficient. In the cases where attention has been paid to the African Diaspora, it has been by and large of a negative nature. A central point of inquiry is why this state of affairs has been perpetuated for such long a period of time? In this paper, the author focuses on several aspects of representation of the African Diaspora in European museums in relation to power construction, which goes hand in hand with racism and social exclusion. The main points of departure in this paper are the articulation and location of representation of the African Diaspora especially from the 19th century to the present day. Additionally, the author raises questions about the ways in which NiNsee (The National Institute of Dutch Slavery Past and Legacy) is developing its own distinctive image of the Dutch slavery past and its heritage and how it is attempting at the same time to foster an alternative representation of the African Diaspora.

wI. INTRODUCTION

Any effort to assess the representations of people of African descent in museums must address a number of key issues and confront a number of problems. Museums in Europe have a tradition of marginalizing representations, images and narratives of people from Africa and the Diaspora. This is often evident in the (in)frequency of appearances and the quality of the presented work. Another point of interest is the manner in which these productions are offered. On one level the question arises regarding the representation of the African after the abolition of chattel slavery to this present age of emancipation. On the other level it has become almost commonplace to

---

Artwell Cain, PhD, is executive director of NiNsee (National Institute of Dutch Slavery Past and Legacy). NiNsee is a knowledge centre for the encouragement of research and the conceptualization and dissemination of knowledge pertaining to the Dutch Slavery in the past and its consequences for contemporary Dutch society. Cain has written various articles and essays on topics relating to multicultural society, race relations, citizenship and the representation of the African Diaspora in European institutions. This paper was presented at the Migration and Museum Maison des Science de l'Homme Conference in Paris 25-26 June 2010.

seek but find little or no positive images of the African Diaspora in these museums. Why has there been such a packaging over the years of the African Diaspora for viewing, displaying and the entertainment of white Europeans? Who gathers and presents African Diaspora cultural artifacts and other material? What criteria are applied during the collection and production of these presentations? And which kinds of museums are inclined to present the African Diaspora in their production?

The representation of persons from the African Diaspora in museums in Europe remains problematic. There are still too many narrow and one-sided representations, with distortions and misrepresentations. One of the major reasons that this is the case is that people of African Descent are not commonly employed as administrators, curators and other stakeholders in these museums. People of African descent are hardly consulted to participate in productions and presentations, even when these are dealing with their way of life or cultural practices. The main points of departure in this paper are the articulation and location of representation of the African Diaspora especially from the 19th century to the present day. Additionally I raise questions about the ways in which NiNsee (The National Institute of Dutch Slavery Past and Legacy) is developing its own distinctive image of the Dutch slavery past and its heritage and how it is attempting at the same time to foster an alternative representation of the African Diaspora.

In assessing the role of NiNsee, it is imperative to locate Ninsee in the context of museum, galleries and exhibits in the Netherlands. NiNsee is not a museum, but rather it has a gallery and exhibit space. This exhibit space is unique. In this respect it is not a classical museum, like those typically found in many of the cities in the Netherlands or for that matter any place else in Europe. European museums are commonly experienced and adept at displaying paintings, material artifacts, a range of physical items, as well as icons, illustrations and other objects which represent the glory of Europe in general or specifically a certain theme in relation to European history, culture, grandeur, taste, personalities, fancy and what else they choose to place on a pedestal. This is tantamount to a distortion of the real range of European societies and experiences. Eichstedt and Small (2002) offer a description of southern plantation museums and history. According to them, what becomes accepted as history is often what comes from the dominant group—whether it be dominance in the arena of class, race, gender, sexuality, nationality or something else (Eichstedt and Small 2002:16). For a long period of time in the modern age the dominant group not only wrote the history but also determined the content of the museums. This dominance has begun to change, especially with the arrival of hundreds of thousands of migrants in Europe from the former colonies in the Caribbean and also from independent African countries. These groups and individuals have questioned the misrepresentations, challenged the assumptions and proposed more accurate representations.

Interest in Europe about Africa and the African Diaspora has always been partial, distorted or deficient. In the cases were attention has been paid to the African Diaspora it has been by and large of a negative nature. A central point of inquiry is why has this state of affairs been perpetuated for such long a period of time? The historical record in Europe provides clear evidence of the various ways in which individuals and groups have tried to influence 'the powers that be' to take a different and more varied outlook of the manner in which people of the African Diaspora are portrayed in their museums and the amount of time this is done (Fryer 1984; Ramdin 1987). These efforts had very limited success. In bringing the representation of the African Diaspora in the European museum into focus, we bring to this discussion a range of historical examples of world exhibitions held in Europe in the 19th and 20th centuries.

In this paper, I focus on several aspects of representation of the African Diaspora in European museums in relation to power construction, which goes hand in hand with racism and social exclusion. This is done by making use of the developments within NiNsee to give the reader an exposé of how one manages the placing of certain information and images into the center of attention, which have been buried for years in the belly and dungeons of large and not so large European museums. Stuart Hall (1994) declares that one needs a change from the struggle over the relations of representation to a politics of representation itself (1994:442). This I interpret as meaning, it is time to stop worrying about their representations of you and begin representing yourself.

II. RACE AND REPRESENTATION

The practice and history of portraying the African Diaspora in a narrow and particular manner is linked not only to the institutions of slavery and colonialism, but also closely to the birth of the new imperialism period 1880–1930, and to the accompanying ideologies of scientific racism (Collins 2000; Brown and Webb 2007). This was a period fuelled by a spirit to conquer, dominate and divide Africa among a few European nations via the deployment of anthropological adventures, which were part and parcel of the mission and submission efforts of Europeans to dominate Africans and people of other continents and cultures. The so-called research findings of these anthropologists were a blessing in disguise for the imperialists. Studies pertaining to physical anthropology and biology were especially used to construct typologies of the 'human' races. During the several centuries leading up to the period of dividing up and distributing African land among European states, the history and experience of the slave trade and chattel slavery provided a clear indication of where whites and blacks were to be located in the racial hierarchy (Banton 1977; Gossett 1965). Racism as an underpinning of racialized enslavement is localized by some scholars as an important factor within the general colonial matrix of power (Grosfoguel 2006; Mignolo 2008).

It has also been recorded that discrimination against Blacks in Western Europe existed well before the introduction of slavery in the Americas and the Caribbean (Gould 1993). It became racism when racial prejudice was combined with ethnocentrism in the service of the slave societies (Lampe 2001:114). Racial subordination and social terrorism were routine and popular instruments of repression during the Atlantic slave trade and chattel slavery. Chattel slavery was irrepressibly and inextricably racialized. Central to this process were legal representations. Every black man, woman and child had to bear evidence on their person to prove that they were not enslaved. It goes without saying that anti-black racism is not just a social construct but a living fact, which has its roots in the 16th century slave societies. The enslavement of Africans from the 16th century to provide free labour in the Americas and the Caribbean area went hand in hand with an ideology of racial superiority and domination (Miles, 1982). In simple terms, it just happened that in the age of the enlightenment and Christian morality, European thinkers had to find a cover for their nakedness in regards to the enslavement of Africans.

The uprisings in Europe of the protestants against the Roman Catholics in the 16th century which led to the protestant reformation is also an important factor that helped to shape the meaning pertaining to racialized enslavement. John Calvin (1509–1564) provided a theological theory of predestination. His teachings specified who was chosen and who was condemned. The holy bible was used as an instrument to certify that Africans were condemned by God to be enslaved in the service of whites. Prior to the European conference in Berlin, Germany, regarding the European expansionist drive in the 1880s to divide and conquer Africa, scientists and other learned persons had already advertised the presumed biological superiority of the white race (Banton 1977). Carl Linnaeus (1707–1778) a botanist and zoologist among other things, presented his colleagues and others research material for the biological definition of the human race in the 18th century. His works next to Charles Darwin's (1809–1882) work were extensively used to justify the ill treatment and dehumanization of those enslaved. The theory was that they were unfit or undeserving of equality. It is rather ironic that the offices and gallery of NiNsee stand today in the 21st century in the Linnaeusstreet in Amsterdam—a street named to honor this very person.

III. THE ESTABLISHMENT AND ACTIVITIES OF NINSEE

The Atlantic slave trade and Chattel slavery in the Caribbean—whether English, Spanish, French, Danish, Dutch or other—are not topics or themes which are popular in the media, academia, in museums or with the general public in European nations. This is especially so in the Netherlands. It took the Netherlands 140 years after the abolition of legal slavery before any serious institutional attention was directed towards public acknowledgment of slavery and its legacies. In all those years silence was the resounding norm. Many scholars have documented the ways in which museums (along with galleries and exhibitions) are sites where knowledge and power are played out (Coombes 1994; Horton and Horton 2006; Eichsted and Small 2002). They view the museum as creative agencies but also as 'contested terrains.' NiNsee operates in the same context.

It took many years before the national monuments pertaining to Dutch slavery in the West were erected. First was the National Slavery Monument in the Eastern park in Amsterdam in 2002. NiNsee as knowledge centre followed in 2003. NiNsee was born out of a struggle by the Afro-Caribbean (Surinamese and Antillean) grassroots individuals and organizations. It was a context in which most institutions, and even schools and educational institutions, provided limited, unsatisfactory and highly problematic representations and/or discussion of slavery and its legacies. The ambitions and aspirations of the communities were high and still remain high in terms of what the expected actions from NiNsee are. They are to a certain degree constantly comparing the mis-representations and or representations of NiNsee of the African Diaspora with those used by the various institutions, museums and galleries in the Netherlands.

NiNsee is involved in a range of activities that create, interpret and disseminate knowledge. At NiNsee we utilize the gallery and exhibit space as educational instruments. In other words as tools to represent the narrative of the Dutch slavery past and its heritage from a different perspective than that which prevails more generally in the Netherlands. Our approach represents a new phenomenon in the Netherlands. The International Slavery Museum of Liverpool in the United Kingdom is different than that at NiNsee. Hence both cannot be compared.

NiNsee as a knowledge centre is structured around five main pillars, these are: 1) The setting-up and conducting of research pertaining to the Dutch slavery past and its legacies; 2) The preparation and development of school and general educational information regarding the same; 3) Using the findings of research and public history to display and share knowledge through exhibitions in the gallery; 4) Creating space to gather all the relevant documents and other sources of information, whether printed and or audio visual works, regarding this history and its heritage; 5) And last but not least, the organizing of the annual national commemoration and remembrance day of the abolition of Dutch slavery in the Caribbean and the breaking of the chains festival on the 1st of July, the commemoration of the Tula uprising in 1795 on the 17th of August and also the commemoration of UNESCO International day for the Remembrance of the Slave Trade and its Abolition on the 23rd of August.

Next to these main activities NiNsee also organizes public lectures, at least twice per month. These lectures are given by local and international scholars, a Summer school program in June articulating Black European thinkers is also a yearly event, which lasts for two weeks. There is also a yearly international symposium. In all these respects, NiNsee plays an important role in the facilitating of the grassroots organizations to undertake their own activities. Another preoccupation of NiNsee is working in cooperation with other institutions and organizations to further realize joint objectives. These are just a few of the endeavors that are generally administered by NiNsee. In essence NiNsee is a certified private foundation with a statuary board of directors. The foundation receives a yearly grant from the Dutch government based on a classified plan and budget.

In the case of NiNsee a wide range of efforts are made to present the African Diaspora in a manner that speaks to the essence of one's own being and viewpoint. This was a conscious decision taken from the moment NiNsee came into being in 2003, and it was a central factor in shaping the first permanent exhibition produced called 'Breaking the Silence.' Having gone through the first development stages we are now bent on revamping the exhibition to meet present needs.

IV. COLONIAL MUSEUMS AND EXHIBITIONS

There exist, according to figures gathered from the Dutch Association of Museums, approximately 1000 museums in the Netherlands. In the case of Amsterdam, the national capital, there are round and about 129 museums. In terms of museums dedicated to exhibiting peoples, cultures and artifacts from the colonial past there are four: The Royal Museum of the Tropics, Amsterdam (KIT) located just across the street from NiNsee; the African Museum in Berg aan Daal; the World Museum in Rotterdam; and another African museum in Cader and Keer in the extreme South of the country. There also exits a Mollocan Museum which, not unlike NiNsee, is administrated and run by the Mollucans.

These four museums focus on the 'other' and are still chiefly interested in presenting the Dutch and or other foreign visitors with a view or an opinion regarding the exotic other. The penchant for presenting the 'other' in large scale exhibitions seems to hark back to the 19th century, when this was envisaged by the powers that be as the obvious thing to do (Blanchard et al. 2008; Coombes 1994). Such exhibits were framed by a crude dichotomy on western and non-western, in order to contrast the civilized world as against the uncivilized world. For example a World exhibition was organized in Paris in 1878 (Nieuwsbrief geschiedenis 2010). It was at that moment the biggest exhibition of natives, these being about 400 colonial subjects from Senegal, Indochina and Tahiti in their makeshift huts. The natives were required to behave and act as if they were in their natural habitats. Next to offering entertainment to the thousands of Parisians, French and other European visitors, it was also an ideological approach to demonstrate the superiority of the colonizer vis-à-vis those who were primitive and had to be colonized.

Another very interesting case, worth relating here, is a book presentation which was done at NiNsee in 2009. This book is called 'De Inboorling' in Dutch, meaning 'the Natives.' It was written by Stevo Akkerman, a Dutch journalist, who is employed at a national newspaper, called Parool which has Amsterdam as its base and brings a great deal of news and opinions having to do with Amsterdam. The writer of the book set out to paint a picture based on historical facts with a mixture of fiction. The narrative has its roots in an exhibition that was held in Amsterdam in 1883. The purpose of the exhibition was not unlike the world exhibition in Paris to have West Indians and Indigenous people displaying themselves to the general public. This was 20 years after the abolition of Dutch slavery in the Caribbean region and also 10 years after the end of apprenticeship in the then Dutch colony of Surinam. Akkerman claims in the book to have found interesting material in one of the larger museums in Amsterdam. This museum and the findings also play a role in the book.

The representation of slavery abolition was that they were made free by the compassionate Dutch King. These ex-enslaved had no notion of the fact that this same King William III was a staunch opponent of their freedom. He was in fact a dedicated slave-owner. He, like the other Dutch slave-owners and planters, demanded financial compensation for giving up of their property. They were compensated at the rate of 300 guilders per enslaved in Surinam (Willemsen 2006). The enslaved got nothing. Neither did they know of the compensation. What they viewed as benevolence was to the King a business disaster. In fact they were brought on a pretense to Europe as representatives of the native, the savage and the uncivilized—i.e., as what it was like to be different from the biological and socially white. Before they left Surinam they were taught songs of praise to the King and were overwhelmed with joy for the opportunity to meet and greet their bogus freedom fighter. One of their foremost wishes was also to complain to the King regarding their social economic position after attaining their freedom. A freedom tantamount to what W.E.B. Du Bois referred to in the context of the United States as a mockery of freedom (Du Bois 1990:107).In fact, the extra semi-enslavement referred to as apprenticeship was actually a new construction fabricated by the planters and the legislature council members to delude many into thinking that this system was meant to teach those Africans who would have attained their freedom from chattel slavery about how to work and become civilized (Willemsen 2006). This was rather ironic because by that particular moment in history the enslaved had been forced and brutalized for centuries into furnishing free labour in the service of western expansion, industrialization and capitalism. In this book dealing with the natives one is told that the Africans and a few indigenous persons of Surinam origin were tricked into making the journey to the Netherlands. The supposed purpose of this trip was to pay their respect and tribute to King William III of the Netherlands and thank him for securing their freedom from slavery.

They were placed in a tent in Amsterdam on one of the squares for months on end, where they remained throughout various seasons. Their temporary dwelling place was also in their show arena. The local populace and other visitors, who could afford it paid one quarter (25 cents) to see, ridicule, mock and scorn them. These natives thought they were waiting for the King to make an entrance. In fact they were part and parcel of a racist circus. In the period of waiting for the King to make his appearance one young man from the indigenous group died. The King did visit the exhibition on the first day and did the ceremonial opening. However, the minute he was finished he disappeared (Akkerman 2009.

Being involved with the organizing of the presentation, I was among those who read the book. We were also able to contact and invite a black woman, Mavis Carrilho as a panelist for the panel discussion. She is a somewhat prominent black businesswoman who moves around in the Dutch business and cultural circles. She had earlier told us that one of the persons brought to the Netherlands to validate white superiority was her great, great grandmother. The picture of her great, great grandmother happens to be pasted against the windows of our building. Actually we have photographs of all of these persons who were brought to the Netherlands, represented separately on the surrounding glass windowpanes of our building. The photograph of her great, great grandmother on the glass was one of the elements that assisted us in arranging a lively panel discussion of five participants. The mere fact that these photographs are displayed on the windows distinguished NiNsee form other organizations in the area. It is also a clear representation and a testimony to those who travel along the building, that somehow there is a connection between the folks on photographs on the windowpanes and other persons in the Dutch society.

We use this example of the book *De Inboorling* to illustrate the historical continuities in misrepresenting Black people as 'the other,' in distorting their lives and experiences for the satisfaction of European audiences. The point is that even though chattel slavery was abolished in the Dutch Caribbean colonies on the 1st of July 1863, exhibits 20 years later continued to objectify and exoticise Black people. And even up to the present the representation of the African has not changed in any fundamental way. Akkerman did not bother himself with any analysis having to do with epistemic racism, domination, colonialism or false representations. What he emphasized was the ambivalent issues that his main character, the black Surinamese civil servant in a Dutch organization, had relating to his identity. This main character thought he had everything, including a white girlfriend and yet he later came to realize that he only had himself and all his identity issues.

The examples just given are not unique or exceptional. In fact, they are indicative of common practices over the last 200 years. The representations in Dutch and European museums, of people of the African Diaspora in these narrow, distorted and peculiar manner continued in fact throughout the 19th and the 20th centuries. For example, in 1897 a large and popular exhibition of 'negroes' was organized in Brussels, Belgium (Nieuwsbrief geschiedenis 2010). This consisted of about 200 Congolese. During this 'negro' exhibition, seven of the persons exhibited died. There were no registered protest or opposition to this exhibition. To compound matters even worse, King Leopold II of Belgium considered the Congo as his personal property and hence claimed the right to do what he wanted with his property. The atrocities, theft and destruction, which had been committed in his name in the Congo were viewed as "collateral damage" in relationship to the civilization of the African 'savages.'

Another example of racist representations is the large 'negro' exhibition held in Rotterdam in 1928 (Nieuwsbrief geschiedenis 2010). A special 'negro' village was built in a Lunapark in Rotterdam to coincide with the Olympic games, which were held in Amsterdam in 1928. The 'negro' exhibition was a section of the industrial exhibition called 'Nenijto,' which aimed at the promotion of national trade. One of the highlights of this negro exhibition was the birth of the child Amadou in this village (zoo). He was the son of Prosper Seek and his wife, who were also held in the village. Commandant Prosper Seek, a Senegalese by birth, was said to have been a decorated captain in the French army. Prosper Seek was compelled to wear his World War I uniform with decoration of valor received from the French government during the period, in which he and his family were being exhibited in the negro village. This state of affair was such that there was not a minimum of protest regarding the manner in which these persons were represented in the early 20th century as animals in a zoo.

V. General Representation of the Black Woman

Actually, the history of European museums can be located and framed in a few words: The glorification of European past and present in terms of history, religion, culture, art, war heroes, pioneers and thinkers. Even though this history is riddled with theft, plunder and the looting of the treasures which rightfully belong to other folks around the world, this was not an attribute in the representation of the European in their museums and galleries. Their story is an imperial narrative of heroism, conquest, civilization and modernity.

Over the years the tendency has been to display people of the African Diaspora in stereotypes meant to buttress certain ill-conceived images based on racialized ideologies. Negative and distorted images of Black women have played a major part in this. Exoticism is frequently used to depict Africans and other women of colour. The so-called Hottentot Venus or Bush woman is a very good example, where the representation was meant to depict the African woman in an inappropriate fashion. The story of Saartje Baartman started with Dutch colonists in 1810 in Cape of Good Hoop. She was a member of the khoi-San tribe of South Africa. She was sold by Dutch colonists to the British who proceeded by taking her to London for exhibitions purposes. It was said that due to her big buttocks and protruding vulva, she was seen and accepted as the living representative of the wild animal inclinations and sexual temperament of the black woman (Wikipedia.org).

Similar representations can be found in today's media, particularly in glossy magazines, television, videos, DVDs, etc. The black woman is still placed out there as being without a true essence of decent womanhood. That is, in the sense of how the Western world interprets and labels true womanhood, in a Eurocentric fashion. One is aware that in Western countries images are created for particular reasons. It is often a question of what you see and how you interpret it. However, the context in which the image is presented is important in relation to the interpretation. So, too, is the context of accumulated knowledge in society regarding certain individuals and groups. The manner in which one looks and interprets is governed by the social laws of race, ethnicity, skin color, gender, sexuality, and a host of other real and imagined factors. If a certain image is presented repeatedly chances are that this image will be seen and interpreted as natural and truthful.

However, in recent years there have been fundamental changes in the manner in which the black woman has been represented. Barson (2010) analyses works of O'Grady on the one hand, and on the other hand, Gilroy to certify that since the 1980s and even before this period, black women artists have been investigating the representation of the black female body and giving them another framing. This conceptualization of Barson was fully evident during the exhibition "Afro Modern: Journey through the Black Atlantic" held at the Tate Liverpool from 29 January to 25 April 2010. In this particular exhibition black women artists such as Tracey Rose, Sonia Boyce, Kara Walker, Ana Mendieta plus others provide a sort of Stuart Hallish self-representation through existing bodies of racism and rationalism. These developments ensued in a context in which African-Caribbeans and others mobilized to protest racist images in the media, in schools and in museums (Small 1997).

To date, we have not been witnesses to large-scale protest or opposition to the representation of the African Diaspora in the Netherlands, whether within or without the museum. One exception was Negrofila (White over Black) done by Felix de Rooy, an Antillean Dutch, who was one of the founders of Foundatuion Cosmic Illusion. This was around the period of 1989/1990. There have been recent exhibitions such as 'Black is Beautiful" in Amsterdam, and in few other museums attention was paid to the presence of the immigrant (the black) in the Dutch society, but these have been scarce productions. It is obvious that if change is going to come and action has to be taken, this has to be the prerogative of Afro-Caribbean persons, those from the African Diaspora and others in the Netherlands. One cannot wait and hope that someone else is prepared and willing to do it on his/her behalf.

VI. NiNsee's Options to Present Another Image

NiNsee has been using its unique position as a centre of knowledge in the Netherlands to make a difference. Our work is driven by knowledge through research and education, learning and making information available throughout the nation and in fact the world. We recognize knowledge production and dissemination as our core business. The main goal is to reach out to educate as many persons as possible about the Dutch slavery past and its legacies. The fundamental assumption is that here lies the key towards influencing the representation of the African on various levels and in different arenas within the society.

NiNsee does not visualize and/or conceptualize the Dutch slavery past and its heritage as an issue that lends itself to entertainment, it is taken more seriously. Enslavement was and remains a solemn history. And it is a history that must be approached with full attention to the facts, and with appreciation of the sensitivity of the issues. In an age when much could be done using the social media and a host of new technological gadgets, the belief is that now more than ever everyone has a responsibility to pay closer attention to the representation of the African Diaspora in Europe, whether inside and outside of the museum. If this means having to refuse to participate in certain preconceived programs or projects produced by others, then so be it. Ninsee will only participate or produce material for its gallery and in other arenas, which does not present persons of the African Diaspora in a manner that depicts black men and women constructively.

At NiNsee we recognize that we are not the only institution involved in a struggle over representations of the past; and we are not the only institution involved in discussions about the many artifacts and precious items acquired during colonialism that are currently housed in museums across Europe. The fact that the British are embroiled with Greece relating to the true ownership of the Elgin Marbles is a good example of vandalism and looting within the European realms. The Elgin Marbles are still in the British Museum and Athens is still waiting for their return. In many European museum depots there are enough African related art, objects and property to full many exhibition halls in Paris and Amsterdam. In the case of Africa there has been numerous plunders and exploitation of people, including the Benin Bronzes (Coombes 1994). This went hand in hand with the theft of artifacts, precious stones and other riches from Egypt in the North to South Africa in the South. However, if Greece, a European country and member of the European Union is having difficulties reclaiming artifacts related to its cultural heritage, what are the chances of African countries to retrieve theirs? The struggle must continue.

It goes without saying that, on its own, NiNsee is not capable of turning around five hundred years of history colored and impregnated with the Caribbean or (better said) the transatlantic slave trade, chattel slavery and colonialism—a history of attempted total and comprehensive domination and misrepresentation. But our endeavors at NiNsee are very important, symbolically, and they also represent in concrete ways a set of initatives that we believe will get the ball rolling and raise awareness and consciousness of the issues. We also believe that our work will lead to new projects and research being carried out, as well as to new frameworks of analysis. We see the framework of the African diaspora as a key feature of this analysis. By this we mean locating the experiences of Dutch slavery in the context of other European nations and slavery, their impact on Africa, the establishment and growth of colonies across the Americas based on enslaved labor, and all the legacies that result from them.

Central to our framework is the identification of commonalities that the Dutch share with other nations, as well as the unique aspects of the Dutch slavery experience. And we insist on examining, representing and highlighting the African diaspora links—political, social and cultural ideologies of Black people across the Diaspora, shared with one another for survival and success. These include resistance and rebellion, maroons, religion, music, political formations and pan-Africanism. The objective is and remains to work with other local, national, and international organizations and institutions to further an agenda geared at gaining and disseminating knowledge regarding the Dutch slavery past and legacies. This is of essential importance to the entire Dutch populace, because the heritage of that slavery past is an everyday experience in the present day society.

And we believe that before NiNsee came into existence there was very little knowledge, information, or analysis of Dutch slavery past and its legacies. We plan to change that because, in a sense, the manner in which individuals and groups see each other and or are represented in the media, academia and in other arenas of the society chiefly determines the ensuring racial and social relations.

REFERENCES

Akkerman, Stevo (2009) *De inboorling*, Nieuw Amsterdam Uitgevers.
Banton, Michael, (1977) *The Idea of Race*, Tavistock, London.
Barson, Tanya (2010)*Introduction Modernism and the Black Atlantic*, in Tanya Barson & Perter Gorschluter (eds.), Afro Modern, journeys through the Black Atlantic, Tate Publishers, Liverpool, p. 8 – 25.
Blanchard, Pascal, Nicolas Bnacel, Gilles Boetsch, éric, Deroo, Sandrine Lemaire and Charles Forsdick, Human Zoos (2008) . *Science and Spectacle in the Age of Colonial Empires*, Liverpool University Press, Liverpool.
Brown, David & Clive Webb (2007*)* *Race in the American South: from slavery to civil rights*, Edinburg University Press Ltd., Great Britain.
Collins, Hill Patricia (2000) *Black feminist Thought, Knowledge Consciousness and the politics of Empowerment*, Routledge, Great Briain.
Coombes, Annie E., (1994) *Reinventing Africa*.

Museums, Material Culture and Popular Imagination in Late Victorian and Edwardian England, Yale University Press, New Haven and London.

Du Bois, W.E.B. (1990) *The Souls of Black Folk*, Library of America paperback Classics, New York..

Eichstedt, Jennifer L. & Small, Stephen (2002) *Representation of Slavery: Race and Ideology in Southern Plantation Museums*, Smithsonian Institution Press, Washington and London.

Fryer, P., *Staying Power: The History of Black People in Britain*, Pluto, London, 1984.

Gould, Stephen (1993) "American Polygeny and Craniometry Before Darwin." In *the Racial Economy of Science: Toward a Democratic Future*. Harding, Sandra, (editor). Bloomington; Indiana University Press.

Gossett, Thomas., *Race. The History of an Idea in America*, Schocken Books, 1965.

Grosfoguel, Ramon (2006) *Decolonizing Political-Economy and Post-Colonial Studies, Transmodernity, Borderthinking and Global coloniality*, in Ramon Grosfoguel, Jose David Saldivar and Nelson Maldonado Torres (eds.), Unsettling Postcoloniality, Coloniality, transmodernity and Borderthinking, Duke University Press.

Hall, Stuart (1996) *Cultural Studies and its theoretical legacies*, in Stuart Hall: Critical Dialogues in Cultural Studies Edited by David Morley and Kuan-Hsing Chen, Routledge, London and New York, p. 262-275.

Horton, James and Lois Horton (editors) *Slavery and Public Memory. The Tough Stuff of American Memory*, New York, New Press, 2006.

Gilroy, Paul (1992) There Ain't No Black in the Union Jack, Routledge, London and New York.

Gilroy, Paul (1993) *The Black Atlantic; Modernity and Double Consciousness*, Verso, London and New York.

Lampe, Armando (2001) *Mission or Submission? Moravian and Catholic Missionaries in the Dutch Caribbean During the 19th Century*, Vandenhoeck & Ruprecht in Gottingen.

Mazrui, A. Ali (1997)*The Muse of Modernity and the Quest for Development*, Africa World Press, Trenton NJ.

Mignolo, D. Walter (2008) *Delinking the Rhetoric of Modernity, the logic of Coloniality and the Grammar of De-coloniality*, in Walter Mingolo, I am Where I Think: Globalization and the De-colonial Option, Duke University Press.

Miles, Robert, (1982) *Racism and migrant labor*, Routledge & Kegan Paul, London.

Nieuwsbrief geschiedenis (2010) *Tentoonstelling van negers in Rotterdam in 1928; op handelstentoonstelling tijdens Olypische spleen*, Vpro.dmd. omroep.nl.

O'Grady, Lorraine (1994) *Reclaiming Black Female subjectivity*, online at http://lorraineogrady.com/sites/default/files/WTTO 2.olympiasmaidfull.pdf.

Nimako Kwame and Stephen Small (2009) *Theorizing Black Europe and the African Diaspora: Implications for Citizenship, Nativism and Xenophobia*, in Hine Clark Darlene, Keaton Trica Danielle and Stephen Small (eds.). Black Europe and the African Diaspora, University of Illinois Press, p. 212—237.

Nimako Kwame and Glenn Willemsen (forth coming in 2011) *The Dutch Atlantic; Slavery, Abolition and Emancipation*, Pluto Press, London, U.K.

Ramdin, Ron., *The Making of the Black Working Class in Britain*, Gower, Aldershot, 1987.

Small, Stephen "Contextualizing the Black Presence in British Museums: Representations, Resources and Response," in Eileen Hooper Greenhill, (editor), Museums and Multiculturalism in Britain, Leicester University Press, Leicester, 1997, pp. 50-66.

http://en.Wikipedia.org/wiki/Saartjie_Baartman.Willensem, Glenn (2006) *Dagen van gejuich en gejubel; over de viering en herdenking van de afschaffing van de slavernij in Nederland, Suriname en de Nederlandse Antillen*, Amrit, Den Haag.

Slavery, Colonialism and Museums Representations in Great Britain

Old and New Circuits of Migration

Stephen Small

University of California, Berkeley

---

small@berkeley.edu

One of the consequences of British colonialism across the world was the appropriation of cultural artefacts, sacred and precious objects; and one of the legacies is their display in British museums. For more than one hundred years the museums of Great Britain have functioned to bolster national (white) pride and glorify British culture by showcasing a wide array of artefacts plundered and looted during European slavery and colonialism. One of the most significant legacies of British colonialism is the migration of minorities to the metropolis, their permanent settlement there and the growth of local-born populations. These groups have mobilized successful challenges to the hegemonic representations of British glory prevalent in museums. At present, dramatic and irreversible transformations in the representations and discourses of colonialism are under way in long-established museums across the nation. And new exhibits, galleries and museums projecting markedly different representations and discourses, and questioning the very foundation of museum principles, knowledge and functions have also emerged in recent decades. None of these developments are conceivable, or their dynamics understandable, outside the framework of international migration and settlement. And at the same time, new circuits of international migration, fuelled by inequalities of wealth and the ravages of war, all in the maelstrom of globalization, have led to the recent arrival of new migrants—and permanent settlers—new artefacts, new debates, and the potential for new transformations.

I. INTRODUCTION

In the 1950s, a majority of white people in Britain had never seen a 'coloured colonial immigrant' in person. The Black[1] population was tiny in number, and concentrated in the historic port cities of Liverpool, Bristol, London and Cardiff (Rose, et al. 1969). But all that has changed. By 2011 the Black population in Britain

---

[1] By 'Black' I am referring to people of African and African Caribbean origin, including people who identify as 'mixed-race' from these groups.

Stephen Small, PhD, is Associate professor of African American Studies at the University of California, Berkeley, and NiNsee Professor of History at the University of Amsterdam. He has taught at the University of Massachusetts, Amherst, and in England at Leicester University. His research analyzes links between historical structures and contemporary manifestations of racial formations, with a current emphasis on museums, public history and collective memory. He was guest curator at the Merseyside Maritime Museum's Atlantic Slave Trade Gallery. He also works on the Black Diaspora in Europe, and people of mixed origins. His next book is tentatively titled "21st Century Antebellum Slave Cabins and Public History in Louisiana." He is co-writing a book (with Dr. Kwame Nimako) on Public History, Museums and Slavery in England and the Netherlands. He published (with Jennifer L Eichstedt) *Representations of Slavery: Race and Ideology in Southern Plantation Museums* in 2002.

numbered more than 1.5 million, and there are sizeable Black populations in all the major cities. At the same time, even larger numbers of immigrants and settlers arrived from India, Pakistan and later, Bangladesh; by 2011 they numbered over 3 million. And in the last decade, Britain has seen the arrival and settlement of hundreds of thousands of new migrants—EU citizens from Poland and Romania, and refugees from nations in Africa that were not part of the British Empire (like Somalia, Congo and Rwanda). There are similar patterns elsewhere in Europe, particularly in former imperial nations, like the Netherlands, France, Belgium and Spain; as well as in Germany and Italy (Hine, Keaton and Small 2009).

In Britain, through the 1950s and beyond, most museums said little or nothing of slavery and empire, and they ignored, downplayed, or marginalized explicit discussion of slavery and its legacy. If they said anything it was to glorify Empire, and/or British abolition of the slave trade, and they focused mainly on material culture, rather than human chattel. They housed objects and art that presented crude and mono-dimensional stereotypes of Africa, Africans and slavery; and almost none had Black people involved as agents, or organisers. They were overwhelmingly visited by white people. This was also the case for the series of world's fairs that took place in Britain (and elsewhere) in the 19th century (Blanchard et al. 2008). And it was true for monuments and statues that memorialized empire (Dresser 2007).

Today (2011) in Britain, if you look in the press, on television, in popular culture, it seems like the legacy of slavery is a key aspect of British museums. There have been temporary or permanent exhibits in the main museums in Liverpool, Manchester, Bristol, Birmingham and Hull (Wallace 2006). And of course, let's not forget London (Littler and Naidoo 2005). Some museums now have permanent exhibits and galleries of slavery, colonialism, or on Africa. Many are rich, textured, progressive even, and have striven to convey a wide range of the Black experience, in Africa and the Diaspora. In several of them there is significant critique of Empire, critique of slavery, even of slave trade abolition. And Black people are more actively involved than ever before—as curators, managers, writers—though still in numbers below their proportions in the population (Tibbles 1994; Visram 2002; Young 2002; Tulloch 2005). And there has been extensive outreach to draw on resources, insights, and information from across the African Diaspora and Africa itself. Some of these activities began several decades ago, but the biggest spur occurred in 2007, which was the 200th anniversary of the legal abolition of the slave trade in the British Empire. The anniversary attracted extensive scholarly interest, a wide range of museum initiatives and significant funds from government (Hilton 2010). Many Black and multi-racial organizations were involved, and there were increased calls for reparations (Brennan 2005, 2008).

Migration and museums brings together two fields of studies for which there are large and fascinating literatures and, which are not usually associated with one another. But with regard to Black people and the legacy of slavery/colonialism and museums in Britain I argue that the two fields are intricately and, in fact, inextricably related, to one another. We know all the reasons migration is important in and of itself, but why are museums important, and how are they connected to migration? Museums are important because they are one institutional site among many where hostile representations, images and discourses of Black people and Africa continue to occur. In fact, historically, museums in Britain have held some of the most reprehensible images of Blacks as barbarians and savages; and the most vicious images of Black women, since the advent of European colonialism (Fryer 1984). Museums are important sites for the contestation of identity and ethnicity, including national and religious identity (Greenhill 1997). They are important sites for contestation over grand narratives of history, especially nationalist and imperial history (Trouillot 1995; Littler and Naidoo 2005). And where you have history you always have memory. This is clearly the case in Britain and elsewhere when it comes to slavery (Nimako and Small 2009). And more generally, museums raise issues of power, inequality and access to resources, just as with so many other racialized institutions, including employment, education and politics (Small 1997). They are one terrain, as elsewhere, in which groups stratified by class, gender, race, ethnicity and nation compete. In what follows my concern is with the connections between museums on slavery, colonialism, and their legacies on the one hand, and the facts, processes, and analysis of migration on the other.

II. Four Overlapping Migrations

In the context of the relationship between the Black experience in Britain, and museum representations of slavery and colonialism, four broad types of migration have shaped the museums that I discuss. The first three have had substantial impact already. The fourth one is more recent and its effects are still yet to be fully felt. Each of these migrations have been and continue to be shaped by class, race and gender.

First, the migration of Europeans to Africa, Asia and what became the Americas, and the establishment of empires (Fryer 1984). Without this migration, conquest and settlement over the last 500 years, many museums of Europe would be dramatically different, or largely empty. For several hundred years the museums of Britain have functioned to celebrate empire, promote imperial glory, bolster national (white) pride and glorify western culture by showcasing a wide array of artefacts plundered and looted during European slavery and colonialism. Gender was also central in the management and representations in these museums. These patterns are also reflected in the various world's fairs in Britain and across Europe (Coombes 1994; Blanchard 2008).

Second, the migration of West Indians and African-Caribbeans to Britain in large numbers since the 1950s—which has both extended and diversified the long-established Black populations of Liverpool and elsewhere (Fryer 1984). There is no need here to discuss the vast details of the migration of Blacks to Britain, but simply to mention that there were small Black communities in the nation going back several hundred years—my home city Liverpool was one of these. And to place them in the context of the much larger populations of Blacks in Britain today, who trace their most immediate origins to post world war II migration—in which a population of less than 50,000 in 1950s had by 2011 grown to more than 1.5 million. This is the one clear example of the direct human legacy of slavery and colonialism (Miles and Phizacklea 1984).

Third, there is the migration of other significant groups from within the British Empire, in particular Asians, from India, Pakistan, Bangladesh, and from East Africa. They too were the victims of colonialism and imperialism (Visram 2002). These populations arrived in larger numbers and are currently larger in size than the Black population, with a population in 2011 over 3 million. Though they have not yet pushed through their issues in terms of museums, representations and exhibits, it is quite possible, indeed quite likely, they will do so. For a variety of reasons, they have relatively greater access to resources—including financial and political—than do Blacks, and this will be a key factor in the competition for cultural representations in the decades to come.

Fourth, dramatically new, demographically large, and politically significant patterns of migration and settlement have unfolded since the 1980s. This involves the large-scale migration and settlement of whites from what used to be Eastern Europe (they joined the already established hundreds of thousands of whites from elsewhere in Europe). And it involves tens of thousands of refugees and asylum seekers from elsewhere, including Africa and Asia, e.g., Somalia. Though their involvement with museums is negligible at present, these groups are significant because as they become established and more indigenous, it is highly likely that they too will demand representations and exhibits that reflect their unique histories. It is possible that these groups will form another collectivity, competing for access to resources to present their own hidden or suppressed histories and legacies.

Needless to say, each of these migrations was and is irrepressibly gendered, and reflects the prevailing divisions of labor, and the differential allocation of men and women to realms of production and reproduction at each stage the migration occurred. Slavery and colonialism involved overwhelmingly white men rather than women, with very low proportion of white women in the colonies (Morgan 2007). The European Slave trade captured and enslaved mainly African men because planters preferred men to women, though over time there were very different patterns in the US than in the Caribbean. And the proportion of white women increased dramatically in mainland USA, while it failed to increase at all in the Caribbean (Morgan 2007). West Indian migration to Britain involved a majority of men, but with significant numbers of women—many of whom came on their own—and others as spouses or children of male immigrants (Miles and Phizacklea 1984). This reflected the significantly independent economic role of Black women in the British Caribbean. Among Asian immigrants, men were very significantly over-represented and Asian women came primarily as spouses, and family members. The gender patterns of other, more recent populations are highly varied, but again reveal higher proportions of men than women.

The precise ways that gender has impacted museums is yet to be fully investigated. But some initial observations can be made. The most important 19th century museums in Britain were articulated through a preoccupation with masculinity as represented in military combat, and have continued to frame subsequent museums development. Sexist stereotypes of women have prevailed from the inception of museums, and stereotypes of Black women have been the most demeaning of all racist representations in museums. Women have been less involved in mainstream museums, though Black women were more active than men in the smaller community organizations involved in commemorations and remembrance of slavery (Bryan 1985; Sudbury 1998). Black women have been active in all the efforts to transform representations of museums in the last two decades and remain at the forefront of efforts today, including reparations. In these ways they seek to ensure that issues of gender, and the distinctive problems confronting Black women, are high on the agenda of museums.

III. Museums and Empire in Britain

In the decades following World War II, museums were not on the radar of the majority of Black people, whether in the long-standing Black communities of Britain, such as Liverpool and Cardiff, nor in the newly arrived and emerging Black communities of London, Birmingham, Manchester and Leeds. Overwhelmingly working class, mostly convinced they were in Britain only for a short while. Black peoples' priorities were jobs and housing. However, as they became settled priorities increasingly focused on education for children, and access to politics. At all times they dealt with racism—because it directly affected them and they most certainly confronted hostile and racist images in television, press and other media. Some campaigns began. But overwhelmingly Blacks did not collectively look at museums or bother with the very explicit racial stereotypes in museums (Sivanandan 1990; Small 1994a; Sudbury 1998).

There were issues of commemoration in Black communities—in churches, in community organizations and groups, including churches. They may have had artefacts, monuments, memorials, but all were on a small scale, and tended to be personal or family based. Rastafarian organizations were central here—especially for the second generation, people like me, born of a West Indian immigrant parent (Campbell 1985). Rastafari brought African images, artefacts, sacred objects, from West Africa and from Ethiopia in particular, to the centre of many Black communities. They also brought images, ideas, icons from Jamaica and the Caribbean (Small 1983). But again these groups did not address museums. They simply set up separate institutional arrangements for commemoration and memorialization. By the 1970s and 1980s, especially as the Black population was being transformed from an immigrant to a British-born population, there was increasing unhappiness in Black communities over the stereotypical representations of Blacks in museums, especially of Africans. Some initiatives to challenge them began in Liverpool, Manchester, Birmingham and elsewhere (Simpson 2001; Rice 2007). And of course, London.

It was the Right Honourable Bernie Grant, MP, who put museums on the agenda of most Black people. And he did so in a direct and innovative way, by linking museums and reparations. Bernie Grant was one of 3 Black politicians elected to parliament in 1987, along with Diane Abbott and Paul Boateng. All three were members of the Labour Party and represented constituencies in London. Born in Guyana, and migrating to Britain as a young man, Grant rose through trade unions, became leader of Haringey Council in London, before being elected to Parliament for a working class multi-racial district—Tottenham—in north London. He was a founding member in 1989 of the Parliamentary Black Caucus, modeled after the Congressional Black Caucus in the United States. His work reflected his priorities in helping working class people, Black and white. He was actively engaged in a wide range of activities, including combating racism and inequality in Britain, and addressing the legacy of slavery and colonialism in the West Indies and Africa. He travelled to Black communities across Britain, and in Europe; he was also involved in Pan-African organizations and conferences. And he initiated and led the largest movement in Britain for Reparations for slavery.

Among the many struggles he mounted against institutional inequality, racial discrimination in employment, housing, education and immigration, he identified museums as an important symbolic issue and he made a big public issue of them. Bernie Grant knew that the British had stolen, borrowed or begged thousands of artefacts from all over Africa, and had them on exhibit across the nation, or locked away safely in the basements of their museums. He identified the Benin Bronzes as one important set of artefacts plundered by the British. The Benin Bronzes included hundreds of artefacts sculptured by indigenous Africans, that were plundered during the British Punitive Expedition in 1897 (Coombes 194). This involved a well-documented incident in which the killing of a white man who trespassed on the land of the Oba of Benin became the excuse for a punitive expedition, the destruction of the city of Benin and the plundering of the Bronzes (Coombes 1994). All of this was just a façade for British imperial aspirations to control the trade and territories of that region. A central controversy associated with the Benin Bronzes involved the reluctance and outright refusal of Europeans to believe that they had been created by Africans. Instead, it was claimed that they had white origins—allegedly Portuguese sailors. Similar doubts had been expressed about other African marvels, such as Great Zimbabwe. Worth millions of dollars at the present time—many of them in the British Museum, Liverpool Museum, and scattered around Europe—the Benin Bronzes demonstrate the ways in which intersections of politics, profits and culture, along with national and racist arrogance, remain one of the direct legacies of slavery and colonialism. The return of the Bronzes is a reckoning that has yet to be assessed; and no doubt there are many more such items hidden in museums across that nation waiting to be accounted for.

One of the first things Bernie Grant did was organize a protest at the British Museum over the many artefacts they had plundered from Africa. He called for precious and sacred artefacts to be returned to their rightful owners. And he highlighted the link between museums and reparations. He began the reparations movement in Britain, mobilised thousands of people to be involved in it and in his capacity as Member of Parliament was able to command considerable public and media attention. He travelled to conferences and activist groups in the Caribbean and Africa and spoke on the topic widely.

In his travels across Britain, one of the trips Bernie Grant made was to Liverpool, to the Charles Wootton Centre, an education and community centre named after Charles Wootton, a Black man murdered by white men in Liverpool in 1919. During that trip he recruited me to work with him. I had already begun working on the Atlantic Slave Trade Gallery in Liverpool (see below), and I was attracted by Bernie Grant's activism and the way he linked Museums, Reparations and more mainstream priorities in the Black community, like employment, education and policing. I knew that the museums in Liverpool had several Benin Bronzes. Many Black people in Liverpool had campaigned for a Black museum, and had argued that the museums had thousands of other artefacts. They had also protested against racism in Liverpool's museums (Gifford et al. 1989). I was strongly attracted to the issue of Reparations—because of the issues it raised about the profits of slavery, and because it promised great potential in mobilizing Black people, and white allies—around the legacy of slavery more generally, especially in the area of education. While working with the organization I made it clear that my priority was never about obtaining cash payments, though it was also made clear to me that for many this was the primary priority. I also urged Bernie Grant to become involved in the Atlantic Slave Trade Gallery that was being developed in Liverpool, and I wrote a chapter on the legacy of slavery in the gallery's catalogue, one that mentioned Bernie Grant and Reparations (Small 1994b).

Over the next decade, I worked as an assistant to Bernie Grant, especially on museums, identifying and summarizing academic studies, gathering information, making assessments and writing speeches. Between 1992-1995, I gave lectures on behalf of Bernie Grant's organization—Reparations UK—at universities around the UK. And I urged him to make museums more central to the debate on Reparations—because museums possessed concrete objects collected during slavery and colonialsm, which we could identify and demand accountability for. He agreed and we did that. For both of us—and Reparations UK generally—museums were more than a matter of changing images and artefacts, nor simply of recovering suppressed or forgotten histories. They were a matter of mobilizing populations to access resources, especially in areas of education and employment. We raised issues about how many Black men and women were employed at museums, questions about portrayals of Africa, about the many lies told about slavery, and we questioned the so-called magnanimity of the British legal abolition of the slave trade. These were concrete questions that arose from museums, but which gave rise to broader, wider and deeper issues to do with slavery and its legacies. It was for many of these reasons that so many people supported the movement. Tragically, Bernie Grant died prematurely in 2000, age 57, of Diabetes. The reparations movement continues—in fact is expanding—but the focus on museums is no longer as central as it was in the past.

IV. THE ATLANTIC SLAVE TRADE GALLERY 1994

While Bernie Grant was active in these issues, there were other developments in British museums that would drag slavery to the front of the public and political agenda. The Atlantic Slave Trade Gallery in Liverpool was one of them. Preparations for this gallery (which in 2007 became The International Slavery Museum) in Liverpool's Maritime Museum became public in 1991 (Tibbles 1994; Small 1997; Wallace 2006). With a large financial donation from a local millionaire, the museum attempted to establish a gallery about the Atlantic Slave Trade that would be based on academic expertise entirely from career historians, and with only token gestures to critical approaches such as Afrocentricity. But the Black community in Liverpool and elsewhere resisted and pushed for the inclusion of more Black scholars, especially women, for Afrocentric scholars, and for significant community involvement. They moved the focus of the gallery in a fundamental way, from an exclusive focus on the slave trade, to a focus on slavery as one phenomenon, in the context of European intrusion in Africa, as well as the legacy of slavery after its legal abolition.

The emergence of the gallery reflected struggles over museums in Liverpool, and elsewhere in the 1960s and 1970s. When the gallery was announced some Black organizations, including the Consortium of Black Organizations, and the Liverpool 8 Law Centre, insisted that the museums on Merseyside were racist, had nothing but stereotypical images of Africans, especially naked women, throughout their museums, did not employ Black staff, and were located in the Albert Dock—a place historically enmeshed in the legacy of slavery, and in the 1990s, hostile to Black visitors (Gifford et al. 1989). Other Black groups in Liverpool, like the Federation of Liverpool Black Organizations and the Merseyside African Council, agreed but wanted to engage with the museum in a struggle over who shapes and controls Black history. I was involved in many of these discussions and I argued that we should be involved in everything the museum planned (Small 1997). I argued that no matter how we responded, the museum was going to go ahead with its plans and so we had to be part of what happened. I had low expectations of what a museum could achieve and I constantly argued that a museum was simply a first step to addressing a much larger set of issues having to do with the legacy of slavery. Some of these bigger issues I described in one of the chapters I wrote in the museum catalogue, and in subsequent publications (Small 1994b, 1997).

The Atlantic Slave Trade Gallery opened in 1994. On reflection it is clear that we had a considerable amount of success. With constant pressure from community groups and others, the museum changed the focus of the gallery from just the slave trade, to looking at African culture and civilization prior to slavery. It also included significant consideration of the legacy of slavery, including reparations (Small 1994b). And the museum increased the number of curators from its original plan of 1 curator to a total of 11, including 7 Black people. None of this would have happened if it were not for the efforts of Black community organizations and our supporters. In the following decade, a range of temporary exhibits took place, and Black people were involved in many of them. In 2007, the gallery opened as the International Slavery Museum covering a much wider range of issues and with very substantial Black representation and involvement. The International Slavery Museum now (2011) attracts thousands of visitors and many of them claim it is the best permanent museum on the subject of slavery in the world. In this way, it is fulfilling an important role in raising awareness of slavery and its legacy in Britain and across the world.

Clearly this is not an unmitigated success but the important thing is that significant changes happened because Black people and multi-racial organizations got involved in the process, in the debates, the discussions, and in the meetings. And the museum now reveals many progressive elements, including the links made between contemporary racial inequality to slavery, and the use of progressive language like 'enslaved' rather than 'slave.' These are elements that came about only after the significant involvement of the Black community. Bernie Grant spoke at the gallery several times, and played an active role in mobilizing populations.

V. Discussion and Some Issues Today

Given all these factors and the rapidly changing context in which museums are being discussed, as just described, I want to raise several important questions. All reflect a concern with how the continuing inequalities in access to resources and power will shape the development of museum representations of slavery colonialism, and their legacies.

First, what is and will be the nature of the stories that museums tell? Now that we have more attention to histories of slavery and colonialism in museums, one challenge will be to prevent the narratives and portrayals from becoming monotonous, anodyne, and devoid of any discussions of the antagonism or conflict and justice at the heart of slavery. I fear the possibility of a drift towards narratives that erase the fundamental violence, brutality and exploitation at the heart of slavery and colonialism. We have seen this pattern become entrenched across the South of the United States where museums that once celebrated and glorified slavery now include passing, facile mention of Black people. In my work in the United States I described this as symbolic annihilation (Eichstedt and Small 2002). I was reminded of this in Veronique's Henelon's presentation on Martinique. This could happen in Britain (and elsewhere in Europe) in particular, because of the financial benefits to tourism from these kinds of museum exhibits, and because of the inescapable power inequalities that continue to shape exhibits. Key here is the national self-referential frame that continues to shape museums. In Britain, of course, this is navel gazing pride about British abolitionism. There remain promising signs that this will be resisted by Black and multi-racial organizations—such as the Franz Fanon Centre in Birmingham, the Kuumba Imani Millenium Centre in Liverpool, and the George Padmore Institute in London. The vibrant reparations movement may also continue to raise questions of the source and legitimacy of artefacts in museums.

As these patterns unfold, I believe that continued engagement with the Diaspora—the exchange of ideas, institutions, ideologies and resources, from the United States and the Caribbean to Africa, should and will play a key role. This has always been the case in Britain. It is increasing the case in other nations, such as The Netherlands and France. It will surely be the case in Spain and Portugal—imperial nations that don't have Black populations of significant size, or community mobilization around museums and related issues—but will surely be drawn into the debates on museums and the legacy of slavery. It is also increasingly the case for Belgium, Germany and Italy.

A second point concerns the potential for reactionary responses. In the context of modern Britain, with the ending of multi-culturalism, the increased emphasis on social cohesion rather than a concern with racial discrimination and inequality, and several instances of celebrations of empire, the legacy of slavery might easily become one in which there is even greater emphasis on the celebration of British abolitionism. The recently changed government (2010) from Labor to Conservative/Liberal Democrats, and the deteriorating economic conditions, and government cutbacks, have already begun to intensify competition over resources. This will directly affect museums too.

A third point concerns the potential challenge that may come from multiple groups in competition for access to museum and gallery exhibits and representations. Blacks alone are not the only ones who want their suppressed and hidden histories told. And as Bob Marley sang 'Every man thinks that his burden is the heaviest,' so with multiple migrant groups from nations around the world—many of whom are arriving from situations of political violence, murder and conflict—there are many stories to be told, each of which is regarded as more important than the others. From the former Yugoslavia to Poland, from Somalia and Congo to Rwanda, there will be competition for resources. Some groups may collaborate; others will compete. As Kwame Nimako said more generally, it is always an issue of resources. While many of these groups have not yet pushed their demands in this domain—because they have other priorities—I suspect that they will become more important as they increasingly demand that their histories are told.

VI. CONCLUSION

After more than one hundred years of museums in Britain that operated as bastions of imperial glory, the last three decades have seen transformations in the nature of representations and discourses of colonialism. Exhibits, galleries and even museums have been established that challenge this mono-dimensional and distorted memory of the past, and significant changes have been achieved (Nimako and Small 2009). We now have a far wider range of representations than ever before. And the transformations occurred primarily because of the migration and settlement of former colonial subjects in the metropolis, and their mobilization along with multi-racial organizations.

Because museums are racialized institutions; because they continue to house so many precious and sacred artefacts that were stolen or illegitimately acquired; because they are one institution among many in which contestations over grand narratives of national history occur; because museums about Black people arose primarily because of multiple patterns of migration; and because they reflect issues of access to resources, of power and inequality, then the link between museums and migration must remain an important issue of concern to social analysts. It is not my intention to argue that museums are the most important issue confronting the Black community in Britain. They are not. Other issues remain far more fundamental—including the entrenched patterns of racial inequality, racial discrimination and continuing conflict with the police. In addition, the narrow and distorted representations of Blacks that one still sees so often in various media—television, films and the press—remain highly problematic. But museums are significant and they require our attention. They still remain important institutions, in terms of the stories they tell about slavery, colonialism, and imperial glory. In this respect they are key institutions that provide large numbers of people in Britain with an important gateway to representations of the past.

Some of the most crude, vulgar and offensive images in museums have been challenged; and some key exhibits have been mounted that offer a more balanced perspective on slavery and its legacies. But they are far from being comprehensive and embedded, and operate currently without any guarantee that they will be developed further. At the same time new migrants and settlers are increasingly making demands. At the very moment that the struggle to challenge historically dominant representations of colonialism in British museums is gaining traction, these new circuits of migration pose challenges to this trend, and could even threaten to undermine it. Whether these developments will stall and curtail the few gains made, or whether they will lead to more fundamental transformations in museum representations is the issue at stake. In this regard, we must continue to be vigilant about the ways in which migration and museums are intertwined.

Works Cited

Blanchard, Pascal, Nicolas Bnacel, Gilles Boetsch, éric, Deroo, Sandrine Lemaire and Charles Forsdick, *Human Zoos. Science and Spectacle in the Age of Colonial Empires*, Liverpool University Press, Liverpool, 2008.

Brennan, Ferne, Race, Rights Reparations: Exploring a Reparation Framework for Addressing Trade Inequality, *Hamline Journal of Public Law and Policy*, Vol 30, Number 1, Fall 2008.

Brennan, Ferne, Are Reparations for Slavery Justified?, Human Rights Global Focus Group, International Human rights Foundation, India, Volume 2, Number 1, March 2005, pp. 5-17.

Bryan, Beverley, Stella Dadzie & Suzanne Scafe, *The Heart of the Race. Black Women's Lives in Britain*, Virago, London, 1985.

Campbell, Horace, *Rasta And Resistance. From Marcus Garvey to Walter Rodney*, A Hansib Publication, London, 1985.

Coombes, Annie E., Reinventing Africa. *Museums, Material Culture and Popular Imagination in Late Victorian and Edwardian England*, Yale University Press, New Haven and London, 1994.

Dresser, Madge, 'Set in Stone? Statues and Slavery in London', History Workshop Journal, Issue 64, 2007, pp. 162-199.

Eichstedt, Jennifer L and Stephen Small, *Representations of Slavery. Race, Ideology and Southern Plantations Museums*, Smithsonian Institution Press, Washington DC, 2002.

Fryer, P., *Staying Power: The History of Black People in Britain*, Pluto, London, 1984.

Gifford, Lord, W Brown and R Bundy, *Loosen the Shackles. First Report of the Liverpool 8 Inquiry into Race Relations in Liverpool*, Karia Press, London, 1989.

Greenhill, Eilean Hooper, (editor), *Museums and Multiculturalism in Britain*, Leicester University Press, Leicester, 1997.

Gouldbourne, Harry, (editor), *Black Politics in Britain*, Avebury, Aldeshot and Brookfield, USA, 1990.

Hine, Darlene Clark, Trica Danielle Keaton and Stephen Small, *Black Europe and the African Diaspora*, University of Illinois Press, Urbana Champagne, 2009.

Littler Jo and Roshi Naidoo, (editors) *The Politics of Heritage. The Legacies of 'Race'*, Routledge, London and New York, 2005.

Miles, Robert and Annie Phizacklea, *White*

Man's Country: Racism in British Politics, Pluto Press, London, 1984.

Morgan, Jennifer L. *Laboring Women: Reproduction and Gender in New World Slavery*, Philadelphia: University of Pennsylvania Press, 2004.

Nimako, Kwame and Stephen Small, 'The Unfinished Business of Emancipation: The Legacies of Anglophone and Dutch Abolition', paper presented at *Unfinished Emancipation and Black European Thinkers Symposium*, National Institute for the Study of Dutch Slavery and its Legacy, Amsterdam, June, 29-30, 2009.

Rice, Alan, 'Naming the money and unveiling the crime: contemporary British artists and the memorialization of slavery and abolition', *Patterns of Prejudice*, Vol. 41, No. 3, 2007, pp. 319-341.

Rose, E. J. B and Associates, *Colour and Citizenship: A Report on British Race Relations*, Oxford University Press for Institute of Race Relations, London, 1969.

Simpson, Mooira G, *Making Representations: Museums in the Post-Colonial Era*, Routledge, London and New York, 2001 (orig. 1996).

Sivanandan, A., *Communities of Resistance. Writings on Black Struggles for Socialism*, Verso, London and New York, 1990.

Small, Stephen "Contextualizing the Black Presence in British Museums: Representations, Resources and Response," in Eileen Hooper Greenhill, (editor), *Museums and Multiculturalism in Britain*, Leicester University Press, Leicester, 1997, pp. 50-66.

Small, Stephen, *Racialised Barriers: The Black Experience in the United States and England* Routledge, New York and London, 1994a.

Small, Stephen, "The General Legacy of the Atlantic Slave Trade," in Tony Tibbles, (editor), *Transatlantic Slavery. Against Human Dignity*, Merseyside Maritime Museum, September, 1994b, pp. 122-126.

Small, Stephen, *Police and People in London. A Group of Young Black People*, Policy Studies Institute, London, 1983

Sudbury, Julia, *Other Kinds of Dreams. Black Women's Organisations and the Politics of Transformation*, Routledge, London and New York, 1998.

Tibbles, Tony (editor), *Transatlantic Slavery. Against Human Dignity*, Merseyside Maritime Museum, September, 1994.

Trouillot, Michel-Rolph, *Silencing the Past: Power and the Production of History*, Beacon Press, Boston, 1995.

Tulloch, Carol, 'Picture this: the 'Black' curator', in in Jo Littler and Roshi Naidoo, (editors) *The Politics of Heritage. The Legacies of 'Race'*, Routledge, London and New York, 2005.

Wallace, Elizabeth Kowaleski, *The British Sale Trade & Public Memory*, Columbia University Press, New York, 2006.

Visram, Rozina, *Asians in Britain. 400 Years of History*, Pluto Press, London, 2002.

Young, Lola, 'Rethinking heritage: Cultural Policy and Inclusion' pp. in Richard Sandell, (editor) *Museums, Society, Inequality*, Routledge, New York and London, 2002, pp. 203-212.

www.ingramcontent.com/pod-product-compliance
Lightning Source LLC
Chambersburg PA
CBHW080401030426
42334CB00024B/2963